THE

Studies in the Anthropology of North American Indians Series

EDITORS

Raymond J. DeMallie

Douglas R. Parks

THE SPIRIT AND THE SKY

LAKOTA VISIONS OF THE COSMOS

MARK HOLLABAUGH

Published by the University of Nebraska Press, Lincoln and London, in cooperation with the American Indian Studies Research Institute, Indiana University, Bloomington

Library of Congress Cataloging-in-Publication Data
Names: Hollabaugh, Mark.
Title: The spirit and the sky: Lakota visions of the
cosmos / Mark Hollabaugh.
Description: Lincoln: University of Nebraska Press,
[2017] | Series: Studies in the anthropology of North
American Indians series | Published in cooperation
with the American Indian Studies Research Institute,
Indiana University, Bloomington. |
Includes bibliographical references and index.
Identifiers: LCCN 2016046918 (print)
LCCN 2016048204 (ebook)
ISBN 9781496200402 (cloth: alk. paper)
ISBN 9781496208231 (paper: alk. paper)
ISBN 9781496201454 (pdf)
Subjects: LCSH: Lakota cosmology. | Astronomy—
Great Plains—History—19th century. | Indian
astronomy—Great Plains. | Indian cosmology |
Cosmology—History—19th century.
Classification: LCC QB32 .H6845 2017 (print) |
LCC QB32 (ebook) | DDC 523.1089/975244—dc23
LC record available at
https://lccn.loc.gov/2016046918

Set in Charis by Rachel Gould.

To Jon

CONTENTS

ILLUSTRATIONS

TABLES

PREFACE AND ACKNOWLEDGMENTS

My interest in Native American astronomy began many years ago when I read John Eddy's *Science* article about the Medicine Wheel in the Bighorn Mountains of Wyoming and subsequently visited the site.[1] When I taught my first college-level astronomy course, I included a five-minute segment on the Medicine Wheel. The following semester, the discussion of Native American astronomy stretched to about twenty minutes. By the time I retired from full-time teaching, I had difficulty containing the topics of ethnoastronomy and archaeoastronomy to a ninety-minute extended class period.

In the summer of 1992 in the bookstore at what was then known as the Sioux Indian Museum in Rapid City, I came upon three books containing the work of James Walker: *Lakota Belief and Ritual*, *Lakota Myth*, and *Lakota Society*. A quick scan of the indexes revealed references to the Sun, the Moon, and the stars. A comment by Lakota elder Ringing Shield, referring to Polaris, caught my attention: "One star never moves and it is *wakan*. Other stars move in a circle about it. They are dancing in the dance circle."[2] I immediately began to wonder about Lakota astronomy and the aspects of Lakota culture that are important to their astronomy. A clue was in the images they left on winter count hides and in ledger books.

In 1996 at the Fifth Oxford International Conference on archaeoastronomy held at St. John's College in Santa Fe, I gave a talk on the images of celestial objects and phenomena (Sun, Moon, eclipses, stars, comets, and meteors) that appear in nineteenth-century Lakota winter counts. My guiding question was "How did the Lakota interpret such events and why did they make note of them?"[3]

In describing the Lakota winter counts in the collections of the National Anthropological Archives, Christina Burke specifically mentions the numerous references in these counts to the Leonid meteor shower of 1833. This astronomical event appears in virtually every Lakota, and other Plains Indian, winter count. Burke notes, "While scholars have mentioned the fact that it appears in every winter count, no one has yet published information on how this event was interpreted by Lakota people."[4]

The phrase "no one has yet published" suggests an opportunity. There has not been a comprehensive treatment of the astronomy of the nineteenth-century Lakota. There has been no unified discussion of winter counts, meteor showers, comets, the aurora borealis, the Sun, the Moon, the stars, and the Sun Dance within the context of Lakota ethnoastronomy. Moreover, very few scholars have attempted to answer the inevitable question, "Why did the nineteenth-century Lakota give so much attention to the heavens?"

One reason for the lack of a comprehensive treatment is the difficulty in locating written sources. The few extant Lakota sources are no earlier than the very late nineteenth century. References to what the Lakota said about the stars are generally lacking in contemporaneous eyewitness accounts of their culture. In other words, a researcher has to dig deeply to find reputable, reliable source materials relating to the astronomy of the Lakota in the nineteenth century.

An astronomer wishing to enter the world of Lakota ethnoastronomy also must be willing to delve deeply into the history, language, culture, religion, and thinking of the Lakota. Misinterpretation, or over interpretation, can be minimized by understanding the Lakota worldview as the context for their astronomy.

I intend this book to be useful to scholars. Hence, there are a large number of references to scholarly articles. However, I have included some background material for readers who may be unfamiliar with astronomy, ethnology, anthropology, or Native American history and culture. I have included many lengthy direct quotations from eyewitness accounts that could require considerable detective work to locate. It is important to have these ethnoastronomy materials assembled in one book.[5]

Chapter 1 is a general introduction to the Lakota's life on the Great Plains, as well as a discussion of the sources for the book. The problem of how to deal with contemporary Native voices in evaluating the material from the past was a particularly difficult and yet important aspect of setting the context for the book.

Chapter 2 is a survey of the astronomical context for the topics of this book. The hybrid fields of archaeoastronomy and ethnoastronomy are relatively new subfields of historical astronomy, and there is a brief discussion of their approach and technique. Positional astronomy is described in detail, explaining eclipses and how we use celestial motions to tell time. Finally, there is a brief introduction to the astronomy of the Plains Indians, of which the Lakota were a part.

Chapter 3 is a discussion of the aspects of Lakota culture that particularly have a bearing on their astronomy. Readers will detect heavy emphasis on numerology, with many references to four and seven, but it will become apparent that celestial phenomena that come in fours and sevens (and 4 × 7 = 28) are central to the Lakota. The concept of *wakháŋ* is crucial to Lakota culture and is introduced.

Chapter 4 describes the repeatable, predictable appearance and motions of the stars and constellations as the Lakota and other dwellers of the Great Plains saw them. The Lakota names for the stars and constellations are discussed with some references to Lakota legends about the stars.

Chapter 5 describes the importance of the two brightest members of the celestial realm, the Sun and the Moon, and their important place in Lakota culture.

Chapter 6 explains how the Lakota used the motions of the Sun and the Moon to keep track of the passage of time. Much of the chapter focuses on Lakota winter counts and their importance for ethnoastronomy.

Chapter 7 looks at spectacular phenomena in the sky: eclipses and the aurora borealis. The explanation of the cause of the aurora that occurred at the death of Black Elk in 1950 is a new contribution to ethnoastronomy.

Chapter 8 is a discussion of the often sudden appearance of meteors and comets. These apparitions provided the pictographs for several Lakota winter count calendar systems, especially the years 1822 and 1833.

Chapter 9 discusses the rich astronomical associations of the most important Lakota ritual, the Sun Dance.

Chapter 10 discusses modern, twentieth-century Lakota ethnoastronomy with an extensive look at *Lakota Star Knowledge*.

Finally, the Lakota are one of many Native American cultures in North America. Chapter 11 places Lakota ethnoastronomy into the wider context of Native American cultures and connects Lakota ethnoastronomy with Lakota culture and spiritual belief. There are comparisons and contrasts to be made between modern science and traditional Native science. Finally, there is an attempt to answer the question, "Why did the Lakota make so many references to the heavens?"

A word about orthography: Lakota was a spoken language for many generations before it became a written language. As with other Native American languages there are several orthographies for writing a Lakota word. For example, one can write *wakháŋ, wakáŋ*, or *wakan*. In direct quotations I have retained the author's spelling and orthography. In discussing the concept, however, I have used the orthography suggested by Raymond DeMallie, *wakháŋ*. Hence, the reader will notice multiple ways of writing one Lakota word.[6]

Starry Night Education of the Simulation Curriculum Corporation produces the excellent *Starry Night* software that I used (available at http://www.starrynighteducation.com). In addition to encouragement for this research, I wish to thank Michael J. Goodman, CEO of Simulation Curriculum Corporation, for permission to use the Starry Night Education graphics explaining geometry of the lunar phases, eclipses, and the orientation of the Big Dipper round the North Star.

I am grateful to my deans and the presidents at Normandale Community College for allowing me to spend two sabbatical leaves working on this project. I especially want to thank librarian Joann Hucko for procuring numerous obscure scholarly materials for me. English professor David Pates edited an earlier version of the manuscript, and his input improved the style and readability.

David Mathieu, former vice president and dean of academic affairs at Normandale, grew up among the Dakota in Minneapolis and became a Lakota language instructor at Black Hills State College. David gave me many insights into the Lakota culture and answered countless linguistic questions. We always greet one another *"Háu kholá!"*

I also wish to thank Claire Hoyum for her eagle-eyed reading of the final manuscript. Every author should have an English major as a friend!

I am indebted to Delores Knipp (Lt. Col., USAF, retired) for providing me with data on the August 1950 geomagnetic storm event. Dr. Knipp, an expert on space weather, was a faculty colleague when I taught at the U.S. Air Force Academy.

Von Del Chamberlain, former director of the Hansen Planetarium, Salt Lake City, brought his important work on Plains Indians winter counts to my attention and gave me permission to copy and to use his 35 mm photo collection of winter count hides and ledger books. I met Von Del at the Fifth Oxford International Conference in 1996. He has been a continual source of encouragement.

Michael Zeilik, another archaeoastronomy colleague, invited me to join this fascinating field, encouraged my work, and made helpful suggestions. Thanks are due Mike for initiating my interest in the diaries of John Gregory Bourke.

The staffs of the following institutions were helpful in locating materials: Western History Department of the Denver Public Library, the Colorado Historical Society, the State Historical Society of North Dakota, the South Dakota Historical Society, and the Minnesota Historical Society.

Some museums and archives are especially rich in Lakota material. Harry Thompson at the Center for Western Studies (CWS), Augustana University, Sioux Falls, graciously invited me to speak at the 1997 Dakota history conference at Augustana University. Harry and his staff also helped me with several inquiries about sources in the CWS collection.

Tom Buecker, curator at the Fort Robinson Museum, Crawford, Nebraska, loaned me microfilm copies of John Bourke's diaries. He also suggested I contact James Hanson in regard to the location of the 1875 Chadron Sun Dance.

Ray Summers and Paulette Montileaux of the Sioux Indian Museum (now at The Journey), Rapid City, were helpful in the early part of my research on celestial images in Lakota winter counts.

Occasionally one meets people who are extraordinary. The late Brother C. J. Simon, S.J., of the Red Cloud School and Heritage Center Museum, Pine Ridge, South Dakota, was such a man. Prior to my first visit to Pine Ridge, a Lakota friend told me, "Be sure to talk with Brother Simon." I made a point of chatting with him, even if only briefly, on every subsequent visit to Pine Ridge. His devotion to Native American arts and the culture and history of the Lakota people led him to take an interest in my research, and he gave me ideas about little-known sources of written accounts about the Lakota. He also made sure I left the museum shop with yet another piece of contemporary Lakota art!

Marie Kills in Sight, current director of the Buechel Memorial Lakota Museum, Rosebud Reservation, South Dakota, gave me many helpful insights into Lakota culture and history. Her interest in my work contributed significantly to my understanding of the Lakota culture. Mike Marshall, formerly of the Buechel Museum, also assisted me in the initial phase of my research.

Sebastian F. Braun, Iowa State University, suggested several revisions to the manuscript, and I appreciate his thoughtful, helpful comments, especially the idea that the differences between Native views and modern astronomy lead to "toleration."

Raymond DeMallie, Indiana University, encouraged me and provided many insights for this undertaking. His vast corpus of work on the Lakota had a strong influence on what I have written. I also wish to acknowledge his assistance with the spellings and orthographies of Lakota words as well as his careful reading and editing of the manuscript. His IU colleague Douglas Parks was instrumental in guiding the manuscript on its journey to the publisher.

Every author needs good editors, and I am fortunate to have worked with Matthew Bokovoy, senior acquisitions editor for Native American and Indigenous Studies at the University of Nebraska Press. Heather Stauffer, his editorial assistant, helped me with everything from documentation to illustration requirements. Project editor Elizabeth Zaleski guided the publication process, and Jane Curran expertly edited the final manuscript.

Father Raymond Bucko, S.J., opened many doors for me and patiently answered countless questions. His access to the Buechel materials enabled me to include some lesser-known and -observed aspects of Lakota culture and astronomy. He introduced me to several scholars and to new Native American friends. His encouragement and challenges spurred me on.

I am deeply indebted to my good friend Martin Brokenleg, former faculty member at Augustana University and the Vancouver School of Theology. Martin took me to family events at Rosebud, strongly encouraged me, and deepened my understanding and appreciation of the Lakota culture. His patience in the face of my endless questions is greatly appreciated. To Martin, my *kholá*, "*Philámayayelo.*"

I have learned much from my Lakota friends and always feel personally drawn toward the Great Plains, where their ancestors lived and flourished, and where today they continue to retell and interpret their rich cultural heritage. It is my hope that *The Spirit and the Sky: Lakota Visions of the Cosmos* will help preserve the rich astronomical heritage of the Lakota people.

1

THE LAKOTA PEOPLE

In the nineteenth century the Lakota, or western Sioux, lived on the Great Plains of what now are the states of Nebraska, South Dakota, North Dakota, Montana, and Wyoming. They are perhaps the best known of the Plains Native American peoples due to their persistent appearance in the popular history of the American West. Historians have tended to focus on the encounters between the Lakota and invading whites, beginning with their first meeting with the exploratory expedition of Lewis and Clark in 1804 and ending with the tragedy at Wounded Knee in December 1890. But this approach ignores the rich history and culture that preceded the arrival of white men on the Great Plains. Petroglyphs and pictographs reveal that Native peoples lived on the Great Plains for countless generations before Lewis and Clark's Corps of Discovery made its historic journey up the Missouri River.

Events tens of thousands, and even billions, of years ago had an impact on Native peoples.[1] The geological and topographical nature of the American West shaped the culture and beliefs of the Lakota. As Colin Calloway states, "West is a land of great scenery, magnificent distances, endless skies, and limited water."[2] The role of the land in shaping Lakota culture cannot be minimized, but the land is only half of the world around us. The investigation, exploration, and interpretation of the Lakota's relationship to the celestial world beneath which they roamed the Plains often were excluded from the non-Native treatments of their culture. What did they do when they saw an eclipse? How did they react when a spectacular meteor crossed the sky? How did they use the Sun, the Moon, and the stars for telling time or for navigation? What role did the sky play in their central ritual, the Sun Dance?

This book explores Lakota ethnoastronomy, that is, the interpretation of celestial phenomena in the context of Lakota culture. To talk about the astronomy of the Lakota requires exploring their culture, including spiritual beliefs and rituals.

Archaeology of the Great Plains

In the southwest United States, the ancient pueblo peoples left numerous physical structures for archaeologists, and tourists, to explore. Sites such as Mesa Verde in Colorado or Chaco Canyon in New Mexico preserve incredible images of the prehistoric Anasazi culture. Artifacts such as rock art, pottery, and adobe structures richly describe the ancient pueblo civilization and its astronomy.

Archaeology of the Lakota, however, can be more difficult to discern due in part to the lack of permanent villages made of materials like stone or adobe.[3] Just as in the Southwest, some evidence of pre-European-contact rock art is found in the Black Hills area. Petroglyphs indicate the Black Hills were occupied as early as 2500 BC.[4] Rock art suggests the Lakota became active in the Black Hills in the early eighteenth century. One painted drawing thought to be from the early nineteenth century shows a crescent moon and star that are similar to those depicted on Lakota winter count calendars.[5]

However, the Lakota, or their antecedent residents on the plains, left only a few artifacts. The Lakota usually anchored the edge of their tipis with a ring of rocks, and rock tipi rings were common on the rolling prairie of the Dakotas.[6] Remnants of campfires were found in the Badlands, and fragments of pottery and flint arrowheads were near the fire pits.[7] Larger structures made of stones placed in the ground in the shape of human or animal figures have been found over much of the Great Plains. Many of these are well over thirty meters long. Their builders and purpose are unknown; none appear to have any astronomical significance.[8]

Lakota History

Linguistic studies place the origins of the Sioux in the northern Minnesota and Wisconsin lake region east of the Mississippi. The first historical mention of the Sioux by Europeans was in 1640. For the next one hundred years they were located in the prairie region from Mille Lacs, Minnesota, westward to the Missouri River. In their oral history, however, the Lakota believe they emerged into the world in the area of the northern Great Plains.[9]

Following the devastating smallpox epidemics that decimated the earth-lodge-dwelling Arikara, whose villages were on the Missouri River, the Lakota crossed the river and began to expand their buffalo-hunting range. By the late 1700s they had acquired horses, introduced to the northern Plains tribes by Native groups living to the west and south. During the brief period from about 1790 to 1850 the Lakota developed the mounted buffalo-hunting way of life that characterizes Plains Indian culture.

The term *Sioux* is derived from an Ojibwe and French term, *nadouessioux*, which means "little snakes" or "enemies."[10] This word usually is thought to reflect the often hostile relationship between the Ojibwe (*Anishinaabe*, also known as Chippewa) and the Sioux.[11] Because the term *Sioux* is rooted in a non-Lakota pejorative word, it is generally preferable to use the self-ascription, namely *Lakhóta*.[12] *Lakhóta* is derived from the verb *lakhólya*, "to be friendly with."[13]

After spreading out on the high plains the Lakota developed into seven distinct tribal groups: the Oglala (*Oglála*), the Brulé (*Sicháŋǧu*), the Hunkpapa (*Húŋkpapha*), Minneconjou (*Mnikówožu*), Sans Arc (*Itázipcho*), Blackfeet (*Sihásapa*), and Two Kettles (*Oóhenuŋpa*).[14] Each had a separate political identity and territory. The Oglala and Brulé lived farther to the south, along the Platte River, the other five ranged as far north as the Cannon Ball River in southwestern North Dakota.

Conflict and Disaster

Although the story of the dispossession of the Lakota of most of their land, and the destruction of the buffalo herds that were the source of their livelihood, is well known and does not require detailed retelling, a discussion of continuity and change in Lakota culture sets the context for Lakota ethnoastronomy.[15] By the terms of the 1851 Treaty of Fort Laramie, signed by the Lakota and other tribes of the northern Great Plains, the U.S. government claimed the right to establish roads across the Great Plains and forts for the protection of travelers heading west.[16] As a torrent of emigrants moved west, tensions with the Lakota over the destruction of game and other resources eventually erupted into full-scale conflict in what is referred to as Red Cloud's War. Some of the bloodiest engagements occurred near the outposts along the Bozeman Trail, which headed north through Wyoming along the eastern flank of the Bighorn Mountains to the gold-mining region of Montana.

Fort Phil Kearny was a frontier outpost constructed along the southeastern edge of the Bighorn Mountains to guard the Bozeman Trail. On 21 December 1866 a company of eighty-one cavalry and infantry under the command of Captain William J. Fetterman raced out of Fort Phil Kearny in pursuit of what they thought was a handful of Indians. Beyond those decoys, over the distant hills, about two thousand warriors awaited the overly confident Fetterman. Fetterman's entire command was annihilated. Warfare continued until the signing of the 1868 Treaty of Fort Laramie and the subsequent abandonment of the forts along the Bozeman Trail. The 1868 treaty established the Great Sioux Reservation, which encompassed much of the plains of South Dakota west of the Missouri River and included the Black Hills.

This second Treaty of Fort Laramie (1868) was very explicit regarding the lands within the reservation: the only non-Indians "permitted to pass over, settle upon, or reside in the territory" were those who were authorized by the government "in discharge of duties enjoined by law" (Article 2).[17] Likewise, the treaty guaranteed the Lakota the right to hunt on the plains north and west of the Black Hills that stretch into Wyoming and Montana "so long as the buffalo may range thereon in such numbers as to justify the chase" (Article 11).[18]

The Black Hills loom over the prairie of northwestern Nebraska, western South Dakota, and southeastern Wyoming like an oasis in the midst of the vast treeless prairie. From a distance the dark green pine trees look black. Although winter in the Hills brings incredible volumes of snow, it generally was a better place to spend the colder months due to shelter from the gale-force winds on the plains and the availability of fuel for warming fires.[19]

The Black Hills were off-limits to settlement by the white man according to the 1868 treaty. The Hills were relatively unexplored until 1874, when a government-sponsored scientific expedition, with a military escort headed by Lt. Col. George Armstrong Custer, surveyed the region and discovered gold in a stream bed. Soon white miners illegally invaded the Hills to search for gold and wealth.[20]

After fruitless attempts to persuade the Lakota to sell the Black Hills to the government, the U.S. Army mounted a major military action in late spring 1876 to confine all the Lakota to their reservation. Although most Americans typically recall only the demise of Custer at the Little Bighorn from this campaign, there were other clashes, and Custer was only one of many participants. For example, on 17 June 1876, along the banks of the Rosebud Creek in southern Montana, troops under General George Crook encountered the Lakota led by Crazy Horse.

Several days later, on 25 June 1876, Colonel Custer divided troops under his command into three units. Custer's column fell into a village of several thousands of Lakota, Cheyenne, and Arapaho. The Indians assembled at least two thousand warriors and thus outnumbered Custer's contingent nearly ten to one. Custer, who retreated to what is now known as Last Stand Hill, didn't have a chance. His two subordinates, Benteen and Reno, survived to fight another day and told their version of events to the world. Reports of Custer's "last stand," reaching eastern cities around 4 July 1876, were not the news the nation wanted to hear on its centennial. For the Lakota and Cheyenne the victory was as much a spiritual victory as a military one. Many Lakota and Cheyenne believed the triumph over Custer was supernaturally foretold. However, their victory was short-lived and may have accelerated their confinement to reservations.[21]

For the next fourteen years government efforts to bring the "hostiles" to reservations met with varying success. Many Lakota, like Red Cloud and Spotted Tail, realized open rebellion was futile and settled for reservation life. Although pressure to assimilate was strong, the Lakota worked hard to adapt and change and yet retain their culture—they were not just victims.[22] In 1883 the government prohibited Lakota religious rituals, such as the Sun Dance, although the Lakota found ways to continue some practices.[23] Sitting Bull and his followers were more resistant to confinement on the reservation and sought temporary refuge in Canada.[24]

The U.S. government had two options: exterminate the American Indians or assimilate them into the majority white culture.[25] Although there were loud cries for the former, political leaders chose the latter. An unusual alliance was forged between government agencies and churches. The government under President Grant assigned churches to select Indian agents for each reservation, together with the charge to civilize and assimilate the Native people.[26] Converting the Indians to Christianity and imposing white man's education would achieve the assimilation goal.[27] In 1879 the first of several off-reservation boarding schools was founded at Carlisle, Pennsylvania, as a means of removing Indian children from the influences of their Native cultures.

A major challenge to the progress of the government's efforts to force Lakota adaptation to reservation life originated far from Lakota lands in Nevada. On 1 January 1889, at the time of a solar eclipse, a Paiute named Wovoka had a vision and was inspired to initiate a sacred dance. The Lakota and other groups learned of his vision and the dance he taught. Ghost Dance fever swept over the Lakota, particularly those who had resisted reservation life and its changes. It was said that dancing the Ghost Dance would bring about the return of the buffalo and send the white man away. Dancers wore Ghost Dance shirts that were believed to make the wearer impervious to the white man's bullets.[28]

Government authorities sought to quell the Lakota's passion for the Ghost Dance and its messianic prophesies, and in late 1890 the Lakota world seemed to be coming to an end. At Standing Rock, reservation policemen murdered Sitting Bull on 15 December 1890. Several days later, a Ghost Dance promoter, Big Foot of the *Mnikhówožu*, was leading his people to the Pine Ridge Agency when they were intercepted by the army and taken to camp overnight along the banks of Wounded Knee Creek, about twenty kilometers northeast of Pine Ridge. Big Foot's camp of some 350 men, women, and children was guarded by the revitalized, and perhaps revenge-seeking, Seventh Cavalry. Commanded by Colonel James W. Forsyth, 500 cavalry and four Hotchkiss cannon opened fire. Who shot first, the Lakota or the cavalry, is still a matter of debate and discussion, but when the shooting ended an hour after it had begun, at least 150 Lakota lay dead, and another 50 lay wounded in the snow. A few weeks later, the remaining "hostiles" surrendered to the military.[29]

The Lakota continue to seek a legal means for the return of the Black Hills. On the Rosebud Reservation in the late 1990s, Doris Leader Charge reminisced about her childhood. She often accompanied her non-English speaking grandmother to the store, interpreting for her. When young Doris, born in 1930, asked for some candy, Grandmother would answer, "When I get my Black Hills back." Later as a grandmother, Leader Charge reflected, "I'm a woman of 70 myself, and we're not any closer to getting back our Black Hills than we were then."[30]

In a ruling released on 23 July 1980 the U.S. Supreme Court ruled the Black Hills had been taken illegally from the Lakota, and they should be paid the value of the Hills plus interest. Principal and accrued interest amounted to over $900 million. Even as this payment for the Black Hills now approaches one billion dollars, the Lakota have refused to accept the settlement, preferring a return of the Hills to Lakota control.[31] In his majority opinion, Justice Harry Blackmun quoted from a previous ruling on the Black Hills: "A more ripe and rank case of dishonorable dealings will never, in all probability, be found in our history."[32] Justice William Rehnquist, who dissented from the majority, found similar words even though he disagreed with the ruling: "That there was tragedy, deception, barbarity, and virtually every other vice known to man in the 300-year history of the expansion of the original 13 Colonies into a Nation which now embraces more than three million square miles and 50 States cannot be denied."[33]

FIG. 1. The Black Hills. The Black Hills, or "the Hills," take their name from their dark appearance from a distance. Perhaps best known for Mt. Rushmore, there also are numerous natural wonders, campgrounds, and trails for horse riders, hikers, and mountain bikers. The Black Hills, *Phahá Sápa*, are sacred to the Lakota people, and visitors to Lakota sites should be respectful. The Crazy Horse Memorial is a must-see stop for visitors. The Needles Highway passes these spectacular rock formations. Photo by Mark Hollabaugh.

From 1851 to 1890 and beyond, in the midst of all this conflict and struggle, the Lakota were doing astronomy. As the story of their astronomy unfolds, we see how astronomical events and phenomena were ingrained in their life. The Black Hills, the center of so much of the turmoil in the Lakota world, would become intimately linked to their astronomy in the twentieth century.

Sources of Information and Limitations

Researchers interested in the timing of repetitive astronomical phenomena such as eclipses, the phases of the Moon, or the seasons have a wealth of data sources on which to draw. Computer programs such as *Starry Night* make the visual reproduction of an event relatively simple.[34] The U.S. Naval Observatory website is a valuable resource for rising and setting data for the Sun and Moon as well as phases of the Moon and seasons.[35] NASA's eclipse website is a primary source for data on every solar or lunar eclipse past and future.[36]

Glimpses into Lakota understandings of astronomical phenomena are harder to come by. The numerous winter counts drawn on hides or in ledger books, which are generally accessible, are a valuable resource. In many cases, digitized images of these pictographs are available via the web. However, finding *written* original source material is challenging. Although numerous eyewitness accounts of nineteenth-century Lakota life exist in diaries, journals, letters, and published accounts, references to the Lakota and the sky are not always obvious or prominent, let alone indexed in these materials. The Lakota were much less precise than white Americans when they kept track of time. Exact dates were not especially important. Hence, finding corroborating astronomical records for phenomena depicted in winter counts or mentioned in written accounts is difficult because of the lack of temporal precision in the Lakota accounts.

Because there is a limited amount of historical material available to document Lakota astronomical beliefs, I have also used material from their eastern relatives, the Dakota (Yankton and Santee Sioux). The close cultural and linguistic relationship among these major Sioux groups and their continuing historical interactions justify this decision to include what has been documented about the Dakota in my study of the Lakota.

Similarly, this book uses a liberal definition of *nineteenth century*; pre-1800 references to the Lakota and Dakota are of interest. Hence, the travels of Jonathan Carver through the eighteenth-century Minnesota frontier are useful.[37] The arbitrary cutoff date for this investigation of Lakota astronomy is 1910, the year Comet Halley appeared. This apparition of Comet Halley was recorded in one of the last Lakota winter counts. Dramatic changes in Lakota culture occurred following the First World War, and so 1910 seems like a reasonable date for the terminus of this research. Even so, listening to late and mid-twentieth-century Lakota voices helps reveal the ongoing meaning of the astronomy, even if direct continuity to past beliefs cannot always be established.

Sources Relating to Lakota Astronomical Concepts

Original written documents that give detailed information on the astronomy of the Lakota are scarce. Some of the difficulty lies in the very nature of the Lakota language—although Lakota is a written language today, it was only an oral language until missionaries translated the Bible into Dakota. DeMallie summarizes the problem.

> Although there are numerous recordings of speeches by Sioux leaders, translated into English and preserved in stenographic reports of talks and councils, most of the contemporary written materials present outsiders' viewpoints on the course of events that, in less than a century, transformed the Sioux from independent buffalo hunters to reservation dwellers. The authors of these documents—travelers, traders, colonial administrators, military officers, missionaries, Indian agents—represented a cultural tradition very different from that of the Sioux. Even when these observers were sympathetic to Indians, they usually failed to understand enough of native culture to empathize with Sioux perspectives.[38]

Thus, this study of Lakota ethnoastronomy is necessarily based on secondhand and translated sources. Even so, many of the observations recorded by travelers, traders, colonial administrators, military officers, missionaries, and Indian agents contribute valuable authentic elements. Often the language they used reflects their biases and interpretations. It is true, as DeMallie states, that "Lakota and non-Lakota documents provide complementary perspectives based on different cultural premises; in a fundamental sense they represent conflicting realities, rooted in radically different epistemologies. The challenge of ethnohistory is to bring these two types of historical data together to construct a fuller picture of the past."[39] This is also the challenge of ethnoastronomy.

DeMallie recounts two gatherings of the veterans of the Custer battle at the Little Bighorn, illustrating a different view of history in the white and Lakota worlds. In response to the white man's necessity to identify Custer's slayer for the history books, the Indians present *elected* Southern Cheyenne chief Brave Bear in 1906 and Minneconjou chief White

Bull in 1926 as the slayers of Custer.[40] In these instances the Lakota and Cheyenne participants essentially told the whites what they thought they wanted to hear, an attitude that may have colored what the Lakota said about the stars in response to some interviewers.

James R. Walker

The richest material on the nineteenth-century and early twentieth-century Lakota life and culture was compiled by James R. Walker, a physician at the Pine Ridge Reservation from 1896 to 1914. Walker, who treated tuberculosis among the Lakota at Pine Ridge, decided to work *with* traditional Lakota healers instead of against them. This cooperative spirit led to a relationship of trust between Walker and the medicine men. Health conditions improved, and the Lakota shared their stories, beliefs, and rituals with Walker. His notes, compiled in *Lakota Belief and Ritual, Lakota Myth*, and *Lakota Society*, are primary sources on the late nineteenth-century Lakota.[41] Walker also wrote an important monograph on the Sun Dance.[42] Perhaps because of his medical training, Walker employed a scientific approach—he essentially reported data.

Walker can be criticized for relying on a small number of consultants, such as George Sword. Sword, who met Walker in 1896, was the president of the Pine Ridge Reservation Council and also a deacon in the Episcopal Church. Sword, who did not speak English, learned to write in the Lakota orthography developed by the missionaries. He noted, "The young Oglalas do not understand a formal talk by an old Lakota, because the white people [i.e., missionaries] have changed [the] Lakota language, and the young people speak it as the white people have written it."[43] Sword also wrote an extensive account of the Sun Dance, translated in 1929 by Ella Deloria from Lakota into English.[44] Sword understood the threats to Lakota culture, and at his funeral he was called "the Abraham Lincoln of the Sioux nation."[45]

To translate Sword's work, Walker "hired Clarence Three Stars, an Oglala who had attended Carlisle Indian School in Pennsylvania," but he "rewrote Sword's texts after his own ideas and translated them in modern reservation-English idiom so that their cultural content was obscured." Walker then relied on Charles Nines, a non-Lakota who produced very literal translations.[46] Ultimately Walker completed the translations himself, illustrating the difficulty in placing the astronomical information Walker collected into a direct cultural context. Thus, for example, when using material on astronomy from Sword via Walker, historians must be alert for the inclusion of white and Christian ideas of that time in the narration.

Other Non-Native Sources

Numerous Army officers of the nineteenth century kept journals or wrote articles about their encounters with the Lakota. Although some military officers showed a vehement bias against the Indians they met, many exhibited sympathy, realizing that the Native Americans were here first, and whites were taking over their homelands and destroying Native cultures. Their observations, journals, and other writings generally supported the assimilation goal of the U.S. government.[47] Officers like John Gregory Bourke were more objective than others.

White traders, travelers, missionaries, and Indian agents also wrote diaries or magazine articles describing the Native peoples they met. Some of these narrations are by persons held in captivity by the Lakota. Indian agents and their wives emphasized politics in their writings. All of these people, army or civilian, mentioned astronomy only in passing. They seldom offered any explanation or commentary.

Early anthropologists such as Alice Fletcher or Clark Wissler rarely discussed astronomy, although they gave some explanation of the months of the year.[48] However, from the viewpoint of ethnoastronomy, Garrick Mallery's work on the pictographs of the Plains Indians is an important and useful early work. More than presenting a collection of images, Mallery interpreted the pictographs based on information from his Native consultants. Fortunately he commented on the symbols representing the Sun, the Moon, and the stars.[49]

Born in Germany in 1874, the Jesuit Father Eugene Buechel lived and worked among the Lakota for most of his adult life. He served at both the St. Francis Mission on the Rosebud Reservation and the Holy

Rosary Mission at Pine Ridge at different times from 1907 until his death in 1954. Although primarily known as the compiler of a widely used Lakota dictionary, Father Buechel also kept many notes and collected many biological specimens and Lakota artifacts during his time at the Holy Rosary and St. Francis Missions. His dictionary definitions often include ethnographic comments. Some of his yet unpublished notes contain additional information useful for ethnoastronomy that is not included in his dictionary definitions. Today the Buechel Memorial Lakota Museum in St. Francis houses many items he collected and serves as an excellent resource for Lakota scholars.

Lakota Holy Men

Although modern society usually views science as objective and removed from other facets of life, ethnoastronomy places astronomical knowledge and application directly into a cultural context. When we consider the astronomy of the nineteenth-century Lakota, the cultural context becomes even more important. Thus even contemporary Lakota practice and thought can help frame questions about the astronomy of the pre-reservation Lakota. The voices of some twentieth-century Lakota holy men are necessary in order to interpret the meaning of the astronomy because their philosophy strongly influenced current Lakota thought and practice.

The Oglala Lakota holy man Black Elk is the single most important source for the content of twentieth-century Lakota religious thought and practice.[50] Born in about 1863, he witnessed the Lakota's triumph over Custer at the Little Bighorn at age thirteen. At age sixteen he had a powerful vision that shaped his life, and by age eighteen it was clear he would become a *wichása wakháŋ*, a holy man. He began his career as a healer of the sick just at the time his people settled on Pine Ridge, after the decimation of the buffalo herds. This was a difficult period of transition from the hunting life to confinement on the reservation.

In 1887 Black Elk accompanied Buffalo Bill (William F. Cody) to England as a performer in Cody's Wild West Show. As a stipulation of the contract he signed, he was baptized in the Episcopal Church, although it is unclear how deeply he embraced Christianity at that time. In December 1904 Black Elk spent time at Holy Rosary Mission near Pine Ridge. He subsequently was baptized into the Catholic Church, given the Christian name Nicolas, and henceforth was known as Nick Black Elk. Over the following decades, he emerged as a catechist not only among the Lakota but also to other tribes to whom he traveled as a missionary. Ultimately he became the head catechist at Holy Rosary Mission at Pine Ridge, and the Jesuits provided him with a house near the mission. Black Elk died on 19 August 1950 at his home in Manderson on the Pine Ridge Reservation. A spectacular auroral display was seen on the night of his death.[51]

In 1930 Black Elk met a white man who changed his life. John G. Neihardt, a well-known Nebraska poet and writer, visited Black Elk. Two books emerged from Black Elk's collaboration with Neihardt, *Black Elk Speaks*, published in 1932, and *When the Tree Flowered*, published in 1951 after Black Elk's death.[52] Another collaboration with Joseph Epes Brown led to the 1953 publication of *The Sacred Pipe*, which is a description of Lakota rituals. A rising interest in the 1960s in all things Indian brought Neihart's words, and thus Black Elk, onto an international literary and religious stage.[53]

The transcripts of the material Neihardt collected are in English. In 1984 Raymond J. DeMallie published these in *The Sixth Grandfather*. DeMallie's publication of the interview transcripts clearly showed what material originated with Black Elk and what Neihardt himself contributed in writing *Black Elk Speaks*. Less clear is the interpretation of what Black Elk actually *said*, which resulted in heated debates over the issue of authenticity.

This dilemma is simply stated: Do the teachings of Black Elk represent traditional nineteenth-century Lakota culture, the teachings of a Lakota who was a Christian catechist, or a blend of both? A simple answer to this question does not exist, and no single answer will satisfy all readers of Black Elk. Indeed, the scholarly and popular presses have produced a plethora of books and articles addressing all aspects of the issue. Of prime importance for a book on ethnoastronomy is whether something Black Elk said about astronomical topics represents traditional nineteenth-century viewpoints or whether the ideas are an interpretation through the filters of a catechist's experience and belief, as well as the reinterpretation of a white author.[54]

Joseph Epes Brown's *The Sacred Pipe* is another source for Black Elk's thought.[55] In 1947 Brown, a college student, traveled to meet Black Elk in Nebraska. He lived with Black Elk and his family on the Pine Ridge Reservation later that winter and wrote down the old man's account of the "Seven Rites of the Oglala Sioux." The account of the sacred pipe and the seven rites, which he volunteered to Brown, had come to Black Elk orally from Elk Head (*Heȟáka Pha*), who was the "keeper of the Sacred Pipe." Black Elk's son Ben assisted Brown with translations and interpretation of his father's narrative. Black Elk's Catholicism is much more evident in *The Sacred Pipe*. In *The Sixth Grandfather*, DeMallie provided a useful analysis of *The Sacred Pipe*.

> These teachings seem to represent the end point in Black Elk's synthesis of Lakota and Christian beliefs, for in them he structures Lakota rituals in parallel fashion to the Catholic sacraments. Perhaps this was Black Elk's final attempt to bridge the two religious traditions that his life had so intimately embodied.[56]

Although the parallels or themes from Christian thought may inform astronomical references in *The Sacred Pipe*, Black Elk's comments on things celestial have a profound impact on twentieth-century interpretations of the sky.

Often called the "Ceremonial Chief of the Teton Sioux," Frank Fools Crow, an Oglala Lakota, was one of the most influential medicine men of the twentieth century. A nephew of Black Elk, he died in 1989 at age ninety-nine. For many years he presided at important ceremonial occasions, bedecked in a traditional double-trailer eagle-feather headdress (and usually wearing sunglasses). He testified before Congress concerning treaties and Lakota rights, helped to negotiate the settlement that ended the Wounded Knee protest of 1973, and was present at the centennial of the Little Bighorn battle in 1976.

Fools Crow related his life story to Thomas Mails, a Lutheran clergy-man. At the time the two met in 1974, Mails already had published his beautifully illustrated *Mystic Warriors of the Plains*, as well as several other books on Native Americans. Mail's *Sundancing at Rosebud and Pine Ridge* is a primary source on the contemporary Lakota Sun Dance.[57] Two books resulted from Mails's collaboration with Fools Crow. *Fools Crow* is a narrated autobiography.[58] Mails's Lakota friend Dallas Chief Eagle assisted with translation. Although Fools Crow lived in the twentieth century, he relates many nineteenth-century customs and incidents he learned from his father and grandfather. *Fools Crow: Wisdom and Power* is a spiritual autobiography of Fools Crow's teachings.[59]

Overt Christian references abound in the Fools Crow books. In his younger years Fools Crow was a member of the Episcopal Church; later in life he joined the Catholic Church. It is impossible to know whether the Christian twist of Fools Crow's words is his own or that of Mails, whose presentation of Fools Crow is in any case romantic and highly subjective. The result is a perennial appeal of Lakota holy men to the New Age movement.[60] Even so, he reported some astronomical concepts he attributes to nineteenth-century sources.

How can the teachings of the Lakota holy men be of use in a study of nineteenth-century Lakota astronomy? Many of these holy men's ideas and traditions on astronomy are rooted in the past. Scholars might learn how Lakota thought has evolved if they could disentangle the new from the old. Moreover, Lakota culture and astronomy are more like a composite collage than a rigid codified body of knowledge. There are no definitive comments on astronomy from truly nineteenth-century Lakota sources—only images and secondhand accounts. Even so, these limited resources can provide valuable insights for our journey into Lakota astronomy.

2

THE SKY

It will be helpful to review some basic concepts from astronomy and, when doing so, to view the sky from the perspective of a nineteenth-century Native American living on the Great Plains. It is necessary to forget the heliocentric universe of Copernicus and Galileo and to adopt a geocentric view of the sky as seen by people who lived between north latitudes 40° and 50° on the vast prairies of what are now Nebraska, the Dakotas, Wyoming, and Montana.

Archaeoastronomy and Ethnoastronomy

Archaeoastronomy combines the sciences of astronomy and archaeology.[1] Familiar archaeological sites with astronomical importance are Stonehenge and the Mayan ruins of the Yucatan.[2] Some of the archaeological sites in the United States that demonstrate ancient peoples' remarkable understanding of celestial motions are in the Four Corners area of the Southwest: Chaco Canyon, Hovenweep, and Chimney Rock.[3]

The archaeoastronomer uses a topographical map, a surveyor's transit, a compass, and personal knowledge of the rhythms of the night sky to probe the astronomical thought of the builders of these sites. However, the lack of written records hampers the archaeoastronomer's work. Names of the people who built the structures are not known, nor are any details of their personal lives recorded. Moreover, the exact purpose and use of a structure are unknown. Everything must be inferred from the buildings themselves or from fragmentary artifacts found in ruins. For example, much has been learned about Mayan astronomy by deciphering their stone calendars. Very often the exact provenance of the artifacts is unknown.[4]

Practices in more contemporary times can help the archaeoastronomer ask the correct questions of the past. Thus archaeoastronomers in North America often rely on reports early anthropologists gleaned from conversations with Native American peoples they met. For example, John Gregory Bourke made extensive notes on the pueblo dwellers of the Southwest in the late nineteenth century. Bourke mentioned that these historic pueblo people made observations of the movement of the Sun along the horizon.[5] Subsequent research has shown their ancient pueblo ancestors made similar observations of the sunrise position on the horizon.[6]

Ethnoastronomy combines ethnography with astronomy. Ethnography describes human cultures in terms of social structure, language, daily life, and religion. The ethnoastronomer is less concerned with physical evidence in the form of ruins but is more interested in myths, legends, religious belief, and even current practices. Although the ethnoastronomer has access to written records, these were often *not* written by the people being studied, but instead are accounts recorded by people outside the culture. Sometimes artifacts in the form of clothing, household items, or decorative art have celestial images that provide valuable data.

The ethnoastronomer must ask the right questions about a culture's past. Attending a pow-wow in 2014 can be relevant to understanding a similar event that happened in 1881 at the Pine Ridge Reservation even though the pow-wow experience has changed in the past one hundred years. The Native American peoples of the present are the descendants of a people with a rich history and culture. Despite westward progression of white, European culture, Native American cultures have survived, although in evolved forms. Learning as much as possible about Native culture is an important step in exploring their understanding of celestial phenomena. An ethnoastronomer listens, literally and figuratively, to the culture because ethnoastronomy is cultural astronomy.

Libraries, museums, and archives house most of the ethnographic materials useful in ethnoastronomy. Yet an ethnoastronomer visits sites of interest armed with a topographical map, compass, GPS receiver, notebook, and camera. What is the direction (azimuth or compass bearing) of the sunrise on the morning of the solstice? Is there an unobstructed view of the horizon? Are there significant landmarks along the horizon? Where could they have built the Sun Dance lodge? Where would the assembled people have camped? These kinds of questions are asked in the context of astronomy *and* the culture.

The Celestial Sphere

A planetarium is designed to project the sky onto the inside of a hemispherical dome because when we view the night sky, it looks like the inside of a dome. This dome-like appearance of the night sky is called the celestial sphere. Only the upper half of the sphere is visible. The celestial sphere, perhaps better called the celestial hemisphere, ends at the horizon because the Earth blocks the lower half of the sphere. A model of the celestial sphere with the Earth inside is often used in astronomy classes to teach concepts about the motions of the sky. Due to the rotation of the Earth, the stars, the Sun, the Moon, and the planets rise in the east and set in the west. There is no sense of the distance to the stars, although it is clear some celestial objects are brighter than others.

Astronomers define several points and lines on the celestial sphere. The point directly overhead is the zenith. The projection of the Earth's geographic equator onto the sky is the celestial equator. Likewise, the projection of the Earth's North Pole onto the celestial sphere is the north celestial pole. Polaris, currently the North Star, is very near the north celestial pole. It is difficult to see that Polaris describes a tiny circular path about the north celestial pole. The meridian encircles the Earth, connecting the north celestial pole, the zenith, and the south celestial pole, which, of course, is unseen in the northern hemisphere. The meridian divides the sky into east and west halves.

The rising and setting celestial objects are not visible all night, but some stars *are* visible all night and are *always* above the horizon. These are the circumpolar stars and constellations. To the unaided eye, Polaris seems to stand still and all the circumpolar stars describe circles about Polaris. Circumpolar stars are very important in the astronomy of the Native Americans. Facing north in South Dakota and looking at Polaris reveals stars moving in concentric circles. For an observer in the northern Great Plains, all stars of the Little Dipper are circumpolar. Alkaid, the last star in the handle of the Big Dipper (Ursa Major), just skims the northern horizon, and the Big Dipper is totally circumpolar at latitudes greater than 49° N, the northern border of North Dakota.

The latitude of the observer is the crucial factor in determining which stars are circumpolar, rising and setting, or never visible. For residents of the Northern Hemisphere, including the Lakota, Polaris provides a very convenient beacon for determining north. Moreover, the relation between Polaris and the horizon can be used to estimate distance from the Earth's equator. The elevation of the north celestial pole above the northern horizon is the same as the latitude, or distance in degrees, of the observer from the Earth's equator.

Latitude also determines the visibility of a celestial object above the southern horizon. A constellation like Sagittarius in the southern sky is very low in the sky for an observer in the Dakotas. In the southern United States, Sagittarius is higher in the southern sky, but Polaris and the Little Dipper are much lower in the northern sky. This means each Native American culture sees different constellations and bright stars, depending upon their latitude. Hence the importance a particular culture places on a given stellar vista may depend on their latitude in North America. Observers who share a *common* latitude, even though separated in longitude, see the *same* sky each night. This suggests Native American cultures at the same latitude may have similar astronomical lore. Finally, when facing south, the direction to the Sun on the Great Plains, the motions of the sky are east to west, that is, clockwise. This clockwise motion is significant to the Lakota.

To understand Lakota ethnoastronomy, it can be helpful to compare the ethnoastronomy of the Lakota with that of their nearest neighbors. While the Lakota developed their own astronomical ideas and names for objects, they did not do so in isolation from their neighbors. Some sharing of stories probably took place. One explanation of this sharing is the idea of proximity. It is reasonable to assume the Lakota may have been familiar with the stories and practices of other Native American groups with whom they either were in cultural proximity or shared a similar geographical latitude. It may be possible to discover similarities with other Native peoples through their myths about the sky. Hence the astronomy of the Cheyenne or Arapaho, for example, may be of interest.[7]

A good example of how latitude determines what a culture holds astronomically significant is the rising and setting of the Sun. The rising and setting horizon locations (azimuth) of the Sun at the time of the solstices and equinox are important in North American archaeoastronomy. However, for the Maya of premodern Mexico and Central America, the rising and setting locations of the Sun on the two days each year when it passed directly overhead through the zenith are also important. An observer must be between latitudes 23.5° N and 23.5° S (the tropical zone) in order to see the Sun at the zenith. The Sun, Moon, and planets will *never* be seen at the zenith from the United States and Canada because both countries are north of latitude 23.5° N. Thus, although Mexican, Mesoamerican, South American, and North American cultures all saw importance in the solstice and equinox, the zenith passages of the Sun and Moon would not be significant to the Lakota because of their northern location.

When a star or planet is first seen on the eastern horizon before the sunrise, it is said to be in heliacal rise. A long-enduring question in ethnoastronomy is the phenomenon known as the Star of Bethlehem, said to herald the birth of Jesus.[8] The phrase that is often translated "we have seen his star in the east" (Matthew 2:2; ανατολη, *anatolē*, Koine Greek for "arising" or "east") could be translated "we have seen his star in heliacal rise." The heliacal rise of certain stars, such as Venus as the Morning Star, was very important to many ancient cultures, including Native Americans on the Great Plains.

Of course, modern astronomy posits that all daily motions of the celestial sphere are really caused by the Earth's rotating on its axis under the sky. Coupling this daily motion with the Earth's yearly orbital motion around the Sun results in a very complex set of celestial motions. These motions kept some of the best minds in human history occupied for a long time. Native Americans tended to look at the effect, whereas astronomers such as Copernicus, Galileo, Kepler, and Newton sought the cause.

The Stars and Constellations

It is a human trait to look for patterns and to give names to objects and creatures in nature. As observed natural objects, the stars are no exception. Every astronomy student learns star names such as Betelgeuse, Rigel, Polaris, Castor and Pollux, or Sirius. Ancient cultures named these bright stars. For example, Sirius is the Roman version of Osiris, an Egyptian deity. The star names used in Western science today are mostly Arabic, Greek, or Roman names. Thus, modern astronomical science has a cultural antecedent.

Stars form patterns in the night sky that excite the imagination: a water dipper, a bear, a hunter, a swan, a lion, a dragon. Most of the familiar traditional constellation names are also very old Roman or Greek names. In the early twentieth century the International Astronomical Union set the number of constellations at eighty-eight as a matter of convenience. Imaginary boundaries between the constellations allow astronomers to say a particular star or other celestial object is "in Virgo," for example. The proximity of stars in a constellation is an illusion due to an earth-bound perspective. The seven stars of the Big Dipper, a smaller portion of Ursa Major, the Great Bear, appear to move together and form a unified group on the celestial sphere. In the reality of three-dimensional space, of course, the seven brightest stars of the Dipper are many hundreds of light years from one another, and each one has motions unrelated gravitationally to any other star of the Dipper.[9]

The constellations through which the Sun passes on its yearly journey around the sky are significant in many cultures. Aries, Taurus, Gemini, Cancer, Leo, Virgo, Libra, Scorpius, Ophiuchus, Sagittarius, Capricornus, Aquarius, and Pisces are the thirteen constellations of the zodiac or celestial zoo. Because the eight planets orbit the Sun close to the same plane as the Earth, the planets and the Moon also pass through the zodiacal constellations. Although the stars making up the zodiac are the same for all cultures, the number and delineation of constellations vary from culture to culture.

Motions of the Sun, Moon, and Planets

The role of the Sun in Lakota culture is based on the Sun's repetitive annual motions in the sky. Over the course of a year, the constellations change their location in the night sky for a given observer. This is due to the annual motion of the Earth around the Sun. From our earth-bound perspective, the Sun appears to move with respect to the background stars. However, pre-Copernican people said the celestial sphere carried the stars, and Sun, around the Earth. With careful observation, it is possible to determine in which constellation the Sun is located on every day of the year. The position of the Sun among the constellations of the zodiac is due in part to the 23.5° tilt of the Earth's rotational axis to the plane of our orbit around the Sun.

The Sun's apparent annual path against the background of stars is called the ecliptic. In reality the ecliptic is the plane of the Earth's orbit, centered on the Sun. But, as seen from Earth, the traditional twelve constellations of the zodiac lie on the ecliptic. There are actually *thirteen* constellations through which the Sun passes—Ophiuchus being the thirteenth one. Most printed star charts and computer programs that generate a view of the sky show a line representing the ecliptic. The Moon also follows the ecliptic, never being more than about 5° away from it.[10]

Complicating the use of the Sun to mark time are the multiple ways to define a year. The simplest definition of a year uses the annual passage of the Sun through the vernal equinox. When the Sun appears to cross the celestial equator, going northward in the sky, it said to be at the vernal equinox, and this occurs around 21 March each year. In June, at the Northern Hemisphere summer solstice, the Sun reaches its highest point in the southern sky, as seen from the Great Plains. The summer solstice is an important celestial event for determining the time for enacting an important Lakota ritual.[11] Around 21 September each year, the Sun crosses the celestial equator, moving south in the sky, and the

Sun is at the autumnal equinox. After the Sun passes its lowest point in the southern sky at the winter solstice in December, the day begins to lengthen on the Great Plains and elsewhere in the Northern Hemisphere. When the Sun returns to the vernal equinox, one year has passed.

Astronomy distinguishes two types of motion, sidereal and synodic. A sidereal motion is a motion with respect to the celestial sphere or the stars. A synodic motion relates to the repetitive appearance of an object with respect to another object in the sky or on the horizon. The word *synodic* comes from Greek words meaning "to travel together" and has the same origins as the word *synod*. The Moon exhibits these two types of motion. The Moon's sidereal period is 27.33 days. This is the time for the Moon to complete one orbit around the Earth.[12] The Moon's synodic period is 29.5 days and this is the time interval from new moon to new moon—that is, the phases of the Moon span the 29.5-day synodic period. This interval is commonly called the lunar month.

With varying success, premodern peoples figured out the recurring cycles of the Sun and Moon and used these cycles to construct calendar systems. The year is based on the motions of the Sun, and the month is based on the phases of the Moon. The day, of course, is defined by the daily passage of the Sun, but really is one rotation of the Earth on its axis. The fact that the Earth rotates once in 23 hours and 56 minutes instead of exactly 24 hours was of little consequence in the nineteenth century. In addition, for each degree of longitude you travel west, the Sun will cross your meridian four minutes later. Standardized time zones were devised to compensate for the four-minute difference when white America used trains to facilitate the westward growth on the continent.[13]

The only planets visible to the Lakota, and indeed to all premodern, nontelescopic cultures, were Mercury, Venus, Mars, Jupiter, and Saturn. Astronomers designate Mars, Jupiter, and Saturn as superior planets because they orbit the Sun beyond the Earth's orbit. Mercury and Venus are inferior planets because they orbit closer to the Sun than the Earth. This affects when and where they are seen in the sky. Native Americans paid little attention to Mercury, which is so close to the horizon at sunrise and sunset that it is seldom seen. Although the planets also rise along the eastern horizon and set along the western horizon, over a longer period of time they move west to east through the constellations of the zodiac due to the Earth's motion round the Sun.

Because Jupiter's sidereal period around the Sun is 11.86 years, Jupiter moves eastward from one constellation to another on the zodiac in about one year. Mars, on the other hand, being closer to the Sun, moves eastward more quickly through the constellations. When Mars, Jupiter, or Saturn transits the meridian at midnight, it is said to be at opposition because it is opposite in the sky from the Sun.[14]

However, Venus and Mercury *never* transit the meridian *at night*. Venus always sets within about one and a half hours of sunset. This is because Venus is in an inferior orbit about the Sun. Suppose Venus is seen in heliacal rise in the morning sky and is the Morning Star. Over the course of the next several weeks Venus is seen on the eastern horizon every morning at dawn, appearing progressively higher in the sky each morning. Finally, it is at its greatest angular distance from the Sun as seen from Earth. This position is called Greatest Western Elongation. Although it is in the eastern sky, Venus is *west* of the Sun as seen from the Earth. Then Venus slips closer and closer to the eastern horizon each morning until it finally disappears. A few days later it appears on the *western* horizon at sunset as the Evening Star, and it is *east* of the Sun in the sky. It begins a slow climb higher and higher in the sky at sunset until it is at Greatest Eastern Elongation. Then it recedes and approaches the western horizon over the course of several weeks, disappears for a few days, and finally reemerges as the Morning Star, and the cycle repeats again. Although Mars, Jupiter, or Saturn can appear in the morning sky as a morning star, or in the evening sky as an evening star, Venus is typically thought of as *the* Morning Star because of its brilliance compared to Mars, Jupiter, and Saturn.[15]

Time and Calendars

There are three motions to consider when devising a time-keeping system. The Earth rotates on its axis once a day, the Moon goes through its phases in one lunar synodic month, and the Sun passes the vernal equinox once per year. A time-keeping system that uses just one of these motions can be relatively simple, but when two or three of the motions are integrated into one system, problems arise.

Most ancient cultures developed calendars based largely on the motions of the moon. The Moon is not visible for about one day when it is near new moon, and so many ancient calendars have cycles of 28 days. A problem emerges when the lunar calendar is merged with a solar calendar. The solar year is about 356.25 days, and leap years account for the extra one-quarter day. Neither a 28-day lunar month nor the 29.5-day synodic month is evenly divisible into 365.25. About 12.4 lunar synodic months fit into one solar year.[16] Yet modern calendars, based on the Sun's motion through the zodiac, have 12 months. The simple solution, employed by some nontechnological societies, including the Lakota, is to use a purely lunar calendar and account for the problem by introducing a thirteenth month when necessary; that is, about every three years.

An even greater problem arises when specific dates are assigned to celestial events. If the vernal equinox occurs exactly at 12:00 noon on 21 March, one year later it will occur eleven minutes earlier. This results in an accumulated error of about two weeks in ten centuries. In other words, a calendar with absolute dates assigned to the seasons will creep "backward" in time. The date of Easter was determined by the vernal equinox. If nothing was done, ultimately Easter Sunday would eventually coincide with Christmas Day, something not acceptable to the Christian church.

Although this drift of the date of the equinox seems like a nuisance, it actually is a useful tool to archaeoastronomers. To understand this tool and the Gregorian "fix" to the calendar, it is necessary to learn some physics that explains the annual eleven-minute discrepancy. When a small child plays with a top, the top wobbles as it rotates on its axis. This wobble, called precession, is caused by the gravitational force between the Earth and the top. The Earth is similar to the rotating top as it orbits the Sun. Due to the gravitational interplay between the Earth, the Sun, and Moon, the Earth wobbles on its axis. However, this wobble is very, very slow. It takes the Earth about twenty-six thousand years to complete one wobble, one precessional cycle! This means a person will not notice any effect from this wobble in his or her lifetime. Indeed, a civilization must use observations made over the course of several centuries to even deduce this motion.

There is another way to visualize the precession motion. Imagine a flashlight's base, attached to the north pole of a globe, in line with the rotation axis of the globe, and shining upward. The light will shine on the ceiling over the North Pole. Now let the globe wobble as it spins. This will cause the light to describe a circle on the ceiling. Imagine the stars are painted on the ceiling. At one time, the flashlight points to Thuban, and Thuban is the North Star. At another time, many, many years later, it points at Polaris, and Polaris is the North Star. Indeed, five thousand years ago Thuban, which figures prominently in ancient Egyptian astronomy, was near the north celestial pole. Moreover, the position where the Sun crosses the celestial equator at the vernal equinox slowly changes over the precession interval of twenty-six thousand years. Over the long term, this has a dramatic effect on the accuracy of calendars when the calendar date of the vernal equinox is based on the Sun's motion.

The precession of the equinox, as this is called, is an important tool in archaeoastronomy. Imagine a structure aligned to aim at some celestial event, such as the heliacal rising of the star Aldebaran at the June solstice. Several hundred years pass. Aldebaran's rising position along the horizon has changed due to precession, and it is not seen rising at the same azimuth (compass bearing). Because the amount of precession is well known, it is possible to "back up" the sky with a computer program until Aldebaran rises in the right place. The date when a particular structure was aligned is then known. This technique has been used in "Old World" archaeoastronomy, as well as in "New World" archaeoastronomy in Central America. Interestingly enough, precession of the equinox does *not* affect the sunrise or sunset azimuth on a particular day, such as the day of the summer solstice. An object aligned with the solstice sunrise will *always* point toward the rising Sun on the day of the solstice. Likewise, regardless of location on Earth, the equinox sunrise and sunset are always due east and west.[17]

Modern calendars, if they are to be accurate, must account for precession. Our Gregorian calendar, adopted in 1582, is such a calendar.[18] The nature of the Christian liturgical year necessitated a precise system of keeping dates. Easter is the first Sunday after the first "ecclesiastical" full Moon after the vernal equinox. That is precise! However, precession is not a concern if exact dates are not important in determining when to hold a particular ritual.

Astrology, an ancient Babylonian religion, attempts to correlate the configuration of the Sun, Moon, planets, and constellations with events in a person's life. That the fundamental premise of astrology is wrong can be seen in a simple example. Consider a person whose birthday is 6 October 1954. He is said to be a Libra, and that is his birth sign. But on 6 October 1954 the Sun was nowhere near Libra but appeared in the constellation Virgo. This is due to precession. In the course of the twenty-six-thousand-year precession interval, the vernal equinox moves through all thirteen constellations on the ecliptic, spending about two millennia in each constellation.[19]

Phases of the Moon

Native Americans of the nineteenth century knew the time from the sky, and the Moon is a fundamental time keeper. The Moon goes through its monthly cycle of phases from new moon to full moon and again to new moon over the 29.5-day synodic period. When it is new moon, the Moon sets at sunset and is not visible due to its position almost directly between the Earth and the brilliant Sun. As the Moon progresses through the waxing crescent phase, it appears more illuminated each night and higher in the sky above the western horizon. The first quarter moon is seen on the meridian at sunset. Astronomy students who are still learning the phases sometimes call this the half moon, but that describes only its appearance in the sky. The waxing gibbous moon appears even more illuminated and closer to the eastern horizon on successive nights. Finally, the full moon rises at sunset.

During the waning phases, the moon rises later and later each night. The last quarter moon rises at midnight and is seen on the meridian at sunrise. Finally, in one of the most beautiful celestial displays one

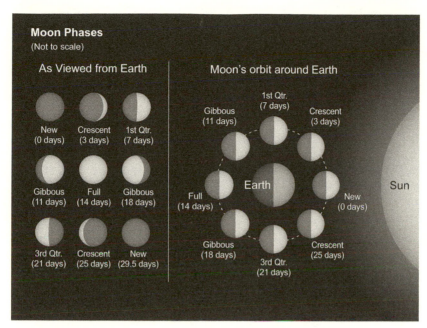

FIG. 2. Moon phases. The set of images on the left shows the appearance of the Moon as seen from the Earth. The images on the right show the orbit of the Moon around the Earth viewed from above the Earth's north pole. The Earth-Sun line is fixed. The side of the Moon facing the Sun is illuminated, the side away from the Sun (the dark side) is shaded. *Starry Night* image courtesy of Starry Night Education, used with permission.

can see, the waning crescent moon hovers above the eastern horizon in heliacal rise just before sunrise. And then the new moon rises and sets again with the Sun. The Lakota have names for each of the phases, usually reflecting the shape of the Moon. For example, *wi mimakanyela*, humpbacked moon, is the waxing gibbous moon.[20]

The phase cycle is caused by the changing location of the Moon with respect to the Earth and Sun. Only the hemisphere facing the Sun is illuminated. So at first quarter moon, when the Moon is on the meridian at about sunset, we see one-half of the illuminated Sun-facing hemisphere.

Eclipses

Eclipses have been observed, understood, and predicted for centuries. Some of the first eclipse predictions go back to the Babylonian culture.

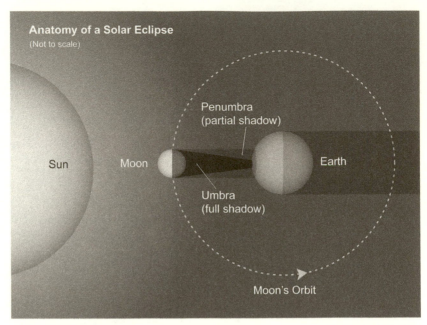

FIG. 3. Anatomy of a solar eclipse. A total solar eclipse viewer in the umbral shadow sees a total eclipse. A viewer in the penumbral shadow sees a partial eclipse. *Starry Night* image courtesy of Starry Night Education, used with permission.

Aristotle, despite his geocentric viewpoint, correctly explained the geometry and cause of lunar and solar eclipses. The nineteenth-century army officers stationed in the West were usually equipped with an astronomical almanac giving the details of upcoming eclipses.

When the new moon is directly between the Earth and the Sun, a solar eclipse occurs. The path of the Sun's shadow during a solar eclipse sweeps across the face of the Earth, and a given location never experiences more than seven and a half minutes of total darkness. The path of totality across the Earth's surface is never more than 270 km wide. Because of the short duration and the highly localized area of totality, very few people actually experience a total solar eclipse firsthand. Hence eclipse aficionados often journey great distances, fly above the clouds along the eclipse path, or travel via a cruise ship to see a total solar eclipse.

Sometimes when the Moon is near its greatest distance from the Earth (apogee), an annular eclipse happens, and a ring (i.e., annulus) of light shows around the Moon. This occurs because the Moon is too small to cover the entire disk of the Sun. Although common, annular eclipses are less dramatic than a total eclipse.

When the Earth comes between the full Moon and the Sun, a lunar eclipse is seen. Because the entire Moon fits within the Earth's shadow, the only requirement for seeing a lunar eclipse is that the observer be on the night side of the Earth. Thus, many more people have seen a lunar eclipse than have seen a solar eclipse. Light is refracted, or bent, when it passes from one medium to another. Moreover, the degree of refraction depends on the color (wavelength) of light. Blue light is more highly refracted than red light, so blue light will come to a focus closer to the refracting medium than red light. Because of the passage of sunlight through the Earth's atmosphere, the sunlight is refracted, and the Moon takes on an eerie orange-red color. Depending on what portion of the Earth's shadow covers the Moon, there are varying degrees of a lunar eclipse. Only when the Moon is completely within the umbral shadow is the eclipse total.

Eclipses are totally predictable by calculating when the Earth, Moon, and Sun will be in a line. Due to a wobble in the orbit of the Moon around the Earth, the regression of the line of nodes, eclipses always reoccur with an interval of 18 years, 11.3 days. This is the saros cycle, first determined by the ancient Babylonian astrologers. This means the solar eclipse on 21 August 2017 visible in the United States will give an encore on 2 September 2035. However, due to the rotation of the Earth on its axis, the eclipse will be seen in a *different* location, namely China, Korea, Japan and the North Pacific. In order to see another eclipse in the *same* location, observers must wait three saros cycles, or 54 years, 34 days.[21]

Because it is possible to predict eclipses, astronomers can calculate when an eclipse occurred in the past, and thus references to eclipses have been used to date ancient writings. For example, in the writings attributed to the Hebrew prophet Amos, there is a reference to a solar eclipse: "I will make the Sun go down at noon and darken the Earth in

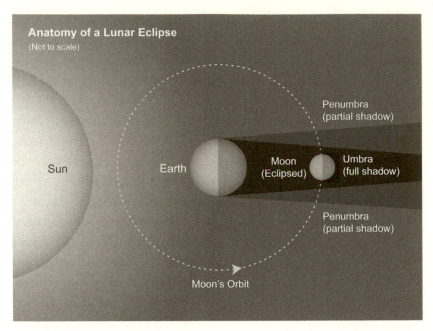

Anatomy of a Lunar Eclipse
(Not to scale)

Sun

Earth

Moon
(Eclipsed)

Umbra
(full shadow)

Penumbra
(partial shadow)

Penumbra
(partial shadow)

Moon's Orbit

FIG 4. Anatomy of a lunar eclipse. Because the entire Moon fits within the Earth's shadow, a lunar eclipse can be seen from anywhere it is night on the Earth. The reddish appearance of the Moon during a lunar eclipse is due to sunlight being refracted as it passes through the Earth's atmosphere. *Starry Night* image courtesy of Starry Night Education, used with permission.

broad daylight" (Amos 8:9, NRSV). This most likely refers to a solar eclipse on 15 June 763 BC that was visible from southern Palestine.[22]

Aurora Borealis

The aurora borealis, or northern lights, occur high in the Earth's atmosphere. Electrons and protons are ejected from the surface of the Sun during a solar flare, which is an energetic disturbance on the surface of the Sun. The solar wind is the stream of these charged particles that eventually encounters the Earth about two days after being ejected. The Earth's magnetic field traps these particles in the radiation belts around the Earth. If the incoming stream of particles is sufficiently energetic, some of the particles can make their way into the upper atmosphere. When the particles interact with oxygen in the upper atmosphere, we see a greenish glow. Likewise, collisions with nitrogen molecules give rise to the red color of the aurora. The aurora borealis is nature's neon sign.

Because of the nature of the Earth's magnetic field, the aurora borealis occurs in the auroral oval, a donut shaped region of space above the north magnetic pole in northern Canada. Traveling north increases the chance of seeing the aurora on a given night. There is, for example, a substantial difference in the probability of seeing the aurora between the Twin Cities metro area of Minnesota and the Boundary Waters Canoe Area Wilderness in the northern part of the state. Thus, most people camping in the Boundary Waters, where it is very dark on a moonless night, bring home stories of spectacular northern lights. Once one gets south of latitude 45° North, the chance of seeing the aurora borealis diminishes greatly.

However, the Sun goes through an eleven-year cycle of activity. When the Sun is more active, the probability of seeing auroras is higher. When the Sun is at the peak of the cycle, more solar flares eject material into the solar wind, and auroras are more common in general and more common at lower latitudes in particular. I have observed the aurora borealis while camping at the Badlands National Park (about latitude 43° N) during a time of maximum solar activity. Did the Lakota see the northern lights?

Comets and Meteors

Comets are the raw materials left over from the formation of the solar system. The long-period comets with successive perihelion passages greater than two hundred years are thought to originate in a vast spherical shell of comets surrounding the solar system. This so-called Oort Cloud is perhaps 50,000 to 100,000 times farther from the Sun than the Earth. Some long-period bright comets in recent history were new to our part of the solar system: Comets Hale–Bopp (1997), Hyakutake (1996), and Holmes (2007). The short-period comets with successive perihelion passages less than two hundred years come from the Kuiper belt of cometary debris between Neptune and Uranus. Comet Halley is the most famous, having shown itself at seventy-six-year intervals in 1834, 1910, and again in 1986.[23]

Many comets are too faint to be seen by the naked eye. Those that do become bright enough to be seen with the unaided eye usually exhibit the distinctive tail of a comet, especially after passing by the sun. A bright comet in the night sky stands out! Comet Halley showed a distinctive tail in 1910. Both Comet Hale–Bopp and Comet Hyakutake became celestial celebrities due to the large number of people who saw them.[24]

A meteor is any space debris that enters the Earth's atmosphere and burns up. This debris can be small chunks of rock left over from the solar system's formation, pieces of cometary debris, or even remnants of rockets and satellites. Of course, the Lakota never saw man-made space junk burn up in the atmosphere in the nineteenth century! Some meteors are sporadic and random. On most clear, moonless nights, perhaps four to five faint meteors are seen every hour. Occasionally a very bright sporadic meteor streaks across the sky leaving a brilliant ionization trail after it that persists for several seconds. These "fireballs" are often seen during daylight hours, and sometimes they even cause sonic booms as they send shock waves through the atmosphere.

A meteor shower occurs when the Earth encounters a celestial debris pile as the planet orbits the sun. A comet that crossed the Earth's orbit left this debris in its wake. When the Earth passes through the debris, a shower occurs, and one may see more than fifty meteor flashes in an hour. These showers are annual phenomena due to the periodicity of the Earth's orbit around the sun. Table 1 summarizes the major showers.[25]

Meteor showers are named for the constellation from which they appear to originate. As many as fifty to sixty meteors per hour can be seen during the Perseid shower in early August. Sometimes meteor showers are even more spectacular. The Leonid shower on 16 November shows a remarkable increase in meteors about every thirty-three years, corresponding to the period of the comet that replenishes the meteoroid swarm. In 1966 observers reported over a hundred thousand Leonid meteors per hour. Although not as spectacular as in 1966, the Leonids put on a good show in the early twenty-first century. In the nineteenth century, 1833 was also a great year to observe Leonids from the Great Plains, as is reflected in many Lakota winter counts.[26]

TABLE 1. Prominent meteor showers

NAME OF SHOWER	DATE OF MAXIMUM INTENSITY	AVERAGE HOURLY RATE	CONSTELLATION OF RADIANT
Quadrantids	3 January	40	Boötes
Lyrids	22 April	15	Lyra
Eta Aquarids	4 May	20	Aquarius
Delta Aquarids	30 July	20	Aquarius
Perseids	12 August	50	Perseus
Orionids	21 October	20	Orion
Taurids	4 November	15	Taurus
Leonids	16 November	15	Leo
Geminids	13 December	50	Gemini
Ursids	22 December	15	Ursa Minor

These basic concepts of astronomy are needed for a fuller understanding of nineteenth-century Lakota astronomy. The emphasis the Lakota placed on them is on the appearance of these celestial phenomena and not on the cause.[27]

Astronomy of the Plains Indians

Archaeoastronomy and ethnoastronomy research spans all continents and all cultures. The astronomy of the nineteenth-century Lakota fits into a larger context. Much of the research in archaeoastronomy and ethnoastronomy in the United States has focused on the pueblos of the Southwest, although numerous sites are located in the eastern United States as well. Chaco Canyon, New Mexico, is the center of the ancient pueblo, or Anasazi, civilization. Chaco has numerous structures that show remarkable alignments with celestial events, such as the summer solstice sunrise.[28] The Chaco culture spread around the Four Corners

FIG. 5. Chimney Rock, Colorado. Chimney Rock National Monument is located twenty miles west of Pagosa Springs, Colorado. It is thought that ancient Puebloans from Chaco Canyon built the village at the top of the mesa. The twin pillars are the remnants, or the chimneys, of an ancient lava flow. This archaeological site is open mid-May through September and is one of the few national monuments managed by the U.S. Forest Service instead of the National Park Service. Visitors must be accompanied by a tour guide to visit the ruins. Because of the nature of the hike to the ruins, visitors should be in good physical condition. Photo by Mark Hollabaugh.

area to other locations, such as Chimney Rock, Colorado. Hovenweep National Monument, straddling the Colorado-Utah border, preserves some remarkably aligned structures from the Mesa Verde culture.[29]

A structure is said to be aligned with the sky when a door, window, or other structural component points, for example, in the direction of a solstice or equinox sunrise or sunset position on the horizon. The "Castle" at Hovenweep has windows that are aligned with the solstice and equinox sunsets. Casa Rinconada in Chaco Canyon shows an alignment with the cardinal directions—north, south, east, and west. Likewise, at Yellow Jacket in Colorado the Anasazi observed the position of the sunrise with respect to a distant object on the horizon. At Chimney Rock (figure 5), the Moon can be seen to rise between the rock pillars

FIG. 6. The Wyoming Medicine Wheel. This archaeological site in the Bighorn Mountains was designated the Medicine Wheel National Historic Landmark in 1969. It has twenty-eight rock spokes, and rock cairns exhibit alignment with the solstice sunrise and sunset. Access is restricted to foot travel due to unfortunate instances of vandalism, and visitors must walk the last mile to the top of Medicine Mountain. Visitors may hike to the wheel from late June until the first significant snowfall in autumn. A special permit is needed to enter the wheel enclosure. There are no nearby facilities, although the U.S. Forest Service Bald Mountain campground is near the turnoff from U.S. Route 14A to the Medicine Wheel. Photo by Mark Hollabaugh.

each time the Moon comes to its northern most rising position along the horizon, about every nineteen years.[30]

The Wyoming Medicine Wheel, a northern plains archaeological site, has been a center of attention for North American archaeoastronomers. University of Colorado solar physicist John Eddy studied this site in the 1970s.[31] The Medicine Wheel lies at an elevation of 9600 feet in the northern Bighorn Mountains. The stone wheel consists of twenty-eight spokes radiating out from a central cairn. Six stone cairns reside on or near the rim of the structure. Pairs of cairns show alignments with the June solstice sunrise and sunset. It makes sense the Medicine Wheel was used only in June at the summer solstice because of the inaccessibility of the top of Medicine Mountain in December.[32]

Using the precession of the equinox to date the structure, Eddy suggested the Medicine Wheel is about three hundred to eight hundred years old. In all likelihood it was no longer used when the use of horses became pervasive among the Plains Indians. The builders of the Medicine Wheel have not been identified. It probably was not the Lakota, although they may have known about it and even visited it. Contemporary Lakota refer to the Medicine Wheel as the "Star-sighting Place."[33] The location is within the traditional territory of the Crow, with whom the Lakota historically were less than friendly. Today, the U.S. Forest Service maintains the site with the cooperation of the Crow people.

A danger faces archaeoastronomers. It is possible to read too much into a site. The caveat is, "If you seek an alignment, you'll probably find it." Archaeoastronomy must be approached with a healthy dose of skepticism if one is to avoid errant conclusions. As an example, consider the case of a stone wall at Blue Mound State Park in southwestern Minnesota. Some writers and the local populace have suggested that an east-west-oriented fieldstone wall is an equinox marker. The evidence supporting this is minimal and perhaps non-existent. Sometimes a stone wall is just a stone wall.[34]

The study of Great Plains ethnoastronomy is active today. The research has focused on Native American legends and calendars. Von Del Chamberlain's important study of winter count calendars included many references to Lakota winter counts. His research provided many ideas for this book. Chamberlain also studied one specific group, the Skidi Pawnee, using the great Leonid meteor shower of 1833 as his focal point.[35] In addition to providing an important summary of North American archaeoastronomy and ethnoastronomy in his book *Living the Sky*, Ray Williamson has also added much to the discussion of legends of the Native Americans related to the sky.[36] The Lakota are discussed in these books, although not extensively.

Only one book has been published specifically on the contemporary astronomy of the Lakota. Ronald Goodman, who was a non-Lakota instructor at Sinte Gleska University on the Rosebud Reservation, edited *Lakota Star Knowledge* after interviewing many late twentieth-century

Lakota.[37] Goodman also wrote an interpretation of the significance of the stars in the Lakota story "The Chief Who Lost His Arm."[38]

Original nonmediated sources on the astronomy of the nineteenth-century Lakota are difficult to locate. Nonetheless, all prior studies have contributed useful material. From Chamberlain to Goodman, from Eddy to Williamson, there have been suggestions where to look for information and how to ask the right questions when new material *is* discovered. Knowing what to research should be based on what we do not know or understand.

Viable Lakota ethnoastronomy must begin with the Lakota culture. Understanding history, culture, religion, and language is the foundation for analyzing nineteenth-century Lakota astronomy. The most important unifying concept from Lakota culture for ethnoastronomy is *wakháŋ*.

3

LAKOTA CULTURE

At its heart, ethnoastronomy is the examination of the role of astronomy in a culture. Raymond DeMallie states why focusing on Lakota culture helps clarify Lakota ethnoastronomy. Although he addresses ethnohistory, his words apply equally well to ethnoastronomy.

> In order to explicate the events of the past we have to explore the mental worlds in which those actions took place, the cultural knowledge on the basis of which choices were made. To attempt an understanding of the Sioux past it is essential to come to an understanding of Sioux culture, which provides the context. The need to understand systems of thought—the norms and values of a particular group at a particular time—involves us in an essentially synchronic reconstruction achieved by building up a picture of component parts (culturally specific symbols and meanings) while at the same time taking it apart to analyze each element separately.[1]

Belief Systems

There is no direct answer to the question, "What did the Lakota believe about the stars?" The question implies there is some sort of *unified* body of knowledge called Lakota astronomy. Western science has codified Newton's laws of motion and universal gravitation, Maxwell's equations of electromagnetism, and the unified theories of particle physics. Although there are as many different ways to teach Newton's laws as there are physics professors, the laws themselves are applicable in all frames of reference, to use the language of physics. The construction of knowledge into physical laws is a Western scientific approach and is not particular to the Lakota ways of looking at the world. Unity in the Lakota world is of a different kind, and Lakota culture actually exhibits diverse beliefs. Diversity of beliefs extends beyond the Lakota and indeed transcends all Native American groups. At the Fifth Oxford Conference in Santa Fe in 1996, George Lankford asked the important question, "How many astronomies are there in North America?" The question points to the variation in practice and belief among North American Native people.[2]

This brings us to an important epistemological point. There is no such thing as one Lakota "system" of "orthodox" belief. Although Christianity organized its beliefs into a set of doctrines, there is still much diversity of belief and practice. However, confessional statements like the Nicene Creed, the Augsburg Confession, or the decrees of the Council of Trent simply do not exist in the traditional Lakota world as unifying dogmas. Lakota belief is not "static" and exhibits diversity.[3]

A twentieth-century noncelestial example illustrates the lack of systemization. A common visual image in contemporary Lakota life, apparently going back to the Lakota holy man Black Elk, is the four-color medicine wheel. The quadrants of the circle are red, white, yellow, and black. Fools Crow also defines these four "spiritual colors" and says he got them from his grandfather.[4] Generally the four colors are fairly constant, but the quadrant location of the red, white, yellow, and black varies. In the symbol of Sinte Gleska University on the back of *Lakota Star Knowledge* and on the SGU website, blue replaces black. However, on the sign for the university on U.S. Highway 18 in Mission, red, white, yellow, and *black* are used.[5]

Although one cannot say, "This is what *the* Lakota believed about the stars," it is possible to discuss what a *specific* Lakota person said about the stars or what the Lakota consistently related. Despite the lack of a neatly described, unified, systematic view, common themes and practices are evident, but variants exist as well in Lakota ways of thinking and doing. Ambiguity and inconsistency, and even outright contradictions, occur in what the Lakota say about the Sun, Moon, and stars. This tension is basic to Lakota culture and to their understanding of the sacred and the natural world.

Lakota astronomy is *not* a separate abstract concept but is embedded in their cultural worldview. This worldview can be expressed in four fundamental themes: the four virtues, the numbers four and seven, the four directions, and the four colors. Seven sacred Lakota ceremonies are an outward demonstration of this worldview. A final crucial consideration is the concept *wakháŋ* as the nineteenth-century Lakota understood it. It is important to note that although the discussion of this worldview is based largely on twentieth-century voices, they can give us insights into how the Lakota may have viewed the heavens in the nineteenth century.

The Four Virtues

A set of deeply held moral values lies at the heart of Lakota society. Contemporary Lakota, drawing on the traditions of their ancestors, enumerate this as the four virtues. Although there are usually four, and the exact names may vary, the Lakota describe positive behavior in the four virtues: wisdom (*wóksape*), bravery (*wóohitika*), fortitude (*wówachiŋthaŋka*), and generosity (*wacháŋtognaka*). Men who exhibited all four of these virtues were extolled as *wicháša wakháŋ*, holy men. Women were expected to demonstrate the virtues of truthfulness and childbearing instead of wisdom and generosity.[6]

As a sign of bravery a Lakota warrior would dash up to an opponent and touch him or "count coup." The war whoops often associated with the Indian in popular accounts served to encourage bravery in one's companions. Bravery was not merely a concept—it was an action. A brave man wasn't necessarily the one who had killed the most enemies in battle, but the one who had sacrificed and endured the most on behalf of the people. Grandparents told children stories to teach the value of bravery. Bravery was closely associated with fortitude.[7]

It probably was the Lakota sense of fortitude that enabled them to survive and keep their culture, language, and spirituality intact. Extreme fortitude is required to endure the pain of the Sun Dance. The stoicism sometimes associated with the Lakota is the visible face of this virtue. A better word than stoicism might be *reserve*, because a Lakota person may hold back a bit.

Generosity is best seen today in the *Naǧí gluhápi* (or *naǧí gluškápi*), the Releasing of the Spirit ritual. This is the "Give Away" that occurs when a person dies and often one year later as a part of a memorial. Not only are the used goods of the deceased given away, but new blankets, quilts, and other gifts are presented to members of the community. In 1998, I helped a Lakota friend by transporting dozens of new quilts and Pendleton blankets from Sioux Falls to Rosebud for a Give Away. A feast of food accompanied the Give Away, and an intentional overabundance of food ensured everyone took leftovers home. Several years earlier, Father Noah Brokenleg, the deceased Lakota elder and Episcopal priest who was being remembered at this event, had provided a good description of this ritual that focuses on the living. "The 'give-away' is a misnomer. It really is a sharing and a remembering of the deceased person. It's a way of beginning over again. You put the past behind you and start over."[8]

The Numbers Four and Seven

The Lakota recognize four virtues, and this may not be a mere accident. Four and seven appear frequently in Lakota stories, rituals, songs, legends, and prayers, particularly in the twentieth century. "[Four] relates to what is perceptually all persons, places, and objects in nature—the four directions, the four seasons, the four stages of life, four kinds of living things, four phases of a plant, and so forth."[9] James Walker elaborated on the fourfold division. Note that he comments this grouping was in "former times." This suggests the concept goes back into the nineteenth century.

> In former times the Lakota grouped all their activities by four's [*sic*]. This was because they recognized four directions: the west, the north, the east, and the south; four divisions of time: the day, the night, the moon [i.e., month], and the year; four parts to everything that grows from the ground: the roots, the stem, the leaves, and the fruit; four

kinds of things that breathe: those that crawl, those that fly, those that walk on four legs, and those that walk on two legs; four things above the world: the sun, the moon, the sky, and the stars; four kinds of gods: the great, the associates of the great, the gods below them, and the spirit kind; four periods of human life: babyhood, childhood, adulthood, and old age; and finally, mankind had four fingers on each hand, four toes on each foot, and the thumbs and the great toes of each taken together are four. Since the Great Spirit caused everything to be in four's, mankind should do everything possible in four's.[10]

The sacredness of the number seven, perhaps not as obvious, may be linked to what the Lakota observed and experienced. First and most importantly, there are the Seven Council Fires of the larger Sioux nation and the seven divisions of the Teton Lakota. According to Black Elk and others, there are seven important Lakota rituals. Astronomically, seven is significant. There are seven stars in the Big Dipper, the most recognizable part of Ursa Major. There are seven bright stars in the Pleiades, also called the Seven Sisters. Contemporary Lakota artist Sandy Swallow-Morgan captured the significance of the number seven in her print titled *Seven Councils*. Hovering above seven teepees are seven moons: three waxing lunar phases, a full moon, and three waning lunar phases.

The number twenty-eight occurs frequently in Native American lunar cycles due to the number of days in the lunar synodic month when the moon is visible. In the early twentieth century Black Elk explained the sacredness of twenty-eight when he commented, "add four sevens you get twenty-eight." He continued:

Also the moon lives twenty-eight days, and this is our month; each of these days of the month represents something sacred to us: two of the days represent the Great Spirit; two are for Mother Earth; four are for the four winds; one is for the Spotted Eagle; one for the sun; and one for the moon; one is for the Morning Star; and four for the four ages; seven are for our seven great rites; one is for the buffalo; one for the fire; one for the water; one for the rock; and finally one is for the two-legged people. If you add all these days up you will see that they come to twenty-eight. You should also know that the buffalo has twenty-eight ribs, and that in our war bonnets we usually use twenty-eight feathers. You see, there is a significance for everything, and these are the things that are good for men to know, and to remember.[11]

But, why is the number seven significant? If the number three was sacred, then the stars of Orion's belt could be a celestial reminder of that number. Or the five bright stars of Cygnus that form the Northern Cross could represent the sacredness of five. Some arrangement of stars can be found to represent any number or object. Meaning can be transferred from earth to sky as well as from sky to earth.

There are probably several reasons for the modern sacredness of seven beyond four sevens equaling twenty-eight, the number of days when the Moon is visible. Today there are seven major groups of the Teton Lakota. Twentieth-century Lakota identify seven sacred sites in the Black Hills, a geographical (and political) reason.[12] There are seven days in the week in the modern calendar. It is possible that late nineteenth-century Lakota saw sacredness in the number seven after learning from Catholic missionaries about the seven sacraments, seven gifts of the Spirit, seven virtues, and the seven deadly sins.

One can construct significance to everything, and these numbers— four, seven, and twenty-eight—keep recurring in Lakota legends and rituals. The number four is typified by the four colors and four cardinal directions.

The Four Colors and Four Directions

Colors are used symbolically in all cultures and especially in religion.[13] The colors red, yellow, white, and black occur frequently in Lakota art and ritual. Sometimes blue replaces black, as was noted earlier. From the Canadian Sioux comes an explanation of the four colors red, yellow, white, and black:

Another important Sioux symbol is the Greek (equal-armed) cross. This symbolizes the four winds or directions, the corners of the universe. Each point of the cross has its own color symbol, white for north, red for east, yellow for south, and blue or black for west. Each of the two arms of the cross is also symbolic. The arm extending from east to west is called the *c'aŋkú dúta*, the "red road," the path of good. The arm extending from south to north is the *c'aŋkú sápa*, the "black road," the path of war and calamity. Both roads are traveled during life, and although the red road is the better and the preferred path, the warrior must travel the black road to protect his family and tribe.[14]

In *Black Elk Speaks* the directionality of the two roads is reversed, red going from north to south and black from east to west. Walker discusses the Lakota ornamental use of colors where red and blue are symbolic instead of red and black:

Men might paint any portion of their persons above or below their hips. All such paintings were either insignia, badges, or symbolic, except such as were placed on the face for mere embellishment. Each of the conventional designs had a conventional signification, the most of them referring to deeds done in war or chase. The badges were insignia of office and were painted on the face. The symbolic were solid colors without figuration. The colors were red and blue. The entire person painted red was symbolic of holiness. Ordinarily only holy men were thus painted, though one who had danced the Sun Dance and lived a life of rectitude according to the ethics of the Sioux was entitled to so paint his body, the scars incurred while dancing the Sun Dance differentiating him from a holy man. A holy man might add the symbolic blue, placed as broad stripes around the head or around the upper part of the chest, which signified that he had communicated with the Great Spirit, the Sky. A red stripe painted across the forehead horizontally was an insignia that a man belonged to the class of ceremonially adopted persons (*Hunka*), the same as the class of women so decorated.[15]

The sky appears red at sunrise or sunset and blue during the day. The name of the famous Lakota chief Red Cloud is *Maȟpíya Luta*, literally "cloud red." The word *luta* is also used to describe the red sky at sunrise or sunset. *Maȟpíya* is the word the missionaries chose to translate the Christian concept Heaven and can mean the night sky or the heavens in an astronomical sense.

It is possible that the codification of the colors red, black, yellow, and white occurred in the 1970s.[16] These colors also have been associated with the seasons in modern times.[17] Powers's assignment of directions to the colors is different from that reported by Howard but follows that given by Fools Crow.[18] This is another good example of the diversity in assigning the colors to the cardinal directions. The actual etiology of the four colors will continue to be the subject of debate and discussion. How important these colors were to the nineteenth-century Lakota is not clear. What is clear, however, is the importance of the circle, colors, and the four directions in the twentieth century.

As James Howard points out, "One of the principal religious symbols of the Sioux, a symbol that illustrates the completeness and interrelatedness of all things in nature, is the hoop or circle." He retells a humorous story about the circle told by a Canadian Dakota, Sam Buffalo:

> The circle is the most *wakan* design of my people. It reflects the way we do things. My people dance in a circle. They used to camp in a circle with the *t'iyót'ipi* ['soldier lodge'] in the center. Indians always sit in a circle when they are counciling [*sic*] or even just visiting. One time I bet a white friend that if we came to the pulp mill [in Prince Albert, Saskatchewan] at lunch time we would find the Indian workers sitting in a circle. Sure enough, there they were, in a circle, and I won my bet.[19]

The circle unifies the directions because "a circle is an emblem of all four of the units of time, each of which, day, night, moon [i.e., month], and year, goes in a circle."[20] The basis for the Lakota ideas of time and the seemingly never-ending cycles of nature are emerging. The circle is inherent in the motion of the sun, the moon, and the stars. The clockwise motion of the Sun (when facing south in the Northern Hemisphere) is

TABLE 2. The fourfold divisions
according to William K. Powers

DIRECTION	SEASON	COLOR
West	Fall	Black
North	Winter	Red
East	Spring	Yellow
South	Summer	White

also significant.[21] The circle is a sacred shape for reasons similar to the sacredness of the number four. As Walker states,

> The Oglala believe the circle to be sacred because the Great Spirit caused everything in nature to be round except stone. Stone is the implement of destruction. The sun and the sky, the earth and the moon are round like a shield, though the sky is deep like a bowl. Everything that breathes is round like the body of a man. Everything that grows from the ground is round like the stem of a tree. Since the Great Spirit has caused everything to be round mankind should look upon the circle as sacred for it is the symbol of all things in nature except stone. It is also the symbol of the circle that marks the edge of the world and therefore of the four winds that travel there.[22]

Fools Crow reports that his father said that in the "early days" the Lakota thought that the "stars were round, and that they turned just like the earth."[23] Although we do not precisely know what he meant by "early days," we could surmise Fools Crow means the nineteenth century, given he was born around 1890. Even though any culture can conclude, as did the Greeks, that the Earth is round, there is no evidence from other sources that the nineteenth-century Lakota knew the Earth rotates about its polar axis.

The night sky is both simple and complex. One could create a complex system to explain what one sees in the heavens, as Ptolemy did. One could look heavenward and see a wholeness and unity in nature: stars dancing in circles around the pole, the Moon going through predictable cycles, the Sun making a clockwise daily journey. The Lakota came to the same conclusions as the ancestors of modern science, the Greeks— it's all about circles. As DeMallie points out,

> The preeminent tangible symbol of traditional Lakota religion was the circle. The Lakotas perceived everything in the natural world as circular (except rock), for roundness was indicative of life itself. For this reason the circle was held to be sacred (*wakan*). Sun, sky, earth, moon, a human body, a tree trunk, day, night, a year, a man's life—all these were sacred circles. In respect for this natural order, the Lakotas made circular tipis, pitching them in camp circles, and sat in circles for ceremonial occasions. The wholeness of the circle, without beginning or end, represented the wholeness and oneness of the universe.[24]

Oneness with the creation does not stop with the design of the camp circle or how one decorates a teepee. The Lakota reached skyward in an endless attempt to comprehend the sacred. They reached for the sacred through ritual experience.

The Seven Sacred Rites

Many accounts have been written of the seven sacred rites of the Lakota. As identified by Black Elk in the twentieth century, those rites are *Nağí gluhápi* (*nağí gluškápi*), Keeping of the Spirit and Releasing of the Spirit; *Haŋblécheyapi*, Crying for a Vision or Vision Quest; *Huŋkáyapi*, The Making of Relatives; *Išnála awíchalowaŋ*, The Young Woman's Puberty Rite; *Inípi*, The Sweat Lodge for Cleansing of the Spirit, also known as the rite of purification; *Thápa waŋkáyeyapi*, Throwing the Ball, also called Making the Choice to Stand and Reach; and *Wiwáŋyaŋg wachípi*, The Sun Dance.[25] While it is not surprising there are seven rites today, we do not know which came first, the sacredness of the number seven because of the seven main divisions of the Teton Lakota and the seven rites, or a prior etiology of the sacredness of seven.

The central purpose of the seven rites is to strengthen the community and the individual's relationship to it. None of the rites is a solitary activity. Even in the Vision Quest, the "lamenter," as Black Elk calls him, goes through elaborate preparations with the "helpers." The rites are not isolated from one another. A "Sweat" is often the prelude to a Vision Quest or the Sun Dance.[26] The Sun Dance, also known as the "Dance Looking at the Sun," is the most important sacred rite of the Lakota. A ritual focusing on the Sun necessarily involves ethnoastronomy. The goal of any of the rites is the physical and moral strengthening of the individual and the larger community to which he or she belongs.

Wakháŋ — The Sacred

Although the most common translation of wakháŋ is "sacred" or "holy," the meaning of this concept is elusive. Wakháŋ also implies "mystery" and must be understood in the cultural context from which the concept takes its meaning. Buechel's Lakota-English Dictionary gives several connotations to the word: "sacred, consecrated; special; incomprehensible; possessing or capable of giving . . . an endowed spiritual quality which is received or transmittable to beings making for what is specially good or bad."[27]

Places like the Black Hills can be wakháŋ. The Hills are isolated from surrounding mountain ranges. The dark pines, appearing black from a distance, stand in sharp contrast to the gray, brown, and pink sandstones of the Badlands to the east. In the 1800s the Lakota often ventured into the Hills to hunt and to spend the winter out of the reach of the frequent blizzard conditions on the prairie. The Hills are geologically and geographically unique, possessing a quality unlike the surrounding plains. In at least one Lakota creation myth the first man is said to enter the world through Wind Cave in the Black Hills.[28] The sacred nature of the Black Hills is the reason why the Hills remain a point of contention between modern Lakota and the U.S. government. One of the most sacred Black Hills sites today is Bear Butte (mahtó pahá), a volcanic outcropping on the northeastern edge of the Hills just north of Sturgis, South Dakota. Bear Butte is the "center of the universe" for many Lakota and Northern Cheyenne. To this day Native Americans in

FIG. 7. Bear Butte. Bear Butte State Park is located 10 miles northeast of Sturgis, South Dakota. The 1.85 mile self-guided trail to the summit of the butte affords spectacular views of the surrounding prairies. Because many Lakota and Cheyenne use this as a pilgrimage site, visitors should respect the privacy of anyone praying and not disturb any cloths tied to trees. Several years ago a wildfire denuded the butte of most trees, and the lack of shade makes for an arduous hike in summer. There is a visitor center open May through September. The park is also the northern terminus of the 111-mile Centennial Trail. Photo by Mark Hollabaugh.

general, and Lakota and Northern Cheyenne in particular, journey to Bear Butte for Vision Quests. Prayer bundles and red, white, black, and yellow ribbons adorn the trees. Walking to the top of Bear Butte is an experience akin to any other religious pilgrimage.

Wakháŋ goes to the very core of what it means to be a Lakota. James Walker offers some valuable insights into the meaning of this concept for the nineteenth-century Lakota. In the following lengthy excerpts, Walker enumerates Lakota elders' examples of what is *wakháŋ*. It is important to realize these are the opinions of the people he interviewed and are not a unified Lakota view. Note the number of references to the Sun, the Moon, and the stars. First Walker begins by relating what he heard from Good Seat:

Wakan was anything that was hard to understand. A rock was some-times *wakan*. Anything might be *wakan*. When anyone did something that no one understood, this was *wakan*. If the thing done was what no one could understand, it was *Wakan Tanka*. How the world was made is *Wakan Tanka*. How the sun was made is *Wakan Tanka*. How men used to talk to the animals and birds was *Wakan Tanka*. Where the spirits and ghosts are is *Wakan Tanka*. How the spirits act is *wakan*. A spirit is *wakan* . . .

A spirit is like a shadow. It is nothing. There are other beings. But they are not spirits. They belong to the world. They are *wakan*. They have power over men and things. They are *wowakan* (belong to the mysterious). They are *taku wakan* (things mysterious).

The *Wakinyan* (Thunderbird) is one. The *Tatanka* (Great Beast [i.e., buffalo]) is one; the *Unktehi* (One Who Kills), *Taku Skanskan* (Changes Things), *Tunkan* (Venerable One), *Inyan* (Stone), *Heyoka* (Opposite to Nature), *Waziya* (Of the North), *Iya, Tate* (Wind), *Yate* (North Wind), *Yanpa* (East Wind), *Okaga* (South Wind), *Iktomi* (Spider-like). These are all *wakan*. The sun, the moon, the morning star, the evening star, the north star, the seven stars [i.e., Big Dipper], the six [*sic*] stars [i.e., Pleiades],[29] the rainbow—these are all *wakan*.[30]

At first glance, it seems as if *everything* was *wakháŋ* for Good Seat. In one sense that is true, because so much of the Lakota world is ex-traordinary, and "*Wakan* was anything that was hard to understand." However, notice the *wakháŋ* or "mysterious" things Good Seat describes are things humans cannot create or control. Good Seat's list of these objects, animals, and phenomena is made up of aspects of the world that have kept the best scientists, philosophers, and theologians busy for centuries. That is, they are extraordinary. Something that is *wakháŋ* does not reach the modern analytical mind but rather catches the spirit of a person and causes him or her to reflect on the meaning of existence. *Wakháŋ* things are those experiences, events, or objects that are worthy of wonder. Indeed, the extraordinary Black Hills are a geographical phenomenon worthy of wonder. One can feel on top of the world when standing at the summit of Bear Butte. Likewise the Moon, planets, and stars, glimmering in the night sky, have fascinated humans since they first looked skyward. A contemporary perspective says *wakháŋ* means "energy" or "power." It is "the power to give life and to take it away."[31] From the viewpoint of a modern astronomer, the wonder one feels when looking at the night sky comes from a realization of the energy of the universe. The carbon, nitrogen, and oxygen atoms so essential to organic life were formed in the thermonuclear furnace of first-generation stars billions of years ago: the stars give life through their power.

Following his transcription of Good Seat's conversation, Walker adds his own interpretation of *wakháŋ*. Here again he draws on his conversations with many Lakota, allowing them to interpret one another:

Long ago, the Lakotas believed that there were marvelous beings whose existence, powers or doings they could not understand. These beings they called *Wakan Kin* (The *Wakan*). There were many of the *Wakan*, some good and some bad. Of the *Wakan* who were good, some were greater than others. The greater were called *Wakan Wankantu* (Superior *Wakan*). The others were called *Taku Wakan* (*Wakan* Relatives). They were not relatives the same as a father or a brother but like the Lakota are all relatives to each [other]. The bad *Wakan* were not relative either to the good or to each other . . .

The old Lakotas also believed that each thing except the *Wakan* and mankind had something like a spirit. This something they called a *nagila* (spiritish). These *nagipila* (spirits-ish) were *wakanpila* (*wakans*-ish). Ordinarily, the people call a *wakanla, wakan*. *Wakan Tanka* (Great *Wakan*) and *Wakan kin* mean the same. In former times the term *Wakan Tanka* was seldom used but now it is used more often than *Wakan kin*. The younger Oglalas mean the God of the Christians when they say *Wakan Tanka*. When a shaman says *Wakan Tanka*, he means the same as *Wakan Kin* as used in former times. This means all the *Wakan* and the *Wakanpila*, both of mankind and of other things, for the old Oglalas believed that these were all the same as one. This is *kan* (incomprehensible, an incomprehensible fact that cannot be demonstrated).

Things other than the *Wakan* are called *wakan* by the Lakotas because they amaze as the *Wakan* do. *A wicasa wakan* (*wakan* man, shaman) is so called because he has marvelous power and wisdom so that he can speak and do as the *Wakan* do. *Mini wakan* (*wakan* water, intoxicating liquor) is so called because its effects are like those of the *Wakan*. *Maza wakan* (*wakan* iron, a gun) is called *wakan* because a shot from it is like the act of the *Wakan* . . .

When an Oglala is amazed by anything he may say that it is *wakan* meaning that it is *wakanla* (like *wakan*). It appears from the above information that "divine" is the proper interpretation of *wakan*.[32]

It is important to note that these characterizations are based on traditional nineteenth-century Lakota beliefs as recorded by white men, such as Walker. *Wakháŋ* interpreted as "divine" shows a later decidedly Christian influence. Encounters with whites in general, and Christian missionaries in particular, have had an effect on modifying the traditional nineteenth-century beliefs. Indeed, George Sword was an Episcopal deacon, and Black Elk was a Roman Catholic catechist. Such relationships certainly influenced the interpretive comments by twentieth-century Lakota elders on older traditions.

Good Seat hints at this when he says, "I am an old man. I know what my father said. I know what his father said. In the old times, the Indians knew many things. Now they have forgotten many things. The white men have made them forget that which their fathers told them."[33] Walker alludes to this modification when he comments, "The *younger* [emphasis added] Oglalas mean the God of the Christians when they say *Wakan Tanka*." The missionaries who translated the Bible into Lakota used *Wakháŋ Tháŋka* to convey the Christian idea of God. Whites usually translated *Wakháŋ Tháŋka* from Lakota into English as "Great Spirit."

Outsiders to the Lakota culture may have a difficult time understanding the meanings of *wakháŋ*. In a white American way of thinking, there are distinctions between the natural and the supernatural, between the secular and the sacred, between the human and the divine, between the spirit and the sky. These distinctions are blurred or perhaps even non-existent in the minds of many Lakota because these dichotomies do not exist. The important traditional distinction for the Lakota was between the ordinary and the extraordinary.

More than anything, incomprehensibility, uniqueness, and wonder characterize the cosmos for the Lakota. Thus, the best interpretations of *wakháŋ* are "incomprehensibility," "that which is different," and "worthy of wonder." The best interpretation of *Wakháŋ Tháŋka* might be "the great incomprehensibility," as awkward as that phrase sounds. The Lakota were able to share in this wonder, mystery, and incomprehensibleness through their rituals and their partnership with the natural world. Interestingly enough, although Lakota *belief* shows many variations, the *rituals* are generally more uniform. This may be because the rituals are a collective, community effort, serving to strengthen kinship ties.[34]

In the following chapters, an ambiguity will emerge in what the Lakota said specifically about the stars. Raymond DeMallie offers an assessment that may explain the tension:

> In the nineteenth-century Lakota system of belief, the unity of *Wakan Tanka* embraced all time and space, together with the entirety of being, in a universe where the place of human beings was minor but well-defined. Because this universe was most fundamentally characterized by incomprehensibility, it was beyond humanity's power ever to know it fully, and perhaps it was this futility that made the quest for understanding of the *wakan* the driving force in Lakota culture.[35]

Ultimately any attempt at understanding the role of celestial phenomena in Lakota culture must also come to terms with an understanding of *wakháŋ*. For us, as for the Lakota, it may be futile to come to any final conclusions that can satisfy a twenty-first-century analytical, scientific mind. Lakota ethnoastronomy remains firmly rooted in Lakota culture.

4

THE STARS AND CONSTELLATIONS

Although the night sky is filled with surprises in the form of comets, meteor showers, and the northern lights, some aspects like the stars' nightly movement and the constellations' annual parade across the sky seemingly never change. Most introductory astronomy students have noticed these phenomena before they actually understand that the cause of celestial motions is the dual motion of the Earth rotating on its axis and revolving around the Sun. Today, living in a technological age centuries after Copernicus and Galileo, people take the heliocentric nature of the solar system for granted. However, in order to fully view the night sky through Lakota eyes, observers must adopt an Earth-centered perspective. The stars, the Sun, the Moon, and the planets move around earthbound people, who are once again the center of the universe.

The Night Sky

To modern city dwellers the air seems fresher, the water purer, and the sky brighter in the traditional territory of the Lakota. The vividness of the stars, Moon, and planets from the western plains and mountains is truly remarkable. This perception is not solely due to a psychological urge by modern city dwellers to experience the wide open spaces. In the western Dakotas, northwestern Nebraska, Wyoming, and Montana the astronomical seeing is optimal.[1]

The officers of the U.S. Army who ventured west after the Civil War were, for the most part, literate, and many became devoted journal writers. Lieutenant Charles H. Springer, an emigrant from Würtemberg, Germany, traveled west in 1865 at age twenty-six. Springer made numerous references in his journal to the appearance of the night sky. "The sky is clear and the heaven covered with stars," he wrote on 29 July 1865. On 8 August, while camped at the Badlands, which he referred to as the "Valley of Death," Springer said he "looked out upon the moon and starlit night." Several weeks later, on 27 September, near Laramie Peak in southeastern Wyoming, he noted that after a storm "the sky was brilliantly studded with a myriad of stars."[2] Springer experienced a common sight in the high plains and mountains of the West—clear night skies with exceptional clarity. This was due in part to the lower moisture content of the air and lack of light and air pollution from cities.

Army officer John G. Bourke also caught some of the beauty of the night sky in the heart of Lakota country, now Wyoming. Bourke's ability to describe his surroundings was first-rate. In this narrative from his diary Bourke vividly captures the allure of the night sky in the open spaces of the West. He mentions the use of the North Star to determine the direction of travel.

MARCH 7TH. [1876] DAY BLUSTERING.

Remained in Camp all day, busy in writing up notes and making the necessary preparations for our movement. At night, about 7 O'clock, by the light of a very fine three quarters moon, commenced our march, which lay to the West for two miles and then moved towards the North star for the remainder of the distance which summed up thirty-five miles.

At first the country had the undulating contour of that near old Fort Reno, already visited, but soon the prairie swells were superseded by bluffs of bolder and bolder character until as we came to the summit of the divide where Clear Fork heads we found ourselves in a region deserving the title mountainous. In the bright light of the moon and stars, our little column of cavalry wound its way up the steep hill-side like an enormous snake whose scales were glittering revolvers and carbines. The view was certainly very exhilarating backed as it was by the majestic landscape of moonlight on the big [sic] Horn Mountains.

Cynthia's silvery beams never lit up a mass of mountain crests more worthy of commemoration upon the artist's canvas.[3] Above the frozen summit of Cloud Peak, the evening star, cast its declining rays.

Other prominences rivalling in altitude this one boldly thrust them selves out against the midnight sky. Exclamations of admiration and surprise were entoned from the most stolid as our column made its way rapidly from bluff to bluff, pausing at times long enough to give every one an opportunity to study some of nature's noble handi-work.

Finally, even the gorgeous vistas I have so feebly attempted to portray failed to assuage the cold and pain in our limbs or to drive away the drowsiness Sleep was placing upon our exhausted eye lids. With no small degree of satisfaction we noticed the signal which at five O'clock in the morning bade us make camp on the Clear Fork of Powder River.

The site was dreary enough; scarcely any timber in sight, plenty of water but frozen solid, and only a bare picking of grass for our tired animals. However, what we most needed was sleep and that we sought as soon as horses had ben [sic] unsaddled and mules unpacked. Wrapped up in our heavy overcoats and furs, we threw ourselves on the bleak and frozen ground and were deep in slumber.[4]

This is Bourke at his best as a diarist. The Moon was full a few days later on 10 March. By a three-quarters moon, he means the waxing gibbous phase. On the night of his diary entry, the Moon was 37° above the eastern horizon at 7 p.m. Venus, the evening star, was 25° above the western horizon, almost due west of his location. Although Bourke does not mention it, Mars, much fainter, was 34° above the western horizon.[5]

The Stars

Giving names to the stars and organizing those stars into patterns called constellations is an ancient enterprise. Most of the modern proper names of the brightest stars have an Arabic origin. Most constellations names are Greek or Latin. The second-century BC Greek astronomer Hipparchus listed the named stars from brightest to faintest and assigned each one a magnitude from 1 to 6. In this system the scale runs backward with a larger positive number indicating a fainter star. In modern times, with the availability of electronic measuring devices, some bright stars and planets have a negative magnitude. Venus had a magnitude of −4 on the night Bourke saw it.

In 1603 German astronomer Johannes Bayer listed the stars in each constellation in order of decreasing brightness and assigned a name combining the possessive form of the Latin constellation name with a letter of the Greek alphabet. Arcturus (magnitude −.04), the brightest star in Böotes, is Alpha Böotis. Sirius, the most brilliant star in the sky (magnitude −1.43), is Alpha Canis Majoris, the brightest star of the Big Dog constellation Canis Major. The North Star, Polaris (Alpha Ursae Minoris), is much fainter than either of these stars, with a magnitude of 1.96.

There is another difference between individual stars besides magnitude. A careful observer of the night sky will notice a slight color cast to the stars, especially the brightest ones. The color of the star is a direct indicator of its surface temperature. Hot stars like Vega or Sirius look bluish; cooler stars like Arcturus or Betelgeuse appear red.[6] Stars of a similar temperature to our Sun appear yellowish. The Lakota noticed these colors. Lakota author Zitkala-Ša (1876–1938) began one of her stories with "overhead the stars were twinkling bright their red and yellow lights."[7] However, the actual color of the Sun may not have been crucial to the traditional Lakota. The spirit *Škáŋ* assigns the color red to *Wí*, the Sun. According to James Walker, the reason is "because *Wi* is the chief of the Gods, red is an emblem of all things that are sacred."[8]

The Lakota and other Plains Indians saw many of the same stars, constellations, and planets as Hipparchus or Bayer. For example, the Lakota called Sirius *Thayámni Siŋté*, animal tail, or the Pleiades star cluster *Thayámni Phá*, animal head. The Lakota shared some of these names with other Native groups, but in many cases each cultural group had its unique name for the star or constellation. Like other common objects, such as particular trees or animals, it would be a simple matter for a non-Lakota to point to the star or draw a constellation pattern and ask the name. Although they were sometimes multilingual, through the medium of sign language Native peoples with differing languages could share celestial concepts. Sign language enabled Native peoples to share ideas with white Americans, too. William P. Clark, who wrote a manual on Indian sign language for military officers stationed in the West, included some gestures that represent various celestial objects. Moreover, he gave a broad summary of the names of planets and constellations.

Make sign for NIGHT; then form an incomplete circle with index and thumb, space of about half an inch between tip of index and thumb; raise the hand upwards towards the heavens. To represent many stars, sometimes both hands are used, and pushed up in different directions. To denote any star of particular brilliancy, such as the morning star, the hand is held towards the direction where the star is supposed to be, and then the tip of index pressed against the ball of the thumb and snapped two or three times to denote the twinkling . . .

The Arapahoes have just enough knowledge of astronomy to name some of the stars and constellations. They call the *Big Dipper* "the broken back." *Mars*, "big fire star." *Jupiter*, "morning star." When Jupiter is an evening star, "the lance". Some call it "the winter star." *Pleiades*, "the bunch." *Venus*, "daystar." *The Hyades*, "the hand."

The Plains Indians have special names for a greater number of stars and constellations than some of the mountain tribes.

The Snakes and Bannacks [*sic*] speak of the morning star and evening star, but, so far as I could learn, have no name for any constellation.[9]

Clark mentions that the Plains Indians have names for more stars and constellations than mountain dwellers. Perhaps this was due to the need for celestial points of reference to aid in navigating across the vast expanse of the plains. Mountain tribes had valleys and peaks to use for landmarks. Those peaks often blocked the view of the whole sky. There are some prominent geographical markers on the Great Plains, such as the Black Hills, Bear Butte, and Devil's Tower, and rivers such as the Niobrara River in Nebraska, the White River in South Dakota, and the Powder River in Wyoming. However, when a traveler on the plains was in unfamiliar territory, without any prominent landmarks, the stars could be a guide for long-distance navigation.

Polaris is especially helpful in determining north/south movement. As latitude increases, the angle Polaris makes with the northern horizon also increases. As the Lakota moved farther to the north, they would have noticed the higher elevation of Polaris above the northern horizon and might have been able to estimate their location. The Lakota name for Polaris, *Wičháȟpi Owáŋžila*, the star that does not move, implies its status as a direction beacon.

One Lakota legend suggests this directional guide role for the stars. Charles Eastman (1858–1939) tells the story of the "Girl Who Married the Star." Two sisters, Earth and Water, marry stars. Earth chooses the brightest star for herself. Once, when digging turnips, Earth digs too vigorously and falls from the heavens to the earth below. Eventually Earth gives birth to Star Boy, who, as the story goes, "grew to be a handsome young man and had many adventures. His guides by night through the pathless woods were the Star children of his mother's sister, his cousins in the sky."[10] This story personalizes the stars. The stars are your guides because they are your relatives and not merely lights in the sky.

In her lengthy discussion of the mythology of the Lakota, Martha Warren Beckwith offers an explanation for all the stories about human women marrying star men.

> The very common Plains Indian theme occurs in which women wish for star husbands, the star men come to claim their brides and carry them to the sky, whence one, having broken a taboo, is let down again to earth pregnant and is killed in the descent, leaving her son a foundling on earth to become the ward of some protecting or unfriendly guardian. In Dakota stories the protecting guardian is stressed, possibly because of the strong social interest in the *hųka'* [i.e., *hunka*] relationship of adoption which is supposed to protect the young from evil influences.[11]

Your cousins the stars are not only your guides through the dark, pathless woods, but they also are your protectors.

Sometimes *stars* aren't really what astronomers call a star. Although *morning star* could apply to any star in the predawn sky, the term is usually reserved for Venus, the brightest planet, or less frequently Jupiter, the second-brightest planet. Wilson D. Wallis, who studied the Wahpeton Dakota at Portage La Prairie and Griswold, Manitoba, discusses their folklore about the morning star. Unfortunately, it is difficult to understand precisely which stars or planets are intended in this narration, and there is apparently no distinction made between stars and planets. Wallis reports,

The morning star appears in April. An old medicine-man said, before dying, that after death he would appear in the heavens early in the morning; that he had come thence and would return in order to prove to the people that he would live there forever. While he was ill he told them to look to the east early on the fourth morning after his death, and there they would see him as he rose, for he would appear in a manner visible to them. He would have with him a large light that would produce all the colors (of dawn). On the day designated, they saw the star appearing in the east. Now everyone believes that story because the star came as the man promised. We call it 'Largest Star' (*witca'pita'ka*). Four stars are called by this name and are said to be brothers, each having prophesied before death his reappearance in the heavens. One of these is the evening star; there is one to the south, and the fourth is seen in the south-east preceding the dawn. The above are said to be the only stars or constellations with which myths are associated. Another version is to the effect that the morning star has more power than either the Sun or the Moon, having once been a medicine man on earth and hence knowing more about human affairs. It is called *wakanopa*. It travels from east to west.[12]

To which stars were they referring? There are no first-magnitude stars on the eastern horizon just before sunrise in April that might have stood out as a morning star. The morning star reference may be to either Venus or Jupiter. The "large light" probably refers to the Sun, which, of course, can produce vivid colors in the sky at dawn, especially if some clouds are present. "Largest Star" may refer to Venus or Jupiter or some first-magnitude star. It is interesting that the east to west motion of the sky is noted.

The Lakota Names of the Stars

Humans have a passion for names. If you know the name of a person or a star, it gives you power, insight, and perhaps an advantage. The Lakota are no exception to this. The *written* forms of Lakota star names, only about a hundred years old, originated in Buechel's notes and eventually appeared in his dictionary. Certainly many of the names and their meanings are much older. Ronald Goodman in *Lakota Star Knowledge* gives contemporary Lakota names for the stars and constellations.[13] Some of the information in *Lakota Star Knowledge* was gleaned from Buechel's notes and some from interviews with late twentieth-century Lakota elders. The star and constellation names (and spelling) in tables 3 and 4 are taken from *Lakota Star Knowledge* as well as entries in Buechel's notes and dictionary.[14] Many Lakota star names, not surprisingly, come from animals such as *Tayamnisinte*.

Other star names involve a concept unique to the star, such the apparent stationary position of Polaris. The traditional Lakota name for Polaris is *Wicháȟpi Owáŋžila*, the star that does not move or the star at rest. As told by Ringing Shield in 1903, "One star never moves and it is *wakan*. Other stars move in a circle about it. They are dancing in the dance circle."[15] The lack of observable motion makes Polaris unique in the sky. It is thus not surprising that a name specifically referring to the star's lack of motion would be used for Polaris. Another name for Polaris is *wazíya wicháȟpi* (or *wazía wicháȟpi*), North Star. This may be an instance of the Lakota adopting and translating the term used by white people, or an influence from their non-Lakota neighbors such as the Ojibwe.[16] German scholar Johann Georg Kohl reported the Lake Superior Ojibwe "all know the polar star, have noticed its fixedness, and call it '*Giwe danang*,'" or the star of the north.[17]

The Constellations

The human mind seeks patterns, and human-devised patterns in the sky are ancient. The Lakota constellations differ from the patterns seen by people in other cultures. Several prominent constellations and asterisms

TABLE 3. Selected Lakota star names

LAKOTA NAME	LAKOTA MEANING	COMMON NAME
Anpo Wicahpi	Morning star	Venus
Anpo Wicahpi Sunkaku	Morning star's younger brother	Arcturus or Jupiter (Buechel)
Ihuku Kigle	Went under it (bird migrations)	Arcturus
Itkob u	Going toward	Arcturus
Tayamnisinte	Animal tail	Sirius (Goodman)
Tayamnitchuhu	Animal outer rib	Rigel
Tayamnituchuhu	Animal inner rib	Betelgeuse
Wicahpi Owanjila	Star that always stands in one place	Polaris

are very noticeable from the Great Plains, and this is reflected in the constellation names listed in table 4.[18]

The Big Dipper asterism is circumpolar in most of the Lakota's territory. The four views in figure 8 illustrate the seasonal variation in the appearance of the Big Dipper above the northern horizon. In winter, as seen from the Pine Ridge Indian Reservation, Alkaid, the star at the end of the handle, just skims the northern horizon. Due to hills and undulating terrain, the end of the handle of the dipper actually appears to dip below the observer's apparent horizon. As James LaPointe reports, "The gradual whirling movement of the Big Dipper was part of [the Lakota's] calendar."[19] This suggests knowledge about the relationship between the orientations of the dipper with the horizon at various times of the year, and the variation is recognizable by comparing the appearance of the Big Dipper above the northern horizon at four times of the year. Careful observation over the course of one night would further reveal the hourly motion of the dipper. This would allow for an estimate of the hourly passage of time.

TABLE 4. Selected Lakota constellation names

LAKOTA NAME	LAKOTA MEANING	COMMON NAME
Chanśáśa ipúsye	Handle of wooden spoon used to take a burning coal for lighting a pipe	Big Dipper, or Triangulum and α, β-Aries (Goodman), Big Dipper (Buechel MS, *Digital Archive*, 102)
Wichákhiyuhapi	Man carriers	Big Dipper (Buechel and Manhart, *Lakota Dictionary*)
Chiŋšká siŋté yukháŋ	Spoon with a tail	Big Dipper (Buechel and Manhart)
Heȟáka	Elk	5 stars in Pisces that outline elk's horns and head
Khéya	Turtle	4 stars of Pegasus square, plus a head and tail of faint and poorly identified stars
Mathót'ipila	Bear's lodge	8 of the 12 stars in Gemini (including Castor and Pollux)
Napé	The hand	Orion's belt, sword, Rigel, β-Eridani
Ochéthi Šakówiŋ	Seven Council Fires	Big Dipper (Goodman, *Lakota Star Knowledge*)
Oglécekhutepi	They shoot arrows	Two stars opposite one another in the east and west (Buechel and Manhart)
T'ayámni siŋté	Tail of *T'ayámni*	(Buechel MS, 102)
T'ayámni c'aŋkáhu	Backbone of *T'ayámni*	Betelgeuse, Rigel (ribs), Orion's belt (backbone), Aldebaran and Pleiades (head), and Sirius (tail)
Thayámnipha	Animal's head	Pleiades (Buechel MS, 103)
Wanáǧi thacháŋku kiŋ	The spirits' road	Milky Way
Wakíŋyaŋ	Thunderbird	13 stars beginning with γ-Draconis, including 2 stars of Ursa Minor's "bowl"
Wichákhiyuhapi	The keeper, the great bear	Ursa Major (Buechel and Manhart)
Wichíŋcala Šakówiŋ	Seven little girls	Pleiades
Zuzéca	Snake	ρ, ξ, γ-Puppis, 7 minor stars in Canis Major, all stars in Columba

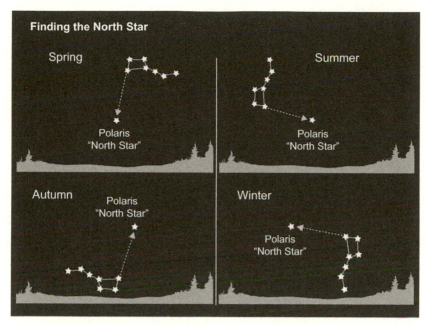

FIG. 8. Finding the North Star. In addition to locating Polaris, the orientation of the Big Dipper can be a seasonal indicator. This diagram shows the orientation of the dipper about an hour before midnight in March at the vernal equinox, at the summer solstice in June, at the autumnal equinox in September, and finally at the winter solstice in December. *Starry Night* image courtesy of Starry Night Education, used with permission.

According to Wallis, the Wahpeton Dakota have a legend about the origin of the Big Dipper that explains its unique name.

> A man went out to hunt. He died suddenly, and his body was found. Four men picked him up. These four are now the four corners of the Dipper (Ursa Major). Of the other three in the group, the first is his wife, the next two are his children. The constellation is called "carrying-the-dead-man" (*witca'kiaha'pi*).[20]

The "other three" refers to the stars Alioth, Mizar, and Alkaid in the handle of the dipper. Peter Iron Shell gave Buechel an alternate name, *Chinšká siŋté yukháŋ*, the Dipper or Big Dipper, and the literal meaning is a "spoon with a tail." The latter definition may refer to the wooden spoon used to carry a coal from the fire used to light a pipe.[21] *Ochéthi*

Šakówiŋ means the Seven Council Fires, and using it to refer to the Big Dipper may have come into use late in the nineteenth century.

The Big Dipper stands out in the northern sky because of the relative brightness of its seven stars compared to the stars around it. A line connecting the two brightest stars, Dubhe (Alpha Ursa Majoris) and Merak (Beta Ursa Majoris), does not point directly at Polaris, the North Star, but it's close enough that these two stars are used as "pointers" to find Polaris (see figure 8). Moreover, Polaris is the brightest star in the Little Dipper, Ursa Minor. Because Polaris is slightly less than two degrees from the north celestial pole; its motion about the pole is barely discernible. The seven stars of the Big Dipper recall, of course, the Seven Council Fires. However, the seven bright stars of Ursa Major are not the only group of seven stars in the sky.

The Pleiades, a small star cluster, are very high in the winter sky and readily observable.[22] The Lakota term *Thayámnipha* refers to this hundred-million-year-old cluster of stars and dust that is 380 light years from our solar system. *Wichíŋcala Šakówiŋ*, seven young girls, is another common Lakota name for the Pleiades.[23] Although the sacredness of the number seven suggests *Ochéthi Šakówiŋ* may be relevant to other cultural patterns, and Walker reports associating the Pleiades with the number seven, *Ochéthi Šakówiŋ* is not used for the Pleiades.[24]

The Lakota paid attention to "star clusters" although it is not clear whether they were referring to true clusters like the Pleiades or just asterisms of apparently close stars.[25] LaPointe reports: "They made vivid and imaginative pictures of the star clusters. They said some of the clusters resembled animals of the earth. One cluster was called *Pa yamini pa*, (a monster with three heads)." He goes on to say the identification of star groupings served a purpose:

> After an evening of casual talk and story telling, it was the custom of the native people to go into the night, singly or in groups, attending to chores before retiring. At this time, if the sky was clear, the wise men who knew the stars gave lessons to the young, and to any others interested in the mysteries of the heavens. Pointing upward into the

scintillating display of heavenly bodies, they traced out the animals portrayed by each cluster.[26]

This description suggests that "cluster" also refers to a constellation and not a true gravitationally bound star cluster like the Pleiades. It is likely the lessons from the wise elders made some point about how things on earth were related to things in the sky. The Wahpeton Dakota have constellation lore that illustrates this, as reported by Wallis.

> A man was erecting a tipi. He made a small round tipi out of eight small poles. Inside were stones. Two men sat within singing. These now make a group of eight stars. They are seen plainly in the summer to the south and west. They change position continually and are not visible in winter. The constellation is called "Sweat tipi" (*i'ni tipi*).
>
> A constellation known as *ta'maopa'*, resembling a kite, is seen overhead in winter. From mid-winter until June it is not visible.[27]

The Wahpeton had their own constellation visualizations, and it is not clear what was meant by the constellations in this account. The "Sweat tipi" (*inithipi*) might be the bright stars of Sagittarius, which easily could be visualized as a sweat lodge and are prominent in the southern sky in summer.[28] However, Sagittarius would be *very* low on the horizon for an observer in Manitoba but slightly higher in the sky from the latitude of the Dakotas. The brightest stars of Cygnus form the asterism the Northern Cross, and this could be seen as a kite, *ta'maopa'* (in Lakota, *thaté kaȟwógyapi*). Cygnus is overhead in late fall, however. Other possibilities include the constellations Auriga or Cepheus.

Collectively the stars and constellations compose the night sky. The same Lakota word for the daytime sky, *maȟpíya*, is also used for the night sky or the heavens. Common to many cultures, the heavens have a unique standing. It was not until the late twentieth century that humans actually ventured into the heavens, that is, outer space. The inaccessibility of the celestial realm makes it a special or mysterious place, even for twenty-first-century star gazers.

The Milky Way

Today's rural dwellers have an advantage over city dwellers: The faint stars of the plane of our Milky Way galaxy are impossible to see from highly illuminated urban areas. Given the optimal seeing conditions of the Great Plains, it is no wonder that the Lakota have legends about the Milky Way. *Wanáǧi Thacháŋku*, the Spirits' Road, is the Lakota name for the Milky Way. This was the path a Lakota followed after death. The Cheyenne had a similar idea but called this path the Hanging Road.[29]

The Milky Way galaxy is disk shaped. More stars are seen when looking into the plane of the disk than when looking perpendicular to the disk. The center of the galaxy is in the direction of the constellation Sagittarius, and one sees an even greater density of stars in that direction. However, from the latitudes of the northern Great Plains, Sagittarius is low in the sky and hence difficult to see. From summer into early fall, the constellation Cygnus is prominent in the sky, and the direction to the plane of the Milky Way passes through this constellation. A person with very good vision is able to discern the various branches in the Milky Way where more stars are seen. Apparently the Lakota noticed these branches and gave them meaning.

According to Wallis, in a general sense the sky above is a place where "everything is wonderful."

> *The heavens.* — All that vast region above us which we call the heavens, the Dakota call *mahpiya* and believe it to be a better land than this earth of ours. There everything is wonderful. Only medicine-men can cross its portals. They have come from there and can go back to it, but no other earthly mortal can do this.[30]

The Lakota connected "a better land than this earth of ours" with the Milky Way. Wallis relates that the Wahpeton Dakota gave an unusual origin for the Milky Way that uses a story involving animals to make the point and perhaps refers to the visible texture of our galaxy.

> *Bado'za* (a bird) and Beaver disputed as to which could dive deeper. Everything clothed in fur and all flying creatures can swim. All of

these gathered together for a contest as to which could dive deepest. All dived. Bubbles came up from them. These bubbles are now the Milky Way. The beaver dived deeper than any other.[31]

Animals are common characters in Native American stories and often serve an etiological purpose. In this story the result of the bird and beaver's contest is the "bubbly" texture of the Milky Way. Moreover, as LaPointe explains, "high in the heavens the Milky Way splits into two parts, one branch continuing endlessly across the sky. The other branch breaks off for a short distance and then fades away in a faint nebula. At this split in the Milky Way, Lakota legend says, there stands a Divine Arbiter of the souls of the dead."[32]

Stories of interactions between stars and humans are common in Lakota legends. The story "Milky Way and Fallen Star," as retold by LaPointe, is the tale of a woman who raises a peculiar boy who has fallen from the sky.

> Fallen Star was a most unusual child; he matured early into a sturdy, healthy boy. He played and hunted with other children, but he seemed to know he was no ordinary boy and was destined for special duties. Soon after attaining manhood, he told his adopted mother that his father was a bright star in the sky and by the command of *Taku Wakan* he must now watch over all the people of the earth. . . . Today, from somewhere near the Trail of the Spirits, known to others as Milky Way, Fallen Star sends rays of hope for his earth people.[33]

Although the story is not further interpreted, it may be that the rays of hope Fallen Star sends out are to assure the people that the *Wanáǧi Thacháŋku* is nothing to fear.

Buechel recorded a version of the Fallen Star story told by Peter Iron Shell in 1904. The theme of the story is that "the wisdom from above is to make good use of one's talents for the sake of those in true need." In this version, the older of two women muses, "My sister, oh how I would love to live with a very brilliant star." The younger woman, perhaps in an attempt to exhibit some humility, replies, "Well, how I would like to live with a star of average brilliance."[34] Each one got her wish, and the older woman conceives and bears the boy who becomes Fallen Star. Although there is little of astronomical significance in this version, it is interesting that the varying "brilliance" or magnitudes of the stars is recognized.

Buechel recorded another Milky Way story told by Lone Wolf and written down by Ivan Stars in September 1919. In this tale, the "Spirit Road is known to be the way to heaven," and the theme is that "a man distinguishes the Two Roads, one from which we would be brought down, the other which serves to lead us heavenward."[35] At the end of the story the narrator says, "the stars collectively carried a message in the heavens in both the winter and the summer. That is why they knew, when it was about to get very cold, when [the Big Dipper and Spirit Road] were close together the weather was cold; and when [they] were far apart the weather was hot and sultry."[36]

This last statement is curious. In early August, when the summer heat can be unbearable at Pine Ridge, Ursa Major is low in the north-northeast in the evening and just skims the northern horizon over the course of the night. It is not particularly prominent in the sky. The Milky Way rises nearly perpendicular from the northeast horizon and ascends through the zenith and into the southern sky.

However, in January Ursa Major is high and prominent in the north-eastern sky, and the Milky Way is setting in the north-northwest. Although they are not necessarily any closer together in terms of angular separation, Lone Wolf may have thought they *looked* closer because of the more noticeable orientation of the Big Dipper. (See figure 8 for examples of the variation in the orientation of the Dipper.)

A theme begins to emerge in Lakota ethnoastronomy: Shapes seen in the sky also appear on earth. Star men marry earthly women. Children are guided by their cousins in the sky. After death, the Milky Way is the path to a world beyond. There is a connection between the earth and the sky, and between the spirit and the sky.

5

THE SUN AND MOON

The Sun and Moon have been significant celestial objects throughout human history. Their status has ranged from being deities worthy of worship to being regulators of time. Indeed the motions of the Sun and Moon are the basis of modern calendars. The Sun and the Moon are of virtually equal apparent size in the sky.[1] This coincidence, of course, makes the spectacular phenomena of solar eclipses possible. The similarity in apparent size may account for the designations of the Sun as the ruler of the day and the Moon as the ruler of the night. This identification of the Sun and Moon as the greater or lesser lights is ancient.[2] However, the awareness that the Sun is a star producing energy and the Moon is simply a rocky body reflecting the Sun's light is not evident in pretechnological cultures. Rather, the Sun and the Moon function as lights for the day and night.

Grandfather Sun

In many cultures the Sun is the master and the Moon is seen as subservient to the Sun. The Moon is less bright, is not seen as much as the Sun, and in fact is not seen at all for about a day each month. George Sword, James Walker's consultant, said the Sun, along with "the Earth, the Rock and the Moon," are material bodies, but the sky and the meteor do not have material bodies. However, Sword also asserted that the Sun, sky, Earth, and rock are superior mysteries (*wakháŋ tháŋka*), and the Moon, wind, and meteor are inferior to them.[3] Thus there is a hierarchy of sorts among the two brightest objects in the sky. A meteor may be considered nonmaterial because it suddenly appears and vanishes, as opposed to the Sun and Moon, which are persistent and predictable in their appearance in the sky.

Charles A. Eastman, the first Native American graduate of a white medical school, wrote several books recounting aspects of the Dakota and Lakota culture that he learned from his Indian relatives. Eastman identifies the Sun as grandfather:

> Before the advent of the white man these people believed that the earth was round and flat, and was suspended in a dark space, and sheltered by the heaven or sky, in the shape of a hollowed hemisphere. The sun was made by the Great Mystery, the father, and the earth, the mother, of all the things that live and grow. But they have been married long, and had become the parents of many generations of races, therefore they were called *Tunkan'sida* and *Uncida*, or *great grandfather* and *grandmother*.[4]

Likewise, in the story "The Beloved of the Sun," Eastman says, "we call the Sun our Grandfather and the Moon Grandmother, and we also believe that the Stars are their children."[5]

Eastman's identification of the Sun as grandfather and Earth as grandmother is not as mythological as it first may seem. The Earth gives birth, literally, to plants. Animals, including humans, are a part of the birthing process, too, and they use the plants and other resources of the Earth. However, without the Sun, there would be no Earth. The energy input from the Sun drives the biological and climatological mechanisms of planet Earth. Today astronomers know that chemical elements, such as oxygen and carbon, were created inside earlier generations of giant stars as they evolved. Native Americans may have philosophically understood that we are literally children of the stars long before the physics of the stars and planet Earth were understood.[6]

The Wahpeton Dakota reverse Eastman's gender of the Sun and Moon, although there is a curious explanation of the genders in this account recorded by Wilson D. Wallis:

The sun. A medicine-man declared the Great Power told him why the sun was made, it was made to furnish light for the whole earth. It comes from the east and sets in the west. During the darkness he travels around by the north to his home in the east. While on his journey home, night comes. The world does not move, it is the sun that moves.

The moon was made for a similar purpose, to give light at night (*hu'towi* = moon; *aupe 'towi*, sun; = night-wi and day-wi). It travels over the same course as the sun. Men travel about at night, but women are afraid to travel about then; hence the sun is female, the moon male. *wi* moon, *apetu* day, *hayetu* night.[7]

Unlike the Romance or Germanic languages, in Lakota only literal gender is used, not grammatical gender, so the genders of the Sun and Moon are literal.[8] Also, in this Wahpeton view the Earth is stationary.

In another Wahpeton story recorded by Wallis, the "sun was once a woman and the moon a man. Hence women were born out of the sun and men out of the moon." The lengthy narrative discusses the relationship between the Sun, the Moon, and their relation to humans on earth. At the end of the story, there is a summary of why the Sun is superior. Its importance is due to the greater effect of the Sun on the Earth:

The Sun and Moon quarreled as to which rendered people the greater service on earth. The Moon declared he had more power than the Sun; the Sun declared she had more power than the Moon. The Moon asked the Sun in what way she possessed more power. The Sun said she gave forth a very bright light all day so that everyone could see what he was about and could see the path when travelling. "Should I, on some days, give them heat all the time they would be sick; on the other hand, too much cold air will make them sick and so I give them a little heat one day, allow it to be a bit cooler the following day, and warm again another day, preserving this alternation of temperatures so that the people may be strong and healthy. The moon does nothing. Those nights while he is full everyone likes him." The Sun told the Moon he could do nothing more than shine at times; he could not furnish abundant light every night as the Sun did every day, neither could he furnish cold or warm days. The Sun declared further that she had more power since no one could look upon her; that the Moon has no power, since everyone can look on him with full gaze. Thus the Sun triumphed over the Moon, for the Moon had no reply to make.[9]

Although we too may see the Sun as superior, the Moon is crucial to life on the Earth. The Moon interacts gravitationally with the Earth and causes the rise and fall of ocean tides, a phenomenon unknown to the landlocked Lakota. Nonetheless, the Sun's superior status is clear in the Lakota mind.

It may at first appear that Native Americans associated the Sun with a god, as did the ancient Egyptians. Worship of Ra, the Egyptian sun god, was central to that culture. Some of the early white observers of Lakota culture thought the Sun and Moon were objects of worship. The following description of the Sun and Moon from James O. Dorsey hints that the Moon is deferential to the Sun and suggests a ritual relationship between humans and the Sun and Moon.

> The sun as well as the moon is called "*wi*" by the Dakota and Assiniboin tribes. In order to distinguish between the two bodies, the former is called *anpetu wi*, day moon, and the latter, *hanhepi wi* or *hanyetu wi*, night moon. . . . The moon is worshiped rather as the representative of the sun, than separately. Thus, in the sun dance, which is held in the full of the moon, the dancers at night fix their eyes on her.[10]

The use of the word *worship* is problematic, however, because there is not any evidence that the Lakota worshipped the Sun or Moon in the sense that Christian missionaries like Riggs or anthropologists like Dorsey would have understood worship. The Sun and the Moon are unique in the sky due to their size and brilliance, and, moreover, the highly repetitive nature of their motions gives them a special importance. What some described as *worship* might better be called *awe, wonder*, or *reverence*. Even the Sun Dance, the central ritual of the Lakota and Dakota, is not the worship of the Sun. Perhaps it is because of the use of these celestial luminaries to regulate and define time itself that the Sun and Moon occupy a special place in Native cultures.

The Moon Watches Over the Earth

The use of symbolic gestures allowed for the communication across Native cultures and languages of ideas like a month or even a week. W. P. Clark's sign language dictionary gives insight into not only time telling but also the meaning of the Moon to the wider cultural context.

> Conception: Night sun. Make sign for NIGHT, and then partially curve the thumb and index of right hand, space of about an inch between tips, closing other fingers, then raise the hand in a direction a little to south of zenith, and well up, the plane of the circle formed with index and thumb perpendicular to the line of sight, from the eye through the incomplete circle of thumb and index to the position in the heavens where the moon is supposed to be. Some Indians, in making the circle which represents the moon, use the index fingers and thumbs of both hands. I have seen a half-month represented by forming a crescent with thumb and index, and usually the moon is represented as full, gibbous, half, and crescent by indicating such and such a portion as dead or wiped out.[11]

Although there is not a specific mention here of the lunar synodic month (29.5 days), the 28-day period when the moon is visible is of central importance to the Lakota, as well as other cultures.

Charles Eastman elaborated on his understanding of the Moon's relationship to the greater Lakota cosmos. Note that the purpose of the Moon is to watch over the Earth at night.

> As far as I can make out the *moon* seems to be their [i.e., the stars'] *servant,* or at least she is required to watch, together with the stars, the sleeping world below; while the *Sun* comes down to sleep with his wife, earth, and his children. The moon is considered a man and the stars are his brothers. In the sense that the *Sun* and *Earth* constitute the parents of the world, they believed that the Great Mystery holds

them responsible. Therefore it was natural for them to appeal to these two, who will in turn appeal to the Supreme Being.[12]

Eastman ties the Sun and Moon to the stars, as well as the Great Mystery. There is an implicit understanding that somehow these celestial objects are themselves a part of the extraordinary. Contrast this with the explanatory notes to the contemporary *Dakota Legend of Creation* in which the Moon is "wife of the Sun; sets the time for important undertakings."[13] Lakota thought is definitely not static, dogmatic, or centralized.

The Sun and Moon in Lakota Designs

As objects worthy of wonder, the Sun and Moon appear often in decorative designs. Ann Coleson, a white woman, was captured on the night of 12 January 1863 near New Ulm, Minnesota, by a Dakota band led by Chief White Eagle. She wrote a lengthy account of her captivity. Coleson refers to the Dakota symbolically "painting" Sun and Moon symbols on their intended "target" before commencing a raid.[14]

In a discussion of the Sun Dance recorded by Richard Nines in 1911, High Bear noted, "In the painting of their bodies they also make a mark on their chest thus: \ | /. This is *wakan*. I believe it indicates the rays of the sun, as the sun is painted on the stomach, and of course all the decorations are *wakan*."[15] The description of these designs as *wakháŋ* is an important clue to the meaning of these images.

Like the Sun, the Moon appears frequently in decorative designs. A shirt reportedly worn by Crazy Horse is in the collection of the Buechel Memorial Lakota Museum in St. Francis, South Dakota. Both sides of the shirt show a crescent moon. Father Buechel's collection notes read: "A war shirt. Old man Red Sack inherited it from the famous chief 'Crazy Horse' who wore it. The tufts of horse hair refer to the number of horses taken from the whites while fighting them or from other Indians. The tufts of human hair (black) were taken from enemies that he killed."[16] Birds and a thunderbird are included with the star, and small dots represent hail. Although not astronomical, birds and hail are in the sky, the same location as the Sun, the Moon, and the stars.

These symbols are said to have protective powers, especially when appearing on clothing or shields. Many of the shield designs came to the owner of the shield in a dream. One shield owner reports "that the moon with its dark color was drawn to represent the night, because that was the time when he had this experience [i.e., the dream]." On another shield four stars—one black for night, one yellow for dawn, one blue for evening, and one red for day—represent the circle of the sky. On this shield we see a confluence of the circle, the number four, and the colors black, yellow, blue, and red.[17]

Stars, along with lightning bolts, can represent the sky. Some stars on these shields are four-pointed. The use of crossed lines, +, or a four-pointed star, ✦, is thought to be more traditional and the manner in which the Lakota drew stars before encountering the American flag and its five-pointed stars, ★.[18]

The symbols on the shields represent particular powers or ideas, but these ideas or powers might have been understood only by the maker of the shield. The round shape of the shield may itself represent the Sun, and feathers suspended from the shield suggest the Sun's rays.[19]

Ghost Dance shirts often contain Sun, Moon, and stars. Shirts in the Buechel collection illustrate this. An upturned crescent on the back of one shirt represents the Moon.[20] Other Ghost Dance shirts are adorned with stars. Buechel made the following note about one shirt.

> Ogle wakan-a ghost shirt. This specimen is from old man "Last Bear." Notice the hole in the back. Last Bear was hunting deer west of the Black Hills in Wyoming. A white man got after him threatening to shoot him; whereupon Lost Bear put on the ghost shirt believing it would make him bullet proof; it did not, however, but went right through. The shirt is said to be about 60 years old. Holy Rosary Mission 3-23-1915[21]

The dragonflies on the shirt in figure 9 represent the emergence of the dancer from a cocoon into the spirit world.[22] The shirt shown in figure 10 has stars and red stripes and was collected by Father Buechel in 1915 from a Mrs. No Ears. These shirts provide vivid examples of us-

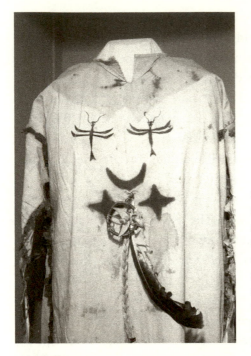

FIG. 9. Ghost Dance shirt. This shirt in the Buechel collection is resplendent with two large four-pointed stars and the crescent moon. Dragonflies are commonly seen on Ghost Dance shirts. This shirt is made of cloth, and although stained and faded, it has retained the original designs. BMLM, photo by Mark Hollabaugh, used with permission.

FIG. 10. Mrs. No Ears Ghost Dance shirt. The stripes on this shirt in the Buechel collection are red, and the stars are blue. The outline of a bird is hidden by the feathers. The top of another shirt is seen in the foreground. BMLM, photo by Mark Hollabaugh, used with permission.

ing celestial images in a highly spiritual ceremony that unites a Lakota person with the sky above and the earth below.

The *heyókha* was a contrary who used his spiritual powers to satisfy the *wakíŋyaŋ* or thunder beings of the west. On the Great Plains summer thunderstorms (and winter blizzards) approach from the west, hence the westerly origin of the *wakíŋyaŋ*. The *heyókha* would dress warmly in hot weather and wear few or no clothes in the dead of winter. The *heyókha* were considered *wakháŋ* and are an example of a person who is different or unusual.

Thunder Bear provided Walker with several drawings of Lakota war insignia. A drawing (no. 8) from his ledger book shows both Sun and Moon symbols (and a thunderbird) on a *heyókha* warrior's body.[23] In a sense the Sun and Moon are opposites or contraries, and hence they are a sort of celestial "joke" when they appear together on the *heyókha*. The significance of the Sun and Moon is that the wearer received a vision from each celestial body. Walker notes in his commentary on the image that it was unusual to paint the symbols on a person but common to place them on a tipi, shield, or even clothing.

These decorations give the wearer a sense of power or confidence. They help unite the wearer with earth and sky. However, the use of the Sun and the Moon in Lakota culture serves an even more pressing need than mere decoration: the necessity of telling time on a daily, monthly, and annual basis.

6

TELLING TIME

A commonly heard question is, "What time is it?" The response may require a glance at a watch or clock. Being on schedule is a preoccupation of modern society. The traditional Lakota were much less concerned with a schedule. A very different understanding of time than that possessed by white Americans or Europeans is seen in how they answered the question "What time is it?" For the Lakota, the time of day is reckoned by where the Sun or Moon is located in the sky. The cycles of nature define the months. Finally, important events in Lakota history recall a specific year.

The Day

The sidereal day, 23 hours and 56 minutes, is defined as one rotation of the Earth on its axis with respect to the stars. A solar day can be defined as a 24-hour interval between successive passages of the Sun across the meridian.[1] In modern usage *day* means the entire daylight and nighttime cycle, that is, a calendar day.

The Lakota, like many cultures, used the daily motion of the Sun to define the time of day. A distinction was made between daytime and nighttime. In a narrative Sword gave to Walker, there are said to be three times: day, night, and the moon (i.e., month). Later in the narrative, the need for a fourth time, the year, is explained.[2] It is not surprising that the Lakota would think of time divided into four.

In many cases, the location of the Sun in the sky is the basis of the word used for the time of day. For example, *wíhinapha* ("sun comes in sight") means sunrise and also the direction east because the Sun can be used to indicate a direction in which one should travel. Likewise when used as an adverb *wiyóȟpeyatakiya* means "towards the west." The subdivisions of the day are based on what the Sun or stars are doing or where they are seen in the sky. "The day is divided into *áŋpao*, [just] before sunrise; *áŋpa*, sunshines, and *htayetu*, fading-time (evening). . . . . Midnight is when the first stars seen in the east are in the middle of the sky, *haŋchókaŋyaŋ* [or *haŋyéchokaŋ*], night-middle-made."[3] This means midnight occurs when the stars seen on the eastern horizon at sunset transit the meridian.

An interesting example of a division of the day using the position of the Sun comes from a participant in the battle commonly known as the Little Bighorn. Iron Hawk, a "Seven Star Soldier," one of the highest among the Lakota, like a general or major general, said the Custer battle was over when the sun was in the "middle of the sky." This astronomical reference corroborates other eyewitness accounts of the battle.[4]

Days could also be described by the visibility of the moon. Jonathan Carver, the explorer of the Great Lakes region, noted that when the Moon did not shine, it was said to be "dead," and that some tribes he encountered referred to the three days when it is usually not seen as the "naked days." The Moon's first appearance typifies its coming to life again. It is not certain whether Carver is talking about Dakota he encountered in Minnesota, the Ojibwe, or perhaps other Indians dwelling in what is now Michigan. He also noted the lack of division of time into weeks. Days were counted simply by pointing to the Sun at noon. Presumably in sign language one could also make a sweeping gesture across the meridian to indicate a day.[5]

Associating the Sun with day and the Moon with night is logical, even though the Moon is often seen when the Sun is above the horizon. Eagle Hawk, an Oglala Lakota, told the story "The Man Who Went After the Buffalo Horn" in 1926. In the course of this lengthy story about acquiring scalps, two old women banter with each other. "One old woman said, 'I am the light of the night; I am the moon,' and the other said, 'I am the light of the day; I am the sun.'"[6]

The Month

The Sun is *aŋpétuwi*, day moon, and the Moon is *haŋhépiwi* (or *haŋyétu-wi*), night moon. However, the word *wi* also means "month." For millennia the Moon has served to mark the passage of time for cultures worldwide. In one form or another, pretechnological societies generally used a lunar calendar. It is not surprising, then, that the Moon plays a central role in Lakota thought.

The lunar month, discussed in chapter 2, has four principal phases. The Dakota and Lakota words for these phases describe whether the Moon is waxing or waning. The waxing gibbous moon is *wí mimákhaŋye-la* and refers to the shape—namely "humpbacked moon" or "near round moon." After full moon, during the waning phases, the Moon rises later and later after sunset each night and is not in the sky at sunset like the waxing phases. It is dark when the Moon rises. This may account for the use of *wímakhataŋhaŋ*, "moon rising from the earth," to describe the phase. Wallis gives only the four principal phases, and he is reporting Canadian Dakota names.

Buechel has an interesting marginal note about the Moon's appearance: "At new moon when the bright crescent lies nearly perpendicular to the horizon, the moon is popularly called a wet moon; and when it is almost horizontal the moon is termed a dry moon."[7] The horizontal or perpendicular appearance of the Moon is due to the angle the ecliptic makes with the horizon. The thin crescent of new moon will be more perpendicular when the ecliptic makes a smaller angle with the western horizon and more horizontal when the angle is greater. For example, a case of the former occurred on 12 September 1915 and of the latter on 7 January 1915 and could have been seen from the St. Francis Mission on the Rosebud Reservation, provided the weather was clear. Although the orientation is not perfect, it would catch the attention and imagination of an observer. Buechel does not give any insight into the meaning of the dry and wet descriptions. Perhaps "wet" moon implies water pouring from a bowl.

When the 29.5-day synodic month interval is known, a calendar based on the phases of the moon can be devised. That is what the Lakota did.

TABLE 5. Lunar phases

PHASE	CANADIAN DAKOTA (WALLIS, "BELIEFS")	LAKOTA (BUECHEL AND MANHART, *LAKOTA DICTIONARY*; BUECHEL MS, *DIGITAL ARCHIVE*)
New moon	*Wi te'tca*, new moon	*Wit'é*, dead moon
Waxing crescent		*Wílechala*, new moon
First quarter	*Wi itca'ga*, growing moon	*Wíokhiseya*, half moon
Waxing gibbous		*Wí mimákhaŋyela*, near round or humpbacked moon
Full moon	*Wi mibe'*, round moon	*Wí mimá*, round moon
Waning gibbous		*Wímakhataŋhaŋ*, moon rising from the earth
Last ("third") quarter	*Wi yespa'bi*, diminishing moon	*Wit'íŋkta khaŋyéla*, near when the moon dies
Waning crescent		*Wit'íŋkta khaŋyéla*, near when the moon dies

However, their lunar months are named for nature's cycles on the Earth and not phenomena in the sky. Walker explained the months (that is, moons) and their relation to seasons of the year:

A moon was the time from the first appearance of the new moon in the west after the sun had set until the last appearance of the old moon in the east before the sun rose. The name of the moon was *hanwi*, night sun, which was commonly abbreviated to *wi*, sun.

There were thirteen moons and four seasons. . . . There were either four or five moons in the winter season. . . . The Discernible-not moon [*Tanin sni wi*][8] sometimes appeared and sometimes did not, and no one could tell for certain whether it had appeared or not until the seasons showed that it had appeared. The year began with the first moon of the first season which ordinarily was when the ducks return together in flocks [*Magaksica agli wi*], but if there was a indiscernible moon, the year began with it.

The winter season completed the year, and in speaking of the past, a winter meant a completed year. For this reason the Oglalas designated the past by winters instead of years. And the nearest that they could specify a particular time was of the moon of a season of a winter.[9]

Table 6 summarizes several different naming conventions.[10] Certain natural events occur at about the same time each year. The ripening of the chokecherries or the birthing of buffalo calves signaled a particular month. Clark notes the surprising variety in his sign language dictionary. He then goes on to list and comment on the months according to the Lakota and Cheyenne.[11]

Some tribes have twelve named moons in the year, but many tribes have not more than six, and different bands of the same tribe, if occupying widely-separated sections of the country, will have different names for the same moon. Knowing well the habits of animals, and having roamed over vast areas, they readily recognize any special moon that may be mentioned, even though their name for it may be different.

One of the nomenclatures used by the Teton Sioux and Cheyennes, beginning with the moon just before winter, is as follows:

1st. The moon, "the leaves fall off."
2d. The moon, "the buffalo cow's foetus is getting large."
3d. The moon, "the wolves run together."
4th. The moon, "the skin of the foetus of buffalo commencing to color."
5th. The moon, "the hair gets thick on buffalo foetus" called also "men's mouth," or "hard mouth."
6th. "the sore-eyed moon" (buffalo cows drop their calves).
7th. The moon, "the ducks come."
8th. The moon, "the grass commences to get green, and some roots are fit to be eaten."
9th. The moon, "the corn is planted."

10th. The moon, "the buffalo bulls are fat."

11th. The moon, "the buffalo cows are in season."

12th. The moon, "that the plums get red."

Lieutenant Scott[12] gives the following as the nomenclature used by the Sisseton and other Eastern bands of Sioux:

January.	Called "very hard to bear."
February.	"the month the coons come out, or Coon's Moon."
March.	"Sore-eyed month."
April.	"the month the geese lay eggs."
May.	"Planting month."
June.	"the month the strawberries ripen."
August.	"Harvest moon."
September.	"The wild rice becomes ripe."
October.	
November.	"Deer-rutting month."
December.	"When deer shed their horns."

Clark's twelfth month, "plums get red," would correspond to August in Walker's list. Note that these lists take cues from the natural world around the Lakota where absolute dates specifying daily, monthly, or annual events are of little importance.

Differences between the Lakota located in western South Dakota and Nebraska and their Dakota relatives in Minnesota are evident in the names recorded by Riggs and Walker (see table 6). Minnesota streams usually begin to thaw in April, strawberries ripen in June, rice harvesting and drying occur in September and October, and deer are mating from November into December. However, for the Lakota farther west, September was "tree-leaves yellow moon," perhaps an allusion to the autumnal aspen in the Black Hills and prairie ravines when the aspen trees appear to be painted a rich yellow.[13]

The inclusion of the "discernible-not moon," *tanin sni wi* (*thaŋíŋšni wí*), is an important concept in Walker's list. This occasional lunar month was needed to deal with a difficulty in coordinating lunar and solar calendars. The problem arises when a lunar calendar and a solar calendar are used simultaneously. There are 29.5 days in the lunar synodic month, the interval from new moon to new moon. But there are 365.25 days in a solar year. Hence, dividing the days in the solar year by the number of days in the synodic month results in about 12.4 lunar months per solar year. About every three years, an additional month is needed to keep the lunar and solar calendar more or less synchronized, so that the months coincide with the natural events they describe.

The modern western Gregorian calendar and its Julian calendar predecessor solved this difficulty by doing away with the lunar calendar altogether and having twelve months of 28, 30, or 31 days. One leap day is added every four years to account for the additional one-quarter day in the solar year. Moreover, the Gregorian calendar compensates for the precessional wobble of the Earth by designating only the century years evenly divisible by 400 as leap years. This more or less keeps the Vernal Equinox at 21 March each year.

How did the Lakota deal with this synchronization problem? They didn't! The Lakota simply adhered to a lunar calendar and added a month about every three years to keep their months synchronized with the seasons. Precise calendar dates were not important. Only natural events were important.[14]

The lack of precision in the Lakota calendar is frustrating to historians who would like to know the exact date when some event occurred. A possible solution to this conundrum is to use astronomy. For example, if an account says something happened during the moon of falling leaves at the full moon, and the year is known, the date can be narrowed down to a few days in October.

Calendar Sticks

Ethnoastronomers are aware of premodern Native Americans' use of calendar sticks to mark the passage of time.[15] A notch cut in a long piece of wood indicated the passage of one day. Every new moon, a special notch could be cut to indicate one lunar month had passed. Calendar sticks apparently were widely used among the pueblo dwellers of the

TABLE 6. The Lakota months

MONTH	WALKER	RIGGS
April	*Maǧaksica agli wi*, ducks together-come moon	*Ma'aokada-wi*, geese lay eggs; *Wokada-wi*, streams navigable
May	*Canwape ton wi*, tree-leaves potent moon	*Wozupi-wi*, Planting moon (cf. *Ćaÿwaptoÿ-wi*)
June	*Tipsinla wi*, prairie-rice-like (wild turnip) moon	*Wasustecsa-wi*, strawberries are red
July	*Canpa sapa wi*, tree-head (chokecherry) black moon	*Caypasapa-wi*, chokecherries are ripe
August	*Kanta śa wi* plums red moon	*Wasutoy-wi*, Harvest moon
September	*Canwape ǧi wi*, tree-leaves yellow moon	*Psiyhnaketu-wi*, rice laid up to dry
October	*Canwape kasna wi*, tree-leaves shaken-off moon	*Wi-wazupi*, drying rice moon
November	*Waniyetu wi*, snow-exists-time moon	*Takiyu-a-wi*, deer rutting moon
December	*Wani cokan wi*, snow-exists midst moon	*Tahecapsuy-wi*, deer shed horns
January	*Tehi wi*, hardship moon	*Wite-I*, hard moon
February	*Wicata wi*, raccoon moon ["dead moon"]	*Wićata-wi*, raccoon moon
March	*Iśta wicayazan wi*, eyes them-suffer moon	*Iśtawicayazay wi*, sore-eye moon
(13th)	*Tanin śni wi*, discernible-not moon	

BLACK ELK	HASSRICK	BELDEN	HERMAN
Red grass appearing	Birth of calves moon	Wild geese lay eggs; rivers flow again	Green grass and budding of trees
When ponies shed	Strawberries moon; moon of thunderstorms	Planting moon	Shedding of ponies
Making fat	Ripe June berries moon	Strawberries are red	Ripening of the June berries
Red cherries	Ripening chokecherries moon	Chokecherries are ripe; geese shed feathers	Ripening of the chokecherries
Black cherries	Ripe plums moon	Harvest moon	Midsummer moon when Indian summer commenced
Black calf; calf grows hair	Moon of yellow leaves	Rice is laid up to dry	Green grass fades away
Changing seasons	Falling leaves moon	Rice drying	Fall of the leaves and fattening of wild game
Falling leaves	Hairless calves moon	Deer killing	Buffalo calf's nose turns brown
Popping trees	Frost in the tipi moon	Deer moon	Frost gets in the eyes of prairie chicken
Frost in the tipi	Tree popping moon	Hard moon	Moon of popping trees
Dark red calf	Sore eyes moon	Raccoon	Moon of the mating of the wolf
Snowblind	Grain comes up moon	Sore eye	(omitted)
		Lost moon	(omitted)

Southwest, and John Bourke reported seeing them in use. The National Museum of the American Indian, Hyde Collection, contains a Pima calendar stick that shows a series of notches carved on the flat side of the stick.[16]

Hassrick gives an account of a Lakota's use of a calendar stick.

Time-reckoning for the Sioux was concerned, however, not only with maintaining a chronicle of the years but with keeping a count of months and days.

According to Iron Shell, the year of thirteen months began in April, and the basis for this was that his father (also named Iron Shell) replaced the moon-counting stick at this time:

In the evenings, when the moon first rose, Iron Shell made a nick in a long pole he kept by the bed for that purpose. Every night he made another nick, until the moon finally disappeared. Then he said "The Moon Died." There were usually 25 or 26 nicks for each month, for there are three days when the moon cannot be seen.[17] On the other side of the pole, Iron Shell marked a single nick to show the passing of a month.

Iron Shell carried this stick wherever he went. He got a new stick each year, cutting it in the moon of the Birth of Calves. It is possible to infer that April, the moon of the birth of calves, was associated with the annual renewal of the Sioux's food supply as exemplified in the calving, combined with the termination of the winter. The important thing is that the idea of a year having a beginning or ending was of little matter to the Indian. The winter served as a designation point in a spiraling series, unmarked by any periods in the sequence.[18]

Calendar sticks were not precise. Samuel W. Pond, a missionary to the Dakota, wrote an extensive narration of his experiences in *Dakota Life in the Upper Midwest*. Pond noted the use and limitation of a calendar stick.

Time was measured by days, or rather by nights, and by moons. None of the Dakotas knew the exact number of days in a year. One of them told the writer that he had tried to ascertain the number by cutting a notch in a stick for each day, but when the year came round he had no means of ascertaining the precise day on which he began to count.[19]

Although calendar sticks could be used to mark the passage of single days or months, they also might serve to keep track of whole years. In 1877 Lt. James Bradley noted such a use by an eighty-four-year-old man at the Red Cloud Agency. He "carried a stick about six feet long, covered with notches, thousands of them. I asked him what it was, and he said it was the history of the world from the beginning, handed down by his fathers."[20]

Even though there are calendar sticks in museums, I am not aware of the existence of any *Lakota* calendar sticks dating from the nineteenth century. The calendar sticks were wood and easily subject to deterioration. Moreover, calendar sticks most likely were seen as sacred objects and might not readily have come into the hands of a white person.[21]

The Year—Winter Counts

Days. Months. Years. These are basic measures of the passage of time. An eclipse occurred on 7 August 1869. Many dwellers on the Great Plains observed a spectacular meteor shower on the night of 12–13 November 1833. These Gregorian calendar dates are precise. However, the determination of dates was less strict for the Lakota.

Certain years stand out in our memory. The years 1776, 1812, and 2001 may cause one immediately to think of the signing of the Declaration of Independence, the War of 1812, and the attacks of 9/11. Likewise for the Lakota, a prominent event provided the mnemonic for an entire year. The event was depicted as a pictograph, a visual representation of the event. The collection of pictographs became a winter count. The keeper of the count either painted the pictographs on a hide or drew them in a ledger book when that medium became available. The record was probably originally an oral history that became iconic when the pictograph was drawn.[22]

The Lakota word *waníyetu* means both winter and year. James Howard noted that the word, "like the English word 'winter,' refers to the cold

FIG. 11. Battiste Good Winter Count. This replica of the Battiste Good Winter Count in the Sioux Indian Museum collection at the Journey Museum & Learning Center is drawn in a ledger book. The icon for 1822 represents the bright meteor discussed in chapter 8. The Battiste Good count is one of the most thorough Lakota winter counts. Mallery gives a complete explanation of the entire count cycle and the individual icons (*Picture-Writing*, 287–328). Photo of replica by Von Del Chamberlain, used with permission.

season of the year. In the other sense it refers to the year as a whole, the Dakota having no other word for this purpose."[23] When inquiring about a person's age in Lakota, one literally asks, "How many winters are you?" Surviving winter was an accomplishment in a climate where winter weather can turn harsh in just a few hours, and the winter winds drive snow across the prairie with deathly force. Physician Walker kept a winter count on the wall of his office and used it to estimate the age of his patients.[24] An elderly patient could point to an icon and tell the good doctor that she was born in the year that Many Stars Fell, 1833.

More than 150 winter counts are known to exist, although some of these are copies of other counts. Many counts are in the National Anthropological Archives, as well as the historical societies of North Dakota and South Dakota.[25] Several winter counts have been published and include both the pictographs and interpretive notes.[26] Other text-only winter counts are less accessible but do provide valuable data.[27] Although winter counts were not confined to the Lakota, the Lakota were prolific keepers of the count.[28]

Winter counts are works of art. Although any large animal hide could be used, a buffalo hide was the preferred canvas for the pictographs. Replicas were often made.[29] The Buechel Museum exhibits two versions of the Thin Elk Winter Count, covering the years 1819–1878. It is obvious from a close inspection of the materials used that one count is older (figure 12) than the other. However, the replica (figure 13) is such a good copy that differences in many pictographs are difficult to detect. The photos of the Thin Elk Winter Count show the 1833 Leonid meteor shower (upper left).

Given the expanse of years most winter counts encompass, it is clear some counts were made by a series of keepers over a length of time. One example of this is the Red Horse Owner's Winter Count covering the years 1786–1940. The count continued after the death of Moses Red Horse Owner (b. 1836, d. 23 July 1908). This count, drawn on fabric, shows the 1833 Leonid meteor shower. The year notations were added to facilitate correlation with the Gregorian calendar.

Paper and pencil were new tools to the Lakota, but when shopkeepers

FIG. 12. Thin Elk Winter Count original. Although some portions of this winter count in the Buechel Memorial Lakota Museum are stained, the images are still very readable. The four-pointed stars in the circle near the top represent the 1833 Leonid meteor shower. BMLM, photo by Mark Hollabaugh, used with permission.

FIG. 13. Thin Elk Winter Count replica. This is a replica of the original Thin Elk count. Notice the attention to detail in copying the original as closely as possible and the repeated use of + to represent the stars. BMLM, photo by Mark Hollabaugh, used with permission.

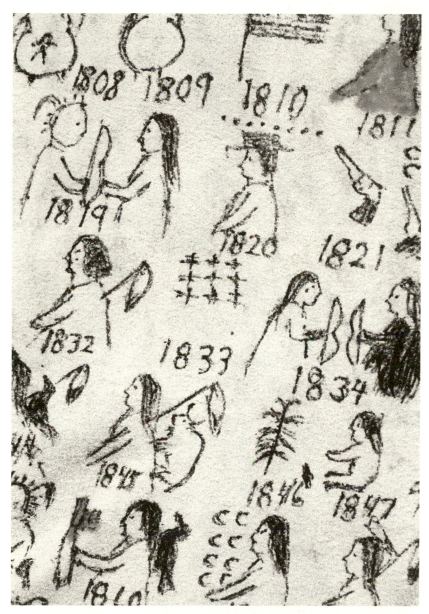

FIG. 14. Red Horse Owner's Winter Count. This count also depicts the 1833 Leonid meteor shower with a series of four-pointed stars, ✦. The use of four-pointed stars in winter counts is most common prior to about 1860. Note the U.S. flag as the icon for 1810. Presumably this was the year the keeper of the count encountered the U.S. Army for the first time. BMLM, photo by Mark Hollabaugh, used with permission.

began trading pencils and ledger books, the nineteenth-century version of the computer spreadsheet, the Lakota found the ledger books excellent media for recording pictographs. These winter counts were also duplicated by hand and could become a source of income when sold to collectors.

Lakota and other Plains Indian winter counts are important objects of ethnographic research. The counts reveal a rich insight into what was important to the Lakota and their neighbors. A cursory examination of any winter count reveals that the Lakota often came to blows with the Crow. In the last two to three decades of the nineteenth century, references to disease and famine were more common as the Lakota suffered more and more under the control of the government. What might be important to white Americans was often of less importance to the Lakota. Very few counts, for example, depict anything about Custer's defeat at the Little Bighorn in 1876. However, many counts recall the murder of Crazy Horse the following year.

Garrick Mallery was a late nineteenth-century expert on Native pictographs in general and winter counts in particular. *Picture-Writing of the American Indians* is the longest report ever published by the Bureau of American Ethnology.[30] Mallery, an army colonel, included not only sketches of the pictographs but also explanatory comments based on Lakota interpretations. He discussed the use and function of the winter count hide:

> The Keeper of the Count was responsible for the perpetuation of the history . . . with this counsel of the old men of his tribe, he decided upon some event or circumstance which should distinguish each year as it passed, and marked what was considered to be its appropriate symbol or device upon a buffalo robe kept for the purpose. The robe was at convenient times exhibited to other Indians of the tribe, who were thus taught the meaning and the use of the signs as designating several years.[31]

The hide or ledger book was a visual prompt for the teller of the band's stories. Today, winter count hides and ledger books are found not only in history museums but also in art museums because they truly are works of art.[32]

Ethnohistorians have used winter counts to chronicle the history of Native peoples.[33] Howard noted, "The counts might be used as a means of studying intertribal intercourse in the protohistoric and early historic periods. They might also be used to determine tribal locations and the dates of the introduction of important features of Dakota culture, such as the earth lodge, the horse, and the Sun dance."[34]

Winter counts are helpful to ethnoastronomers as well. Von Del Chamberlain completed an excellent study of Plains Indian winter counts on hides and in ledger books that specifically refer to astronomical events. His work remains the best summary of use of winter counts in ethnoastronony. Chamberlain's cataloging of celestial events portrayed on Lakota winter counts provided a road map for the specific phenomena I investigated.[35]

Establishing absolute dates for events chronicled in a winter count can be problematic, however. Consider the dramatic Leonid Shower on the night of 12–13 November 1833. Winter began in the autumn of 1833 and ended in the spring of 1834. This shower might be recorded in a count as occurring in 1833 or 1834, or even 1832, depending on when the keeper of the count made the record. Knowing the exact Gregorian calendar date of an event can help identify the winter count reference. For example, both transient phenomena and predicable astronomical events like eclipses or annual meteor showers were recorded in the winter counts. A transient event, discussed in chapter 8, is the bright meteor that suddenly flashed across the sky on 20 September 1822. The exact date was recorded, but is this the event on the winter counts?

Eclipses are predictable phenomena. The *Rocky Mountain News* provided excellent documentation of the widely seen 7 August 1869 eclipse, which was visible in Lakota country. Note, however, that the three winter counts listed in table 7 give 1870 *or* 1871 as a date for a solar eclipse. Gregorian calendar dates now affixed to winter count events are usually plus or minus one or two years.

Winter counts are valuable for ethnoastronomy. The meteor of 1822,

TABLE 7. Selected astronomical events appearing in winter counts

EVENT	BIG MISSOURI	LONE DOG	WOUNDED BEAR
20 September 1822 meteor		A ball of fire flew across the sky	*Wicahpi wan hoton hiyaya,* a star went by loudly (1821–1822)
12–13 November 1833 Leonid shower	The winter the stars fell	Many stars fell (1834)	*Wicahpi ota hinhpaya,* many stars fell
7 August 1869 solar eclipse	The winter the sun was eclipsed (1870)	Eclipse of the sun (1871)	

the 1833 Leonid meteor shower, and the 1869 eclipse caught the attention of some bands of the Lakota and were important enough events to be used as the pictograph for that year. The winter counts are a starting point for research on the meaning of these celestial events for the Lakota.

The Seasons

Closely linked to the concept of the year is the division of the year into four seasons. The modern calendar marks the beginning of the four astronomical seasons with astronomical events: the vernal equinox, summer solstice, autumnal equinox, and winter solstice. The date of 1 January as the beginning of the year is arbitrary. Astronomically, it would make more sense to use the vernal equinox as the beginning of a year, but because of the slight fluctuations in the Gregorian calendar date of the equinox, it would be confusing to do so.

A Lakota child may have heard a grandparent relate a story intended not only to teach why things are the way they are, but also to impart some moral idea. This is the case in a story about the seasons that Charles Eastman related, "North Wind and Star Boy." Star Boy goes

HARDIN	WHITEMAN STANDS IN SIGHT	GARNIER	MAKULA
Star passed by with loud noise	*Wicahpi wan hoton hiyaya u*, a star came producing a loud voice as it goes (1821)	*Wicahpi wan hoton heyayeci*, a moving star roared	A star sang across the sky
Storm of stars	*Wicahpi okicamna*, star it storms	*Wicahpi okicamna*, the stars fell	The stars fell (1834)
			There was an eclipse of the sun (1870)

about helping those in some kind of need, and he eventually reaches people in a northern land. They are in great distress "because they feared Wazeya, the North Wind, who drove away the buffalo herds so that they had no meat." Star Boy eventually subdues North Wind, who "made a treaty of peace with Star Boy, promising to come to earth for half the year only, and to give timely warning of his approach, so that the people might prepare for his coming and lay up food against the day of scarcity." Eastman concludes, "By this means the winter and summer were established among us."[36] The seasonal variations in the weather are not due to the tilt of the Earth's axis with respect to the ecliptic plane, but rather to an agreement between a malevolent force and a hero looking out for his people.

The four seasons in Lakota culture, according to material collected by James Walker, relate closely to the four directions. In two stories collected from George Sword and in Walker's own retelling of similar stories, the four winds, personified by four brothers, engage in a struggle, and the result is the yearly passage of the seasons, one following another.[37] The most intense struggle, not surprising to anyone familiar with living on the prairie, is between the South Wind (*okáǧa*) and the North

Wind (*yata*).[38] Like the months, the seasons of the year also take their cues as much from the environment of the plains as from the sky above.

Time in Lakota Culture

The Eurocentric view of time could be characterized by the ticktock of a grandfather clock, the radioactive decay of cesium, or the successive passage of numbers on a modern digital clock, which often contains a small radio receiver that nightly synchronizes the clock with a time signal from the U.S. Naval Observatory. Society is obsessed with time but relies subtly on astronomy to know the time or date. Modern Americans tend to think of time, and thus history, as a sequence of events, and this view of history embodies events and progress.

The daily celestial events that the Lakota used to tell time were adequate for them, as well as for white immigrants traveling by covered wagon, but things changed with the construction of the railroads. It is possible that the modern preoccupation with time owes its origin to the westward expansion of the United States. Time zones were invented in the late nineteenth century to facilitate travel and commerce. Time signals sent daily by telegraph from the Naval Observatory in Washington synchronized time zones and allowed the trains to coordinate their schedules.

The goal of "ethnohistory is to write Indian history in a way that incorporates Indian cultural understanding,"[39] and the goal of ethnoastronomy is to incorporate that same cultural understanding into a Lakota view of the cosmos and time. Although the Lakota use repeating cycles of nature to give names to the passage of time and used past events as mnemonics for a whole year, they have a continuous, harmonious, balanced view of time. In the nineteenth-century Lakota mind, history seemingly would never end, at least as long as the buffalo roamed the earth. DeMallie's assessment of the Lakota view of time is useful:

> In Lakota culture time was not conceived of as a causal force; history was not directed nor did it embody that notion of progress and change which is so fundamental to European culture. Instead, the universe

was perceived as existing in harmonious balance. As Ella Deloria once put it, "You see, we Indians lived in eternity."[40]

DeMallie and Parks echo Deloria's insightful comment: "The yearly pictographs . . . were a record of equilibrium, providing chronology in a culture that did not embrace time as a relentless, forward-moving force impinging on human life."[41] Likewise Hassrick noted: "The important thing is that the idea of a year having a beginning or ending was of little matter to the Indian. The winter served as a designation point in a spiraling series, unmarked by any periods in the sequence."[42]

The nineteenth-century Lakota, living in a moment of eternity, were suspended in time. Although they faced many hardships on the Great Plains, they existed in harmony with the cycles of nature and life. The motions of the Sun, the Moon, and the stars provided regularity and order to the Lakota cosmos. The signs of nature on earth and the phases of the Moon above marked the passage of the months. The passage of a bright meteor, an eclipse of the Sun, or a meteor shower interjected extraordinary events into the Lakota cosmos. These were yet another connection for the Lakota between the earth and the sky, between the ordinary and the extraordinary.

7

ECLIPSES AND THE
AURORA BOREALIS

Although celestial displays that occur over repeated and easily measured time intervals are the basis of time-telling systems, some celestial
wonders are less frequent and less predictable than the daily motions
of the Sun, the Moon, and the stars. Eclipses and the aurora borealis
often were held in awe by premodern peoples. When a culture lacks
the ability to predict or explain these phenomena, its people are more
likely to feel a sense of fear or wonder in the presence of such events.[1]

Eclipses

A solar eclipse occurs at new moon and is seen over a limited area,
whereas a lunar eclipse occurs at full moon and is generally visible over
a much larger region. Usually there are two pairs of lunar and solar
eclipses each year. Although eclipses are totally predictable, it takes
many years of careful observation and record keeping to identify the
18-year- and-11.3-day saros eclipse cycle. It may take a generation or
more to identify the full 54-year cycle. The nineteenth-century Lakota
did not know this eclipse cycle.

Images of both partial and total eclipses, while not uncommon, do
not appear in all nineteenth-century Lakota winter counts. This may
be due to more pressing matters on the minds of the keepers of the
counts or to cloud cover at the time of some of the eclipses. Most likely
the Lakota, lacking the instruments to peer directly at the Sun, made
lesser note of partial eclipses when only a small fraction of the Sun's

disk was covered. Nonetheless, some eclipses were noted in the winter counts. More importantly, white observers who were present recorded the Lakota's reactions to the eclipses. Lt. William Clark did not give a sign language gesture for eclipse.

It is possible to examine the details of historic eclipses, as well as to forecast those in the future. The NASA Eclipse Web Site contains a wealth of information on all eclipses past and future, including detailed data on all annular and total solar eclipses for 1851 to 1900 visible in North America.[2] A computer program like *Starry Night* can simulate the appearance of an eclipse.[3]

Several eclipses are referenced in Lakota winter counts. This study does not include all eclipses or non-Lakota winter counts.[4] In table 8 accurate dates are given for the eclipses that can be documented. An eclipse with only a year assigned is a date based on the best evidence, and thus these winter count dates are not precise.

References to the actual appearance of an eclipsed Moon are lacking. This may be due to the less dramatic appearance of the Moon during a lunar eclipse compared to the intense changes accompanying a solar eclipse. The reddish appearance of the Moon ("blood moon") may have been seen as an omen.[5] However, the lunar and solar eclipse pairs, occurring about two weeks apart, are not always visible from the same region of the Earth. Hence, the Lakota may not have associated the lunar eclipse with the corresponding solar eclipse.

An icon on the Short Man Winter Count for 1888 (figure 15) depicts an eclipse, possibly representing a lunar eclipse that occurred on 16 January 1889. However, James Walker's interpretation of the count says this was a solar eclipse.[6] Neither identification is definite. Aaron Beede's interpretation of the High Dog Winter Count says, "There was an eclipse of the sun. The Sun turned black and died."[7] Howard's interpretation of High Dog's count also is, "There was an eclipse of the sun 'The sun turned black and died.'" Howard then gives the Lakota text *Wi-sápa t'a*, which, according to Howard, means the "Moon (or sun) black died." In other words, it could be the Moon that "died." Further complicating

TABLE 8. Some nineteenth-century eclipses in Lakota territory

SOLAR ECLIPSE	DESCRIPTION	WINTER COUNT REFERENCE
19 October 1865	Annular solar	No specific reference
7 August 1869	Total/partial solar	*Rocky Mountain News*, "Great Eclipse"; Mallery, *Picture-Writing*; Poole, *Among the Sioux*
1870	"The Winter The Sun Eclipsed"	Big Missouri Winter Count (1869?)
1870	"There was an eclipse of the sun"	Makula—Mrs. J. F. Waggoner (1869?)
1871	Eclipse of the sun	Lone Dog Winter Count—Susan Bordeaux (1869?)
29 July 1878	Partial solar	*Rocky Mountain News*, "Denver Eclipse"; Scott, *Some Memories*
16 March 1885	Annular solar	No specific reference
1888	"The sun was eclipsed"; *Anpa wi wan te*	Short Man Winter Count—James Walker, *Lakota Society* (1 January 1889?)
28 January 1888	Total lunar	No specific reference—Shortman Winter Count (?)
22 July 1888	Total lunar	No specific reference—Shortman Winter Count (?)
1888–1889	"The Sun turned black and died"; *Wi-sápa t'a*	High Dog—James Howard, most likely solar eclipse of 1 January 1889
1 January 1889	Partial solar	No specific reference
16 January 1889	Partial lunar	Shortman Winter Count (?)

FIG. 15. Short Man Winter Count. This count may represent a lunar eclipse that occurred on 16 January 1889. Photos of a drawing of the icon show a red star and black crescent. Photo of painting on wood by Mark Hollabaugh, based on Walker, *Lakota Society*.

the correlation between the counts is Howard's comment that "Black Moon was a man's name, and in this year he died."[8]

There was a solar eclipse on 1 January 1889. The path of totality traversed northwestern Wyoming, southeastern Montana, and northwest North Dakota. The eclipse maximum at Williston, North Dakota, was at 3:07 p.m. Mountain Time. Observers at Pine Ridge would not have seen this as a total solar eclipse. Even the partial phase would have been unremarkable and perhaps not even noted unless someone with an almanac had mentioned the occurrence. It is possible the keeper of the Short Man count heard about this eclipse but did not see it personally.[9]

If this indeed is the lunar eclipse that followed the solar eclipse, the crescent represents the eclipsed Moon. A five-pointed star is used as an icon in this pictograph for a star or planet that would be more visible near the darkened Moon. The 1889 lunar eclipse was at a maximum around 10:30 p.m. at Pine Ridge on 16 January 1889. The Moon was below Castor and Pollux and above Procyon. Saturn shone lower in the eastern sky. Each of these three stars and one planet would stand out due to their brilliance. The star in the pictograph could represent any of the three bright stars or Saturn, although none of them was particularly close to the Moon. It is unlikely this was the 28 January 1888 eclipse because that eclipse ended at sunset. It could be the 23 July 1888 lunar eclipse that began after sunset on 22 July and ended after midnight when the Moon was low in the summer sky between Capricorn and Sagittarius. However, there were no bright stars or planets near the Moon during that eclipse. Does the Short Man Winter Count record a lunar eclipse? Possibly, but a definitive answer is elusive.

Fortunately the winter count data for solar eclipses is more robust. Two solar eclipses, for which we have narrative accounts of Lakota and Cheyenne reactions to the events, passed through Lakota territory. Denver's *Rocky Mountain News* also reported extensively on both eclipses.[10] The newspaper's accounts reported negative results in the search for the supposed planet Vulcan, lying between Mercury and the Sun in both years.

In 1869 the *Rocky Mountain News* reported on observations from Des Moines of the total solar eclipse on 7 August 1869.[11] The path of totality was 254 km wide, and the maximum duration of totality was only 3 minutes and 48 seconds. The path of totality passed over Des Moines, and the partial phase also caught the interest of observers in Denver.[12]

Garrick Mallery includes an image (figure 16) and an extensive narration about Lakota reactions to this eclipse from Fort Rice, which was about twenty-five miles south of Bismarck on the west side of the Missouri River. The maximum of this eclipse at Fort Rice was in the late afternoon, around 4:50 p.m. Central Time.[13]

FIG. 16. Lone Dog Winter Count. Mallery includes a full-color reproduction of this winter count hide. The Sun in this icon is black, and the two stars are red. Mallery provides annotations for the icons he records and reports, "This device has been criticised because Indians generally believe an eclipse to be occasioned by a dragon or aerial monster swallowing the sun." He further notes that the Sun indeed appears dark in an eclipse, and the stars are bright (i.e., red). Photo of painting on wood by Mark Hollabaugh, based on Mallery, *Picture-Writing*, 286.

An eclipse of the sun. This was the solar eclipse of August 7, 1869, which was central and total on a line drawn through the Dakota country. This device has been criticised because Indians generally believe an eclipse to be occasioned by a dragon or aerial monster swallowing the sun, and it is contended that they would so represent it. An answer is that the design is objectively good, the sun being painted black as concealed, while the stars come out red, i.e., bright, and graphic illustration prevails throughout the charts where it is possible to employ it.

Dr. Washington Matthews, surgeon, U.S. Army, communicated the fact that the Dakotas had opportunities all over their country of receiving information about the real character of the eclipse. He was at Fort Rice during the eclipse and remembers that long before it occurred the officers, men, and citizens around the post told the Indians of the coming event and discussed it with them so much that they were on the tip-toe of expectancy when the day came. Two-Bears and his band were then encamped at Fort Rice, and he and several of his leading men watched the eclipse along with the whites and through their smoked glass, and then and there the phenomenon was thoroughly explained to them over and over again. There is no doubt that similar explanations were made at all the numerous posts and agencies along the river that day. The path of the eclipse coincided nearly with the course of the Missouri for over a thousand miles. The duration of totality at Fort Rice was nearly two minutes (l′ 48″).[14]

D. C. Poole, an Indian agent and captain in the Twenty-Second Infantry, relates a humorous incident about this eclipse, which was retold by many other authors. The Indian agency to which Poole refers is the Whetstone Agency in south central South Dakota.

Some days before the great eclipse of August, 1869, Dr. C—— [sic], physician for the Indians at the agency, concluded to try his skill as a magician, and impress the Indians with his magic art, inseparably connected in their minds with the healing art. The doctor announced to some of the principal chiefs and warriors the coming event, telling them the precise time (taken from an almanac) when the sun would be obscured and darkness follow, until he saw fit to have it pass away. When the day and the hour arrived, the doctor had his audience in readiness, duly armed with smoked glass. Being within the line of totality, and having a cloudless sky and the clear, delightful atmosphere of the plains, the phenomenon was observed under the most favorable circumstances. There was no mistake as to time; the moon gradually crossed the disc of the sun, a black, spherical mass, surely putting out its light. The Indians were impassive lookers on, until, as the eclipse reached its culmination, leaving only a narrow, bright rim around the outer edge of the sun, the deepening steel-gray shadows attracted their attention, as well as that of beasts and birds. Then, concluding that the exhibition had gone far enough, and that they must drive away the evil spirits, they commenced discharging their rifles in the air. The light of the sun gradually returning, they were thoroughly convinced that it was the result of their efforts, and that the Indians' medicine was better than the white man's. The doctor could predict the eclipse, but they could drive it away and prevent any evil consequences arising from it. So the doctor failed in fully establishing himself as a big medicine man.[15]

Chamberlain notes: "This was the only total solar eclipse which passed clearly through Teton and Yanktonai Sioux country during the period covered by the winter counts. The Moon's shadow passed close to the west of Sioux country on 30 November 1834, to the south on 16 January 1806 and just through the north of Sioux country on 1 January 1889."[16] The maximum of the eclipse at the Whetstone Agency was just a bit later in afternoon than Fort Rice, around 5:00 p.m. Central Time. Late afternoon thunderstorms are common in August in South Dakota. This day must have presented clear skies. The Big Missouri Winter Count shows an eclipse for 1870, which actually may be a reference to this August 1869 eclipse. While the Swan count records an eclipse of the Sun, the Flame Winter Count says there was an eclipse of the Moon, again demonstrating slight discrepancies among counts.[17]

Another spectacular solar eclipse occurred on 29 July 1878. The *Rocky Mountain News* coverage was even more extensive than in 1869 and included a photograph of the eclipsed Sun.[18] The path of totality passed right over Denver and the populated central Colorado mining towns. With a mere three minutes and eleven seconds of maximum totality and a path 191 km wide, Denver was fortunate this time. Those living in Lakota territory were not so lucky—they only saw a partial phase.[19]

However, Hugh Lenox Scott, a young army officer, was traveling with a group of Cheyenne when they camped at Bear Butte in the summer of 1878. Based on other comments he makes in the same chapter of his book, a July 1878 date is reasonable for his stop at Bear Butte. Scott probably saw the partial phase of the 29 July 1878 eclipse, which was partial in the Black Hills area, with the eclipse maximum at 2:47 p.m. Mountain Standard Time. If the Cheyenne camp at Bear Butte was near the bend in Spring Creek to the north of the Butte, the Sun would have been well to the west and about 40° above the Butte. Without a doubt Scott and the Cheyenne could have seen this eclipse easily. He reports that the Cheyenne reacted to the eclipse in a fashion similar to the Lakota at the Whetstone Agency in 1869.

> Our camp was immediately under and north of Bear Butte, a single peak some miles east of the Black Hills range, which was regarded by the Cheyennes as their principal medicine place. Many of them climbed to the summit, where they left presents to the medicine that inhabited the mountain. Some would go to the top, about twelve hundred feet above our camp, and stay there three days and nights, without eating, drinking, or sleeping, believing that the medicine would help them get horses or perhaps to strike their enemy.
>
> While the Cheyennes were still in that camp an eclipse of the sun took place that was announced by the public press. I told the Cheyennes to expect it several days beforehand, but they did not believe me. They became very much excited when the eclipse began, shooting off guns and making every sort of noise they could to frighten away the bad medicine which they thought was destroying the sun. Their treatment was highly successful—the sun recovered.[20]

One event in western history may have a relationship to a solar eclipse in 1888 recorded on the Short Man and High Dog Winter Counts. Roberta

Carkeek Cheney indicates that Lakota medicine man Kills Two connected the 1869 eclipse and the 1888 eclipse to Wovoka's establishment of the Ghost Dance that ultimately led to the Wounded Knee massacre.[21]

1870 THE WINTER THE SUN ECLIPSED.

During this winter, a Paiute shaman, named Tavibo, had a vision and prophesied to his Nevada tribe the end of the world and sure destruction of the hated white aggressors. The earth would be reborn and dead Indians would return to help the living ones establish an Indian paradise on earth. Using another eclipse of the sun (1888) and his foreknowledge of it from the white man almanac, Tavibo's son, Wovoka, pointed to the great sign from the Heavens to stir his tribe into action. The frenzied Ghost Dance that developed and spread to the other tribes reached the Sioux Nation, and was later to trigger the Sioux Uprising of 1890 [Wounded Knee].[22]

Did the Lakota see meaning in the occurrence of an eclipse? In the following explanation from Wallis, the Wahpeton Dakota said an eclipse was a warning to prepare for some calamity.

An eclipse of the sun, some say, betokens the approach of the end of the world; some say it means war soon in some part of the world. After one eclipse, news came that there was war in Mexico and soon, after another eclipse, came news of the great European War [World War I]. The only explanation given of eclipses is that the sun and moon being friendly toward the Dakota give them this warning to prepare them for the catastrophe. In case the sun does not exhibit the warning sign, the moon will show it, eclipses of the moon meaning the same as those of the sun.[23]

Whether eclipses were an omen of bad times or a sign of powerful medicine, the Lakota saw them, remembered them in winter counts, and related them to other events. More importantly, the Lakota's interest in the Sun was more than astronomical—the *Sun* is the central astronomical body in their most important ceremony, the Sun Dance.

Aurora Borealis

Although the aurora borealis, or northern lights, occur high in the Earth's atmosphere, they typically are treated as a part of astronomy because the aurora are a solar-terrestrial interaction. Aurora are rare in the traditional Lakota lands of northern Nebraska and southern South Dakota due to the lower magnetic latitude.[24] They are only a little more common in western North Dakota, northeastern Wyoming, and eastern Montana. The Lakota nevertheless observed these colorful celestial displays.[25]

Buechel gives the words *mahpíya thaŋíŋ*, "sky shows itself,"[26] for the aurora borealis: "The northern lights, the aurora borealis. When this sort of event took place, the Indians would paint their faces, sit up all night and burn leaves as incense."[27] The roots of this word are *mahpíya*, the sky or cloud, and *thaŋíŋ*, which conveys the sense of flickering. The same phrase is used in the Dakota dialect.[28]

Clark's sign language gestures communicate the flickering of the aurora as well. Although his symbolic language is not specifically Lakota, it does reflect a widespread understanding of the aurora on the Plains in the 1800s.

> Hold both hands, back down, well out in front of body at height of wrist, hands partially closed, ball of thumb pressed against nails of fingers; raise the hands, at same time extend and separate fingers and thumb with a partial snap, to indicate the flashes of light in the northern sky; and, unless in conversation where the sign is readily understood, it is better to face towards the north. . . . Some Indians make also the sign for *medicine*, calling it the mysterious light or fire of the north; others call it the light of the northern dancers; while still others call it the "White man's fire," or "Sacred cloud."[29]

This view of the aurora as "the light of the northern dancers" is telling. Walker also recorded the idea of the flashing of lights and dancers in *Lakota Belief and Ritual* in a passage attributed to Red Rabbit. The spirit *Wazíya* takes his name from *wazíyata*, "at the north." *Wazíya* presides over snow and ice and guards the entrance to the dance of the shadows of the north, the aurora borealis.[30]

> The land of the spirits is far beyond the place of the pines. When the *wasicunpi* dance and *Wohpe Wakan* dances with them, the light of *Wohpe Wakan's* hair flashes through the air and men can see the light as it dances far beyond the pines. When *Woziya* [*Waziya*] dances with them, his breath comes, cold and disagreeable.[31]

Walker also relates that the role of *Waziya* is linked to the aurora: "The aurora are new born clouds, but *Waziya* kills them as fast as they are born."[32] The Lakota may have helped *Waziya* kill the aurora. Mary Eastman, writing of her Dakota relatives, said, "The appearance of a brilliant aurora borealis occasions great alarm. The Indians run immediately for their guns and bows and arrows to shoot at it, and thus disperse it."[33]

An explanation given by John Blunt Horn suggests the aurora are ghosts dancing. The wispy, ethereal appearance of the flickering aurora can appear very ghostly.

> Then they went into the council lodge and stayed there two days and two nights. The council lodge was in the center of the camp. No one would go near it. And many persons saw ghosts the first night. The second night the ghosts danced so that it was light like the moon (the Aurora Borealis). While the ghosts were dancing, the old men and the wise men and the medicine men came out of the council lodge and danced in a circle around it. Many saw ghosts dancing with them. So all were afraid and went into their tipis. In the morning one of the old men called aloud to the people to come out of the tipis and look on the sun when it was rising. And all the people came out and stood looking at the sun, and while it was rising, the old man cried in a loud voice that the spirits were pleased, that they had told them how to perform the ceremony of the *Hunka* in the right way.[34]

Note that the ghosts weren't dancing just for the sake of dancing but were telling the people how to do the *Hunka* ceremony (*huŋkáyapi*, "making of relatives") in the proper way. Characteristically, the "old men and the wise men and the medicine men" danced in a circle, the perfect image of the celestial harmony.

These explanations of the aurora link what one sees in the sky and what one does on earth. The most important celestial object in the Lakota cosmos, the Sun, was responsible for the extraordinary display of northern lights, but the Lakota did not know that it is a solar-terrestrial interaction that causes the aurora, namely particles emitted from the Sun striking our atmosphere and causing the bright spectacle.

Solar activity waxes and wanes with an approximately eleven-year cycle, and aurora are more frequent, and intense, during times of maximum solar activity. The periodicity of solar activity has been monitored for almost two hundred years, since long before scientists knew the reasons for the cycle. Observers simply counted sunspots—sunspots are more numerous during solar maximum. Historical sunspot data is readily available from the National Oceanic and Atmospheric Administration's website. With this information, it is possible to determine when the aurora borealis were more likely to occur in the nineteenth century.

The nineteenth-century peaks in solar activity occurred in 1804, 1817, 1829, 1838, 1849, 1860, 1871, 1883, and 1894. Did winter counts within one year of those years depict a display of the northern lights? Would an Indian agent, soldier, or anthropologist make reference to a specific night when the aurora were visible? Unfortunately, no specific, datable references to nineteenth-century aurora were found, only the general comments about the visual appearance of the aurora borealis.

Although it occurred fifty years after the end of the nineteenth century, one remarkable aurora display was observed at Pine Ridge in 1950 at the death of Nicolas Black Elk. His daughter, Lucy, related to Fr. Michael Steltenkamp that her father had said something remarkable would happen when he died.

The night of his wake was one I'll never forget. Others saw it that night, but they don't seem to talk about it. My father said toward the end that "I have a feeling that when I die, some sign will be seen.

Maybe God will show something. He will be merciful to me and have something shown which will tell of his mercy."

What we saw that night was the sky in a way we never saw before. The northern lights were brighter than ever, and we saw those figures—the number 8 and a ring, or circle. They were separated by a short distance, but they were there—an 8 and a circle. I always wondered what that meant.[35]

Steltenkamp also shares a vivid description of the aurora from William Siehr, a Jesuit brother at the Holy Rosary Mission near Pine Ridge, who knew Black Elk and had attended his wake.

Well yes, I remember old Nick, he was the medicine man Neihardt talks about in *Black Elk Speaks*. He was also a zealous catechist from Manderson. He had quite a bit of influence with the people, old Nick did. He was the old medicine man who, in the old days, was considered something like our priesthood. That is, they respected him for the authority he had, especially in religious matters. He was considered to be quite a noted man among the tribe.

Anyway, I was with Father Zimmerman that night, and we went over to the wake. It was in the old house that's still standing there as you approach Manderson. There were many people sitting nearby the coffin, like they do at all the wakes, but this was a large assembly. There wasn't so much auto traffic in those days, but there were quite a few cars around, and it was impressive to see so many people there. We stayed there and spoke to many of the mourners, and it must have been around 10:30 when we started back up to the old Manderson road.

When we left the place, we noticed that light. The sky was just one bright illumination. I never saw anything so magnificent. I've seen a number of flashes of the northern lights here in the early days, but I never saw anything quite so intense as it was that night.

When we came back from the wake, the sky was lit up, and you could see those flames going into midair. It was something like a light being played on a fountain which sprays up. It seemed like it was rising and moving. There would be some flames going at a great distance way up into the sky above us. And others would be rising and coming into various groups and then, all of a sudden, spurt off on this side and then another side and then off to the center again. It was almost like day when we returned.

Everything was constantly moving. As I said, it was something like a display on a fountain of water where you see light reflecting on the water as it's being sprayed up. That's the way the sky was illumined — something like that — but it was all in every direction. That is, it was all coming up from the east and the south, the north and the west. And they'd all converge up to the top where they'd meet — rising up into the sky, and it was a tremendous sight.

They weren't stars or meteors, but rather, well, they were beams or flashes. And there was a variation of color effect in there — the whole horizon seemed to be ablaze. That's the first time and the only time I ever saw anything like it.

There were different formations in the sky that night which, to me, looked like spires, like tremendous points going up — then flashes. And it seemed like they were almost like fireworks in between. It was something like when a flare goes off in the sky — some sparkle here and there, but spread over such a vast area. And it was not just momentary. We all seemed to wonder at the immensity of it.

I don't recall just what anybody else said, but I know it was something I'll never forget. It was something I rather associated with the old man as he was buried at his funeral. Some sort of heavenly display, a celestial presentation — that's the way I looked at it. It was sort of a celebration. Old Nick had gone to his reward and left some sort of sign to the rest of us. With the Indians here, it seemed like it had a real significance. I think it was symbolic. There was something there.[36]

What might have caused this brilliant, spectacular aurora? Although records of sunspots go back to the mid-nineteenth century, solar flare and aurora data are less common until the late 1950s when the military began to closely monitor the Sun. The U.S. Air Force and U.S. Navy need-ed to know how solar flares and auroral activity would affect radio communications with their newly formed strategic nuclear forces. In 1950 it was known that auroral activity could cause serious disruptions in some types of radio communications.[37] On the night of Black Elk's wake, 19 August 1950, radio disruptions were so severe, that communications between the United States and Korea were knocked out for several hours.[38]

The few available scientific reports of this event point to a solar flare. Although the sunspot cycle was beginning its decline in mid-1950, and flares would have been less common, sudden outbursts could have happened and did happen. An observatory in Japan recorded a complex sunspot group on the Sun at the time of the radio disruption, and a sudden solar flare could have caused the aurora. Furthermore, the solar radio noise spiked and several European magnetic observatories reported "a sudden and rather long lasting commencement of magnetic disturbances."[39] These scientific accounts of the disruptions and Brother Siehr's description point to a massive solar flare as the cause of the geomagnetic storm and aurora on the day Black Elk died.

Solar and lunar eclipses became the subjects of legend and even the icons for an entire year in a winter count. The aurora borealis, dancing like ghosts on the northern horizon, filled the Lakota with awe. The phenomena of eclipses and the aurora borealis caught the attention of the Lakota and still intrigue us today. Rather than cowering in fear of these celestial displays, they faced them with ritual, linking the sky to life on earth. Somewhat predictable, yet always spectacular, these events are worthy of wonder. The extraordinary is central to the Lakota cosmos.

8

METEORS AND COMETS

Comets are the remnants of the raw materials that formed the solar system. A falling star, a meteor, is any piece of rocky material that burns up in the Earth's atmosphere. A meteor shower occurs at about the same date annually, when the Earth encounters dust left in the wake of a comet's passage through the solar system. The physical relationship between meteors and comets was probably not clear to Native peoples, although they had similar reactions to random meteors, meteor showers, and comets.

In his sign language dictionary, Lt. Clark summarized the attitude many Plains Indians had about the meteors and comets.

> Make sign for STAR, and with hand in that position make sign for FIRE, and then let it drop with a wavy, tremulous motion. Meteors and comets cause great uneasiness in Indian camps. Guns and arrows are sometimes fired at comets, and pieces of flesh, cut from the arm of the man who is firing, are placed with the bullet, or attached to the arrow, as gift or sacrifice to the mysterious power. Some disasters having followed soon after the appearance of comets and meteors, they look upon them in superstitious dread as the harbinger of bad luck.[1]

Random Meteors

One of the most notable unpredicted meteor appearances occurred in 1822. Legends abound concerning this "falling star," including the suggestion that Chief Red Cloud, born sometime around 1822, was named in honor of the event.[2] There are numerous reports of this bright meteor in the autumn of 1822. The Battiste Good Winter Count, one of the most important winter counts, documents this meteor.

Garrick Mallery records many of the reports of this bright "fireball" in his definitive work on Plains Indian winter counts. Mallery reproduces several icons for this meteor. Three of these icons are shown in figures 17, 18, and 19. Furthermore, Mallery provides some analysis of the event:

> A large roaring star fell. It came from the east and shot out sparks of fire along its course. Cloud-Shield's Winter Count, 1821–'22. Its track and the sparks are shown in the figure. White-Cow-Killer says "One-star-made-a-great-noise winter."
>
> [The figures] evidently refer to the fall of a single large meteor in the land of the Dakotas sometime in the winter of 1821–'22. The fact cannot be verified by scientific records. There were not many correspondents of scientific institutions in the upper Missouri region at the date mentioned.[3]

Nine of the Lakota winter counts in the Smithsonian collection make reference to this event. The counts show slight variations in the manner in which the meteor is depicted, as can be seen in the three Mallery figures. The sputtering sparks and booming or hissing noises are not uncommon with bright meteors. When a meteor passes through the atmosphere, the frictional heat causes air to superheat and rapidly expand. Thus, when the meteor appears, there may be a sonic boom as well as bits of debris breaking away from the meteor.[4]

Colonel Josiah Snelling wrote an eyewitness account of a bright meteor that fell in September 1822. It is possible that this observation is the same as those in the winter counts, although there is no definitive evidence of this.[5] On the evening of 20 September 1822 the Moon was a waxing crescent with 26 percent of the Moon's visible disk illuminated. Moonset was at 8:16 p.m. and sunset was at 6:15 p.m., with twilight lasting about one-half hour. Snelling relates the incident in his report to his superior.[6]

FIG. 17. Flame Winter Count 1822 meteor. Like most of the counts depicting this meteor, the meteor is shown as a star with a long tail. Mallery's annotation says, "Large ball of fire with hissing noise (aerolite). The Flame's Winter Count, 1821–'22." Rendering by Mark Hollabaugh, based on Mallery, *Picture-Writing*, 723.

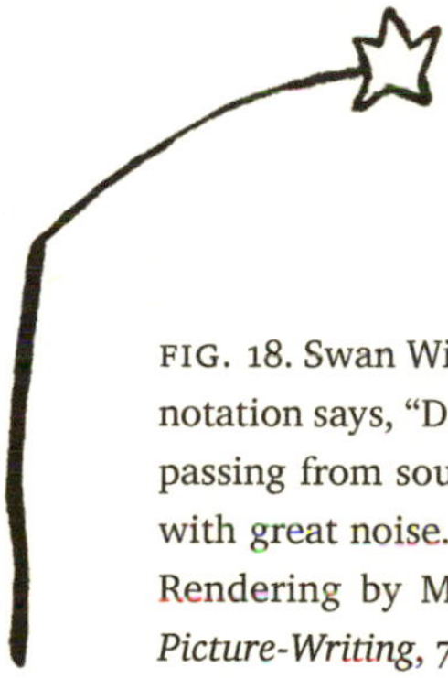

FIG. 18. Swan Winter Count 1822 meteor. Mallery's annotation says, "Dakota Indians saw an immense meteor passing from southeast to northwest, which exploded with great noise. The Swan's Winter Count, 1821–'22." Rendering by Mark Hollabaugh, based on Mallery, *Picture-Writing*, 723.

FIG. 19. Battiste Good Winter Count 1822 meteor. Mallery's annotation says, "Battiste Good says for the same phenomenon: 'Star-passed-by-with-loud-noise winter.' His device [shows] the meteor, its pathway, and the clouds from which it came." Rendering by Mark Hollabaugh, based on Mallery, *Picture-Writing*, 723.

TABLE 9. 1822 meteor in Smithsonian winter counts

COUNT	EXPLANATION	ICON TYPE
Lone Dog	Falling to earth of a very brilliant meteor	Five-pointed star ★ with long tail
The Flame	Large ball of fire with hissing noise	Eight-pointed star ✳ with thin tail
The Swan	Dakota Indians saw an immense meteor passing from the southeast to northwest which exploded with great noise (in Dakota Territory)	Five-pointed star ★ with thin tail
Major Bush	Saw very large meteor going S.E. to N.W.	(No drawing)
Long Soldier	Rock Creek. Time comet fell on the ground with loud noise	Five-pointed star ★ with broad tail. No other count mentions the location or the meteor hit the ground
Cloud Shield	A large roaring star fell	Five-pointed star ★ with long thin tail and streamers emanating from the head. Corbusier notes, "It came from the east, and shot out sparks of fire along its course. Its track and the sparks are shown in the figure."
Battiste Good	Star-passed-by-with-loud-noise winter	Four-pointed star ✚ with tail and the cloud from which it came
No Ears	A moving star roared/ *Wicahpi wan hoton hiyayeci*	(No drawing)
Rosebud	Moving star made loud noise	Five-pointed star ★ with braided tail

Source: Greene and Thornton, *Year the Stars Fell*, 169–71.

Fort St. Anthony, July 8th, 1823.

Sir,

On the evening of Sept. 20th, 1822, while crossing the parade [grounds] of this post, from the store to my own quarters, I was startled by a brilliant light in the atmosphere, and looking up, saw a meteor passing in a direction nearly from north-west to south-east, and as well as I could judge at an angle of about fifty degrees with the horizon; it appeared of uncommon magnitude, and passed so near me that I distinctly heard its sound, which resembled that of a signal rocket; in its descent my view of it was intercepted by the Commissary's store, but I heard it strike the ground, when it sounded like a spent shell, though much louder. I went immediately to the sentinel at the corner of the store, and asked him if he had seen any thing extraordinary; he replied that a large *ball of fire* had passed very near him and struck in the public garden which borders the river St. Peter; he appeared much agitated; after requesting him to mark the spot where it fell, I proceeded to the other sentinels, whose accounts, as far as their stations allowed them to judge, agreed with his. The next morning I went early to the spot where the meteoric stone was supposed to have fallen, but could not find it; the ground is alluvial and much broken into holes or hollows. I continued my search until the breakfast hour: but my ordinary avocations called off my attention, and I did not look for it again; which I have since regretted, as I think it might have been found by going to a greater depth in search of it. The evening was uncommonly fine, and the concurring testimony of all the persons who saw it, with my own observation, I presume, will be sufficient evidence that it was no illusion. I have communicated this incident, as the question whether meteoric stones do or do not fall from the atmosphere has recently excited much interest, and it may be deemed in some measure of importance in support of the affirmative proposition.

Respectfully,
I am, sir, your obedient servant,
J. snelling
Col. U.S. Army.

The reason Snelling could not find the meteor is that it fell much farther away than he estimated.

William Hypolitus Keating commented on Snelling's meteor, as well as the general reaction of the Dakota to meteors. Geologist Keating focuses on the petrologic details.

An object, which had appeared to us worthy of inquiry long before we visited the Indian country, was to ascertain whether the natives, who are accurate observers of every natural occurrence, had any tradition or recollection of having witnessed the fall of meteoric stones. Since the fact of the fall of these heavy bodies from the atmosphere has been proved to the satisfaction of the most skeptical, numerous observations, recorded by ancient historians, have been collected to prove that the occurrence is much more frequent than one would at first be led to expect. On being informed of the existence of a painted stone, which was held in great veneration by the Indians of the Mississippi, we entertained a hope that it might prove of this nature; we experienced, therefore, no slight degree of disappointment in finding it to be merely a boulder of sienite [sic].[7]

We have, as we think, in our intercourse with the Indians, been able to trace an indistinct notion on the subject of meteorites. The following belief, which is common to several nations, but which principally prevails among the Sioux, appears to bear upon this point. They state, that whenever a tree is affected by lightning, a stone of a black or brown colour may be found at its foot; it is said to be very heavy, and to have been, in some cases, picked up while hot: several of our guides stated that they had seen them, and had owned some of them. These stones are held in some esteem, as being uncommon, but no supernatural or mysterious property is attached to them. We think it probable, from the respectable sources from which we received this report, that the Indians may have mistaken the phenomena which attend the fall of these aerolites for the effects of lightning, and having, in a few instances, observed these stones and picked them up while still hot, been led to consider them as the usual attendants upon lightning. There seems to be reason to believe that an aerolite fell a few years since at St. Anthony; but all attempts to find it proved fruitless.

We have, with a view to obtain further information on the subject, examined every stone which we observed as having been held in veneration by the Indians, but in no case have we been able to detect any meteoric appearance in them.[8]

Another resident of the Minnesota fort, Mary Eastman, chronicled the life of her husband's Dakota relatives in *Dahcotah, or, Life and Legends of the Sioux around Fort Snelling*. In a lengthy retelling of a legend about a meteor that fell to earth, she gives an insight into the way in which the Dakota personified celestial phenomena.

The Dahcotahs say that *meteors* are men or women flying through the air; that they fall to pieces as they go along, finally falling to the earth. They call them "Wah-ken-den-da", or the mysterious passing fire. They have a tradition of a meteor which, they say, was passing over a hill where there was an Indian asleep. The meteor took the Indian on his back, and continued his route till it came to a pond where there were many ducks. The ducks seeing the meteor commenced a general quacking, which so alarmed him that he turned off and went around the pond, and was about to pass over an Indian village. Here he was again frightened by a young warrior, who was playing on the flute. Being afraid of music, he passed around the village, and soon after falling to the earth, released his burden. The Indian then asked the meteor to give him his head strap, which he refused. The Indian offered him a feather of honor for it, and was again refused. The Sioux, determined to gain his point, told the meteor if he would give him the strap, he would kill a big enemy for him. No reply from the meteor. The Indian then offered to kill a wigwam full of enemies—the meteor still mute. The last offer was six wigwams full of dead enemies for the so much coveted strap. The meteor was finally bribed, gave up the head-strap, and the Sioux went home with the great glory of having outwitted a meteor; for, as they met no more, the debt was never paid.[9]

The central character in this story eventually outwits or gains control over the meteor. Having subdued the meteor, the hero is honored. A person on the earth gained power over an object in the sky.[10]

Wallis has a discussion of the significance of a meteor that gives meaning to what is observed. The meteor may be a portent of ill luck or disease, or an indication of the impending weather.

A man saw some shooting stars fall on top of a hill. When he went to the place he found that the fragments were several stones. These he took home and carefully kept as being wonderful. According to another informant, the falling of a larger star will be seen by some and not by others, though all have equal opportunity. It means bad luck for him who sees it, indicating that a death may be expected in his family or among his relatives. If a small star is seen falling, the direction taken by it heralds a wind going in that same direction. If all in the party see the falling star, some kind of fever will visit the people.[11]

Recurring Meteor Showers

Meteor showers are annual phenomena, but in some years a shower is more spectacular than in others. This is due to the replenishment of the celestial debris by the comet responsible for the shower. The November 1833 Leonid shower was widely observed on the Great Plains. It was "the night the stars fell." The best estimate suggests 100,000 to 240,000 meteors streaked across the sky every hour on the night of 14 November 1833, roughly 30 to 60 meteors *per second*![12] The moon was a waning crescent and would not have interfered with observations. The probability of scattered clouds in November in the area in which the Lakota were living ranges from 40 percent to 60 percent.

There are numerous records of the Lakota reaction to the shower.

TABLE 10. 1833 Leonid meteor shower in Smithsonian winter counts

COUNT	EXPLANATION	ICON TYPE
Lone Dog	"The stars fell," as the Indians all agreed	Numerous small ovals with a moon-like object
The Flame	Many stars fell (meteors)	Six black four-pointed stars above a concave moon
The Swan	Dakotas witnessed magnificent meteoric shower; much terrified	Dots with small lines, concave moon
Major Bush	Witnessed a magnificent meteoric shower, scared nearly to death	(No figure)
Long Soldier	Stars shoots off	Six-pointed star with circular center
American Horse	The stars moved around	Large four-pointed star at center surrounded by numerous four-pointed stars
Cloud Shield	It rained stars	Numerous four-pointed stars
Battiste Good	Storm-of-stars-winter	Tipi surrounded by four-pointed stars
No Ears	The stars fell/ *Wicahpi Okicamna*	(No figure)
Rosebud	The year the stars fell	Numerous five-pointed stars

Source: Greene and Thornton, *Year the Stars Fell*, 193–95.

George E. Hyde reports:, "[In] November 1833 when Spotted Tail was ten, the stars fell. The entire sky was streaked with fire as myriads of meteorites flashed across the heavens, and the frightened Indians thought that the world was coming to an end."[13]

Mallery recorded several Lakota observations of the 1833 Leonid Shower and offered this explanation:

The five winter counts next cited all undoubtedly refer to the magnificent meteoric display of the morning of November 13, 1833, which was witnessed throughout North America and which was correctly assigned to the winter corresponding with that of 1833-'34. All of them represent stars having four points, except The Swan, who draws a globular object followed by a linear track.[14]

Three of Mallery's pictographs are shown in figures 20, 21, and 22. It is interesting that the "stars" in these winter count pictographs often are represented as a + instead of a five-pointed star, ★. This may be due to the less common sight of the American flag and its five-pointed stars in the first half of the century.[15] Flame's pictograph places the meteors with the stars in the heavens. The Swan count icon emphasizes the ionized trail left by some meteors. Battiste Good scatters star-like objects around a tipi.[16]

The dates of astronomical phenomena like the 1833 Leonid shower are precisely known. If a celestial display for which a date is known appears on a winter count, the absolute date of the count can be estimated. Knowing that the meteor shower pictograph represents an event in 1833, it is a simple task to count forward and backward from that pictograph. Russell Thornton dated other pictographs that appear on the Rosebud Reservation Winter Count, using the pictograph for the 1833 Leonid shower as a starting point.[17]

The Thin Elk Winter Count in the collection of the Buechel Memorial Lakota Museum at Rosebud contains an icon (figures 12 and 13) that represents a meteor shower. However, little is known about this count, and hence the year of the depicted shower cannot be precisely determined; but, based on similar iconography, it most likely represents the 1833 Leonid shower. The Red Horse Owner's Winter Count (figure 14) at the Buechel Museum also shows the Leonid shower.

James Walker offers an insight into the impression meteors made and their relation to the sacred. In a letter to Clark Wissler, Walker reported a conversation with Finger, an Oglala Lakota holy man who spent an entire night instructing Walker in the sacred ways of the Lakota.[18] Walker

FIG. 20. Flame Winter Count Leonid Shower 1833. Mallery comments, "Many stars fell. The-Flame's Winter Count, 1833–'34. The character shows six stars above the concavity of the moon." Rendering by Mark Hollabaugh, based on Mallery, *Picture-Writing*, 723.

FIG. 21. Swan Winter Count Leonid Shower 1833. Mallery comments, "Dakotas witnessed magnificent meteoric showers; much terrified. The Swan Winter Count, 1833–'34." Rendering by Mark Hollabaugh, based on Mallery, *Picture-Writing*, 723.

FIG. 22. Battiste Good Winter Count Leonid Shower 1833. Mallery comments, "Battiste Good calls it 'Storm-of-stars winter' and gives as the device a tipi with stars falling around it. . . . The tipi is colored yellow in the original and so represented in the figure according to the heraldic scheme." Rendering by Mark Hollabaugh, based on Mallery, *Picture-Writing*, 723.

often asked several people to give their opinions, and he attempted to corroborate the information he received from Finger with other Oglala Lakota. This passage hence indicates how Walker approached his task of determining the meaning of these concepts and events:

A few days before leaving the Pine Ridge Agency, I had an interview with Finger, an old and conservative Oglala, which was of much interest to me, and of much value relative to the mythology of the Oglala.

It came about in this way: I was at the house of Finger in the evening, and when starting for the agency, all were out in the gloaming, and a very brilliant meteor fell. Finger exclaimed in a loud voice, "*Wohpe. Wohpe-e-e-e.*" He then harangued for a short time and the women built a fire and when it had burned to coals, Finger burned a quantity of sweet grass on it, evidently with forms and ceremonial mutterings.

I asked him the meaning of this, but he would tell me nothing. I then offered him pay, and he agreed to come to my office and tell me what he knew of the mythology relative to his performance. About thirty days afterwards on the 25th of March, he came for this purpose and I secured an interpreter of unusual ability for grasping the concept of the Lakota language and translating it. The interview lasted nearly all night, and I believe the old man tried honestly to give the concepts of the shamans relative to the matters discussed. The most of the matter discussed was relative to *Taku Škanškan*, or *Škan*, to *Wohpe*, and to the immortality of the *Wakan*. I left the Agency on the first of April, so had no opportunity of reviewing the matter with Finger or of submitting it to others of the Oglala for their discussion.[19]

Woȟpé, the Lakota word Finger uses for the meteor, derives from the verb *woȟpá*, "to make fall by shooting" or "to shoot down."[20] *Woȟpé*, also associated with the White Buffalo Calf Woman, is a prominent figure in the Lakota creation story. The burning of sweetgrass is a characteristic Lakota ritual that accompanies many spiritual activities. "Good" spirits savor the smell of sweetgrass, and the burning of the grass is a means Finger employed to bring the good spirits to him.

Marie Kills in Sight, director of the Buechel Memorial Lakota Museum, recounted a story about the 1833 Leonid shower passed on to her by her paternal grandmother Laura Hollow Horn Bear: "The Lakota fired their weapons into the air when they saw the meteors falling."[21] Presumably grandmother Laura meant they shot arrows due to the scarcity of fire-arms among the Lakota in 1833. The response to the shooting down of the stars was to shoot back with arrows. Although you can't personally reach out to catch or touch the falling stars, you can shoot arrows up to their realm. The motivation might have been to scare away whatever agent was causing the stars to fall.

Comets

Throughout human history comets often elicited terror and fear. These infrequent interlopers were feared due to their unpredictable appearance. It was easy to blame bad luck on an apparition. Bright, naked-eye comets are somewhat rare. Although dozens of new comets are discovered every year, very few become bright enough for the average person to notice them in the sky without binoculars as an optical aid. One new bright comet may appear every ten years. The waning years of the twentieth century were an exception to this, when Comet Hale–Bopp and Comet Hyukatake both appeared within the span of a few years. The Lakota also noticed comets and apparently distinguished them from meteors. Buechel's dictionary gives *wicháȟpi siŋtéthuŋ* "star with a tail," for comet.

Comet Halley is perhaps the best known comet of all time, appearing every seventy-six years. Its appearance has been recorded since the time of Julius Caesar. The appearance of Comet Halley in 1066 was said to cause the defeat of King Harold at the Battle of Hastings. On the other hand, William of Normandy, who ascended to the English throne, probably saw the comet as a harbinger of good luck! It is a once every generation event.[22] Some feared the Earth's passage through the comet's tail in 1910 would result in death from the cyanogen present in the gasses, and enterprising entrepreneurs sold gas masks to ward off the effects.[23] There was a great deal of publicity surrounding the appearance of Comet Halley in 1910, and this may in part account for the appearance of Comet Halley on the Lakota winter counts for 1910.

The Swift Dog and High Dog Winter Counts in the collection of the State Historical Society of North Dakota depict the Comet Halley apparition. The Swift Dog count chronicles Lakota history from 1797–98 to 1911–12. The High Dog count, from the Upper Yanktonai Dakota band, also depicts events from 1797–98 to 1911–12 and is thought to be a copy of the Swift Dog Winter Count. They both show early nineteenth-century meteor pictographs and also a comet.[24]

The third-to-last entry in the Swift Dog count probably depicts Comet Halley's 1910 apparition. Beede notes the icon for 1910 indicates "there was a comet." Likewise, in 1912 "children had measles and the [the following words added in script] same year a star burned up."[25] This again illustrates that exact Gregorian calendar dates may not always coincide with dates given for a particular pictograph. The Swift Dog Winter Count icon clearly shows a star with a tail, as a comet would appear. However, it also could represent a meteor.

What did a cometary show mean to the Lakota? The unpredictable nature of a new comet suggests it would catch them by surprise and be seen as the herald of some important event. Wallis indicates the Wahpeton Dakota saw several possible outcomes from a comet's passage.

When it [a star] is seen with a long "tail" (i.e. as a comet) it indicates war and means that the Dakota will kill Cree. It makes a slight sound resembling thunder. When it travels toward the south, all pray to it and offer it thanks, knowing they will defeat the Cree. If it is in the west and travels east the Dakota will be beaten. On such occasions they pray to it saying they wish to live, and asking it to assist them in the coming fight. They fill pipes with tobacco and offer it these.[26]

Because the *wicháȟpi siŋtéthuŋ* has a tail, the direction of travel is probably indicated by the long wispy tail. However, comets are not in the atmosphere and do not produce audible sounds, so this description may actually refer to a meteor.

The phenomena of meteors and comets caught the attention of the Lakota. The Lakota faced them with ritual and links to life on earth. Meteors and comets are worthy of wonder; they are extraordinary. They are the heavens falling down to earth, yet another connection between the earth and sky in the Lakota cosmos.

9

THE SUN DANCE

In most cultures, astronomy often determines the timing of important religious rituals and, in some cases, of civil events. For instance, Easter is an annual event for Christians, and Passover is an annual event for Jews. The date of each is determined by astronomical phenomena. When Pope Gregory XIII needed a calendar that would keep the date of Easter synchronized with the time of the spring equinox, he consulted an astronomer.

The Sun Dance, also partially tied to celestial events, is a ceremony that has been repeated many times by most of the Plains Indians and remains to this day the most important ritual of the Lakota. Based on a statistical analysis of common Sun Dance features, the Sun Dance probably originated with the Arapaho or Cheyenne and spread to the Lakota.[1] Perhaps no Lakota ceremony was studied in the nineteenth century as much as the Sun Dance.[2] The interest may have been due in part to the practice of piercing the dancers' flesh, particularly the chest. The attention also may have reflected the large numbers of Lakota who congregated to observe or participate in the Sun Dance. The widespread participation in the Sun Dance continues into the twenty-first century, suggesting the Lakota themselves place primary importance on this ritual. Because the nineteenth-century Lakota Sun Dance is related to astronomical phenomena, the seasonal timing of the Sun Dance is important. The details of two specific Sun Dances show a special astronomical connection. The orientation of Sun Dance structures also shows an astronomical alignment.

The Lakota Sun Dance

Ceremony, tradition, spirituality, and astronomy come together in the Lakota Sun Dance, or in Lakota *wiwáŋyaŋg wachípi*, "dance looking at the Sun." It is one of the seven sacred rites of the Lakota. The purpose of all seven rituals is to strengthen the *thiyóšpaye* ("community" or "extended family") and to further a sense of interrelatedness or, as the Lakota say, *mitákuye oyás'iŋ* ("all my relatives").[3] A Lakota man does not undertake the Sun Dance or become a "pledge" for his own glory or prestige. Rather, the dancer endures the ritual on behalf of the people. Although women participated as helpers and observers of the ceremony in the nineteenth century, it was then a male activity.

The Sun Dance was widely observed and chronicled by white soldiers, traders, Indian agents, and anthropologists. Unfortunately, the very nature of the Sun Dance led non-Indian descriptions of the Sun Dance in the nineteenth century to concentrate on the "barbarism" or "horror" of the "torture" and ignore any coincident astronomical phenomena.[4] Modern observers use nonjudgmental language when describing the Sun Dance and have concentrated on relating the Sun Dance to the larger spiritual and cultural life of the community.[5] Indeed, a Lakota view says the ceremony's importance "lies in the importance given to various phases of the ceremony . . . and in the prayers and songs."[6] Walker's treatise on the Sun Dance, although seen through the lens of his culture, is an exceptional account of his impressions of events at Pine Ridge in the late nineteenth century.[7] Black Elk gave a detailed explanation of the Sun Dance in *The Sacred Pipe*.[8]

A helpful late twentieth-century description of the Sun Dance from a Lakota perspective is by Arthur Amiotte, a Lakota author and artist who resides in the Black Hills. Amiotte is quick to point out that the modern-day Sun Dance has evolved from nineteenth-century practices: "no longer is the favorite horse attached to the tipi, but rather the favorite car." Nonetheless, the "sacred intent" of the Sun Dance has remained. To say the Sun Dance is the center of Lakota spirituality is perhaps an understatement. Amiotte eloquently makes the case: "Inherent in the Sun Dance itself is the total epistemology of a people. It tells us of their values, their ideals, their hardships, their sacrifice, their strong and unerring belief in something ancient."[9]

Captain George W. Hill, an officer of the Twenty-Second Infantry Regiment, observed a Sun Dance at Fort Sully.[10] It is likely this Sun Dance occurred in June 1866, and Hill wrote the account several years later. The Lakota told Hill that the purpose of the Sun Dance was for the payment of "vows" made the previous year, for initiation into the band of "strong hearts," or as penance for some act of deliverance. Hill's use of religious language from his own culture to explain the Sun Dance is common in contemporaneous accounts.[11]

W. P. Clark, the sign language chronicler, observed a Sun Dance held in 1877 in Crazy Horse's camp. His opinionated explanation of the reasons for the Sun Dance is similar to Hill's discussion:

The Sun-Dance is a religious ceremony, the fulfillment of a vow made to some mysterious force in nature. If an Indian be surrounded by his foes, he promises the God in the sun or the Great Spirit that if he be delivered from the hands of his enemies he will, when the time comes (usually full of the moon in June), dance the Sun-Dance. If some friend or kin is at the point of death, he makes the same vow: if the Great Spirit will restore his friend or kin to health. In time of sore need he calls on the greatest and most mysterious force of nature for aid, and promises that he will subject himself to physical suffering and torture, fasting and mutilation, if succor is accorded him.

This dance partakes as strongly of a religious character as any custom which the Indians have preserved since the invasion of the white race; and to my mind, gives evidence that before our Christian religion was disseminated among these people by the missionaries they worshipped the sun more than anything else in nature. This view seems to have support in the fact that today, after some hundreds of years of contact with our religious views, they still worship the mysterious and unknown in nature.[12]

Although he was mistaken in viewing the Sun Dance as worship of the sun, Clark did sense the goal of the dancer to partake of the incomprehensible mystery, *wakháŋ tháŋka*.

According to Hassrick's anthropological study, there were four reasons for undertaking a Sun Dance. First, and most common, was to fulfill a vow made in return for a favor granted in time of need or distress. Second, men would dance to secure supernatural aid for themselves.[13] Third, dancers occasionally endured the ceremony on behalf of another. Finally, a Lakota seeking a vision or desiring to become a *wichása wakháŋ*, "holy man," would dance to secure the necessary power.[14]

Explaining the Sun Dance through modern Lakota eyes, Amiotte links the ceremony with the Lakota sense of self and goes beyond pragmatic reasons to the spiritual reasons. The purpose of the Sun Dance is to strengthen the four "souls" of a person. The *niyá*, or life breath, ties the body to the innermost being of a person. The *nağí* is a ghost and is very capricious. The *nağíla* is the little ghost that is a part of the *tákuškaŋškaŋ*, that which causes all things to move in the universe. The Lakota phrase *mitákuye oyás'iŋ* expresses the interrelatedness of one person's *nağíla* with that of another. Finally, there is *šichúŋ*, the power that comes through the intervention of the supernatural.[15]

The summaries of Walker and Fletcher add to the diverse opinions about the purpose and meaning of the Sun Dance in the 1800s. The common thread, however, is the strengthening of the dancer's relationship to himself, to the creation, to the community, and to the creator. Beneath this is a connection between earth and sky: astronomy is an integral, yet subtle, part of the Sun Dance.

Conducting a Sun Dance

The first step in holding a Sun Dance in the nineteenth century was to locate the Sun Dance camp, a site flat and open to accommodate a large number of people. Control of the event was turned over to the *wichása wakháŋ*, holy men, and men's societies, called *akíchita*. In modern times it is common to hold a Sun Dance at a public pow-wow arena or in a private location on a reservation.

FIG. 23. Montana Sun Dance site. The structure at what is thought to be a Sun Dance site near Lame Deer, Montana, is similar to the shelters found at many contemporary pow-wow grounds. Contemporary pow-wow structures usually retain the circular shape and entrance on the east side of the Sun Dance lodge, and today the bough-covered shelters serve as a shady sitting area for tribal elders. Photo by Mark Hollabaugh.

After some preparatory activity the Sun Dance lodge was construct-ed. Hill says it was about twenty-five feet in radius, and he makes special note of the east-facing entrance. Central to the lodge was the erection of a large pole, typically cottonwood. The selection, cutting, and erection of the tree that served as the pole were key parts of the preparation for the Sun Dance, and much ceremony accompanied these activities. Other poles were erected around the circumference of the dance circle to form an arbor and often were covered with willows (or pine boughs) woven together. Hill suggests this was for privacy, but the covering would also provide spectators with some protection from the blistering June sun.

A site in Montana about five miles west of Lame Deer along U.S. Highway 212 is thought to be the location of a Sun Dance in 1875. A much more recent structure, presumably used for a Northern Cheyenne pow-wow, sits on the site. The entrance to the structure (left of center and in line with the access road in figure 23) faces east.

An important feature of the Sun Dance is the preparation of the dancers. Each dancer has a principal mentor and other assistants. While some of the preparation is physical, much of it is spiritual in nature. The Sweat Lodge ceremony often precedes participation in a Sun Dance.[16]

Many eyewitness accounts place important Sun Dance events at dawn. Walker describes similar predawn beginnings of another ceremony, the Buffalo Dance.

> At dawn the next morning the people were astir and as the eastern sky grew red the shaman[17] who was to conduct the ceremony came from his tipi and facing toward the east sang this song: —

"A voice, *Anpeo*, hear it.
Speaks low, hear it."[18]

According to his interpreter, *Anpeo* is the red aurora, the forerunner of the sun, a God who should be invoked by song to secure a pleasant day, and this song was such an invocation. In this description Walker does *not* refer to the aurora borealis, but to *maȟpíya luta*, the red sky.[19] When he says *Anpeo* is the *akíchita*, or forerunner of the sun and the red aurora, he is describing the red sky at sunrise and not the northern lights.[20]

One particular practice of the ceremony led to its suppression by the U.S. government and the Christian missionaries: some dancers' chests were pierced with skewers, and they were attached to the Sun Dance pole by long thongs. Dancers moved around the Sun Dance pole until either their flesh gave way or the thong itself broke. Frequently they blew on a small whistle, often made of a goose leg bone. The sign language gesture for Sun Dance combined the motions for *dance* and *whistle*. Clark indicates, "Some add signs for the enclosure, and putting of skewers in muscles of [the] breast."[21] The decorated skull of a buffalo was often attached to the back muscles by similar thongs and dragged about the Sun Dance lodge.

As the Sun Dance progressed, the dancers kept an eye skyward. The dancers at a Yankton Sun Dance looked "directly at the sun by day, and at the moon by night."[22] This recalls the Lakota name for the Sun Dance, *wiwáŋyaŋg wachípi*, "Dance looking at the Sun." Walker gives an interesting interpretation of this skyward gaze:

> The sun is a material god. The sky gave him his power, and can withhold it, but he is more powerful than the sky. Daily he makes his journey above the domain of the sky and at night He resides with his people in the regions under the world and there communes with his comrade, the Buffalo.
>
> The [sky] is the source of all power and motion and is the patron of directions and trails and of encampment.
>
> The Moon is a material God whose substance is visible or partly visible [i.e., phases of the moon], as She wills.[23]

The rhythms of the Sun and Moon are connected to people on earth. The sky is connected to the earth, the earth to the buffalo, and the buffalo to the people. The Lakota's emphasis on the Sun, Moon, and stars in the Sun Dance is an attempt to bring the incomprehensible mystery to earth through the ritual of the Sun Dance.

This earth and sky connection is further seen in their choice of adornment and decoration of the Sun Dance lodge during the Sun Dance. A statement from High Bear about the Lakota's use of celestial symbols during the Sun Dance emphasizes the sacred nature of the symbols:

> In the painting of their bodies they also make a mark on their chest thus: \ | /. This is *wakan*. I believe it indicates the rays of the sun, as the sun is painted on the stomach, and of course all the decorations are *wakan*.[24]

Black Elk also gives an explanation of the celestial symbolism in the Sun Dance. It is significant that he places this in the context of the *wakháŋ tháŋka*, the incomprehensible mystery:

> A *hanhepi wi* [night sun, or moon] should be cut from rawhide in the shape of a crescent, for the moon represents a person and, also, all

things, for everything created waxes and wanes, lives and dies. You should also understand that the night represents ignorance, but it is the moon and the stars which bring the Light of *Wakan Tanka* into this darkness. As you know the moon comes and goes, but *anpetu wi*, the sun, lives on forever; it is the source of light, and because of this it is like *Wakan Tanka*.

A five-pointed star should be cut from rawhide. This will be the sacred Morning Star who stands between the darkness and the light, and who represents knowledge.

A round rawhide circle should be made to represent the sun, and this should be painted red; but at the center there should be a round circle of blue, for this innermost center represents *Wakan Tanka* as our Grandfather. The light of this sun enlightens the entire universe; and as the flames of the sun come to us in the morning, so comes the grace of *Wakan Tanka*, by which all creatures are enlightened.[25]

Black Elk's use of the word *grace* and reference to the enlightenment of all creatures by the light of *Wakan Tanka* sound like phrases from one of his catechism lessons. This most likely is an example of the Christian influence upon Black Elk.

Clark noted celestial imagery as well: "I was told by a Sioux that the enclosure was a church; their Grandmother (the Earth) was represented by the grass and sage, and 'a cross was made at the foot of the pole to represent the sun and stars.'"[26]

Seasonal Timing of the Sun Dance

The Lakota Sun Dance is typically held in the late spring or early summer, usually in June. The Lakota generally took cues from nature to determine the time to begin preparations for their central ceremony.

Alice Fletcher, in one of the earliest written accounts of the Sun Dance in the late 1800s, said the dance occurred when the prairie sage bloomed.[27] Typically this is in June. Other sources report the rite taking place when the chokecherries ripen.[28] This would place the Sun Dance later in the summer, perhaps July or August, depending upon the local climate. Prairie sage is common throughout western North America. Fletcher may have confused this species with the other varieties of sage found in the western Great Plains, but all bloom in the late spring.[29]

Black Elk links terrestrial phenomena with celestial events when he ties together the blooming of plants with the phase of the Moon:

> It [the Sun Dance] is held each year during the Moon of Fattening (June) or the Moon of Cherries Blackening (July), always at the time when the moon is full, for the growing and dying of the moon reminds us of our ignorance which comes and goes; but when the moon is full it is as if the eternal light of the Great Spirit were upon the whole world.[30]

Likewise, James Walker in his monograph on the Sun Dance gave four criteria that combine earth and sky for the timing of the ritual:

1. When the buffalo are fat.
2. When new sprouts of sage are a span long.
3. When chokecherries are ripening.
4. When the moon is rising as the sun is going down. [i.e., full moon][31]

Walker's set of natural events appears to merge Fletcher's and Black Elk's criteria.

Most of the nineteenth-century Sun Dances for which accurate dates are known occurred in June. Clark notes the Sun Dance usually occurred during "full of the moon in June."[32] Other accounts also say the Sun Dance took place in June at the "full of the moon" or at the moon of ripening chokecherries and lasted twelve days.[33] Lakota artist Amiotte commented, "The Northern Lakota tradition, that of the Hunkpapa and Sihasapa (Blackfoot Sioux) bands, is to have the Sun Dance take place around the summer solstice, when the June-berries are ripe."[34]

Determining the precise date of the summer solstice merely by watching the movement of the sunrise along the eastern horizon is difficult. Sunrise at the equinox is always due east, and the azimuth of the rising Sun moves quickly along the horizon at that time of the year. Unlike the equinox events, the azimuth of the sunrise in June changes very slowly.

One actually may not know the solstice has occurred until it is past and the sunrise position begins to move south along the northeastern horizon. Anticipating the solstice can be crucial. Observing the sunrise, or sunset, position with respect to horizon landmarks may help.

Amiotte reports a tradition involving the use of a calendar stick to predict the time of the summer solstice:

> The old-man-who-counts watches the sunset, cutting notches in his stick, even though with calendars this is no longer necessary. The old man watches until the sun sets on a well-known landmark. When finally it reaches the appropriate place, the time has come to make the sacred lodge.[35]

Thus, marking the movement of the sunrise *prior* to the solstice may be of paramount importance for the Lakota, as it apparently was for the pueblo dwellers of the Southwest.[36] Amiotte told me in 1996 that Sun watching was practiced at the time of the winter solstice. He mentioned that although nomadic, the Lakota did return to the same location each year for their "winter camp," and hence they would recognize familiar horizon landmarks. However, the use of a landmark for the summer solstice Sun watching would require the Lakota to return to the same place each June, an unlikely occurrence as they roamed the plains. Amiotte also said he knew of no Lakota calendar sticks in existence today in any private or museum collection.[37]

Black Elk stated that the "Morning Star brings wisdom."[38] One might expect that the appearance of the Morning Star (Venus, or perhaps Jupiter) in the predawn sky signaled the time for a Sun Dance, but this was probably seldom the case because Venus is not always the Morning Star in June. While it is possible for Venus to appear low on the horizon in June at the time of the full moon, it does not do so every year. The synodic period of Venus is 584 days. This is the time interval between successive appearances of Venus above the horizon at the *same* place *and* time with respect to the Sun. If the Sun Dance occurred at about the same time in June each year, there would be an interval of almost eight years (2,920 days) between successive apparitions of Venus in the

June predawn sky.[39] If one is not particular about Venus being in *exactly* the same place in the *June* sky, reappearances as the morning star are much more common, due to the 584-day interval that it takes Venus to be above the eastern horizon at western elongation. In all likelihood, any appearance of Venus in the morning sky at the time of a June Sun Dance was merely a happy coincidence.

Buechel has a reference to holding a Sun Dance at the time the morning star is visible. He also indicates the dancers faced east when they began the ceremony.

> The sun dance lasts for 2–4 days. In the morning when the morning star is still visible, they begin the ceremonies. They face the east with their hands lifted. Have no clothes on. While they move rhythmically up and down they blow the *šiyót'aŋka* keeping time — ho-ho-ho—eagle bone and feather bound tight to the lower end of the flute. The women have the *wíŋyaŋ wic'áglata* in their right hand and move it up and down while they move up and down with their bodies (see specimen).[40]

Although Venus as the Morning Star is not always visible in the morning sky in June, the symbolic representation of the Morning Star on the body of a dancer is a part of the Lakota attempt to grab onto a part of the cosmic mystery. It is yet another example of the quest to bring the extraordinary down to earth.

These comments suggest that the nineteenth-century Lakota preferred to have the Sun Dance during a full moon near the time of the summer solstice in June. However, attempting to correlate specific Sun Dances with astronomical phenomena is difficult due to the lack of reliable information of specific dates on which the ceremony occurred. In some cases white observers of the event made notes and wrote down the date, but in many cases there are only vague references, such as "late June."

The four modern-day Rosebud Sun Dances observed by Thomas E. Mails took place in July, two of them during the extended Fourth of July holiday and none of them at full moon.[41] A more recent analysis of the Sun Dance suggests late July or early August for holding the ritual.[42]

Of six nineteenth-century Lakota Sun Dances for which there are specific dates, four occurred at the full moon. The two exceptions are noteworthy: Sitting Bull's Sun Dance of 1876 took place under a waning gibbous moon, and a 1881 Sun Dance at Pine Ridge occurred at a waning crescent, almost new moon.

The 1876 Sitting Bull Sun Dance

If the Sun Dance must be held at the time of the full moon in June, one might anticipate a Sun Dance in which Sitting Bull participated to have followed this tradition in 1876. However, Lakota thought and practice is fluid: no rubric or dogmatic rule governs the timing of any event. The Sun Dance happens when the holy men deem it is the right time.

The Sun Dance was held on Rosebud Creek near Lame Deer, Montana, in mid-June 1876, just prior to the Lakota's encounter with General Terry at the Battle of the Rosebud, and about two weeks prior to Custer's demise along the banks of the Little Bighorn River. It was at this Sun Dance that Sitting Bull had his famous vision of soldiers falling into the Indians' camp. A few days after this Sun Dance, Custer's troops, hot on the trail of Sitting Bull, camped at the same location. A small stone monument along Montana Highway 39 about nine miles northeast of Lame Deer marks the location today.[43]

The moon was full on 6 June 1876. Sitting Bull danced in this Sun Dance around 15 June, when the moon had just passed from a waning gibbous phase to a waning crescent. On 15 June 1876 at sunrise the moon was about 28° above the southeast horizon, and Saturn, 29° above the horizon, was about 10° farther south in the sky than the moon. Saturn probably didn't make much of an impression due to its low altitude and relative dimness compared to Venus, which also may be why Saturn was not considered the morning star. Neptune, also in the sky at sunrise, was invisible to the naked eye. There were no other significant astronomical displays at sunrise in mid-June 1876.

Sitting Bull had more on his mind than what was in the sky. For the Lakota, the victory at the Little Bighorn was religiously sanctioned.[44] Spiritual and pressing military concerns seemed to be the determining factor in the timing of this Sun Dance, rather than astronomical considerations. This may not have been the case for two other noteworthy Sun Dances.

The 1875 Chadron Sun Dance

In June of 1875 a great Sun Dance was held near the present city of Chadron, Nebraska. Lieutenant Frederick Schwatka, an army officer, observed this dance, and his account shows the importance of the Sun's position in the sky for the Sun Dance. The site of the Sun Dance is thought to be at the location of the modern-day Chadron airport. One remarkable aspect of this Sun Dance is that the Oglala at the agency near Fort Robinson, twenty miles to the southwest, joined forces with the Brulé from the Spotted Tail Agency, located about twenty miles to the northeast on Beaver Creek.[45] Schwatka notes,

> In general it is almost impossible for a white man to gain permission to view this ceremony in all its details; but I had in Spotted Tail, the chief, and in Standing Elk, the head warrior, two very warm friends, and their promise that I should behold the rites in part slowly widened and allowed me to obtain full view of the entire proceedings.[46]

Schwatka reports between fifteen thousand and twenty thousand Lakota were present at this event, and if this is the case and not an exaggeration, then it must have been one of the biggest tribal events recorded. Unlike Hill, he does not relate or even speculate on the reason for the Sun Dance, reporting only what he saw.

Schwatka does not give an exact date for this Sun Dance. In fact, he does not even say it was in 1875. But near the end of his article he says,

> Within a year they had checked, at the Rosebud Hills in Montana, the largest army we had ever launched against the American Indians in a single fight; had retired successfully to the Little Big Horn, a few miles away, and there, a week later, had wiped Custer's fine command from the face of the earth; had held Reno for two days upon a hill.[47]

This comment suggests a mid-June, 1875, date for this Sun Dance.

The full moon was on 18 June 1875, three days before the solstice.

An hour before sunrise Venus, the Morning Star and brightest celestial object that morning, was a mere 8° above the east-northeast horizon, and the Pleiades were visible just above Venus. Saturn, brighter than any nearby star, was 32° above the southern horizon. Mars, hovering on the southwest horizon, was probably too low to be seen. Neptune would not have been visible to the naked eye. For this Sun Dance at least, the full moon and the Morning Star were opposite one another in the morning sky.

Unfortunately Schwatka, perhaps caught up in the spectacular events he witnessed, makes no mention of the planets or the moon. He does, however, report one very significant action preceding the felling of the tree for the Sun Dance lodge. In typical nineteenth-century fashion Schwatka's entire account is peppered with language that irritates our modern ears.

> Not far away, on a high hill overlooking the barbaric scene, was an old warrior, a medicine-man of the tribe, I think, whose solemn duty it was to announce by a shout that could be heard by every one of the expectant throng the exact moment when the tip of the morning sun appeared above the eastern hills. Perfect quiet rested upon the line of young warriors and upon the great throng of savage spectators that blacked the green hills overlooking the arena. Suddenly the old warrior, who had been kneeling on one knee, with his extended palm shading his scraggy eyebrows, arose to his full height, and in a slow, dignified manner waved his blanketed arm above his head. The few warriors who were still unmounted now jumped hurriedly upon their ponies; the broken, wavering line rapidly took on a more regular appearance; and then the old man, who had gathered himself for the great effort, hurled forth a yell that could be heard to the uttermost limits of the great throng. The morning sun had sent its commands to its warriors on earth to charge.[48]

Schwatka was not an artist, but the editors of *Century Magazine* enlisted Frederick Remington to draw a sketch of the old man watching the sun. One of Edward Curtis's photographs (*Invocation—Sioux*) shows a

Lakota man greeting the morning sun. That photo may record the sight that comes closest to what Schwatka observed.[49]

George Hill's Sun Dance account also noted that the Sun Dance began in earnest "at the first appearing of the sun":

> Just outside of the inclosure [sic] on a little elevation stood the medicine-man, a powerfully built Sioux, rather more than six feet high, straight as an arrow, he had an intelligent face, dressed in his official robes, beside these he had on a buffalo robe with the skin of the head attached and worn as a hood which was fastened under his chin, hanging down his back ending in a trail some three or four feet long. Thus caparisoned was he who was to give the signal to start the dance. As he stood there, the centre of all eyes, with his extended palm over his eyes to catch the first glimmer of the morning sun, as its golden edge showed itself above the horizon he waved his hand and gave a shout which was taken up and echoed by a thousand voices who had been waiting quietly for the signal, so too, the orchestra struck in with their tomtoms and those who were in the circular line led off in the dance.[50]

The difference between Hill's account of the "medicine-man's" action and Schwatka's report is when this proclamation occurred. Hill places it at the beginning of the dance proper, but Schwatka places the announcement of the sunrise before the felling of the tree for the Sun Dance pole.[51] Although Hill might have been overcome with excitement, or he recalled the event later, his observation may be accurate in spite of this apparent discrepancy.

The 1881 Pine Ridge Sun Dance

Due to government intervention, the last great Sun Dances that drew thousands of people occurred in early 1880s.[52] Captain John Gregory Bourke was present at the Sun Dance held in June 1881 at the Pine Ridge Reservation. Bourke the soldier was also a writer, a self-taught anthropologist and ethnographer. His journals, diaries, and books provide valuable and important insights into the Native American culture in the western and southwestern United States in the late 1800s. Following the Civil War, he was nominated to West Point, from which he graduated in 1869. His first assignment was in the Southwest. Almost immediately upon his commissioning, Bourke emerged as a soldier-scholar.[53]

In the fall of 1871 Bourke had the good fortune to become an aide-de-camp to General George Crook. Crook, other military leaders, and political authorities began to rely on his copious notes and diaries. Bourke was present with Crook at the Battle of the Rosebud in June 1876, and although Bourke functioned as a soldier in this encounter, his writing about the event sounds more like that of an ethnographer than that of a military historian.[54]

By the early 1880s Bourke had established himself as an expert on Indian culture.[55] On 31 March 1881, under orders from General Philip H. Sheridan, Bourke left Omaha for Santa Fe, where he undertook extensive observations of pueblo dwellers.[56] Bourke essentially commuted between Santa Fe and Omaha over the next several months. His diary is filled with accounts of encounters with all sorts of people, as well as his impressions of the landscape.[57]

On one trip he took time to stop at Fort Robinson, Nebraska, where he learned of a Sun Dance to be held some fifty miles to the northeast at the Pine Ridge Agency. His notes on this Sun Dance are some of the most extensive Sun Dance observations in existence.[58] Bourke had the support of both Chief Red Cloud and Indian agent Dr. Valentine T. McGillycuddy to observe this Sun Dance, which he did on 22 June 1881, the day of the summer solstice.[59]

What lunar phase was visible for this Sun Dance? On 22 June the Moon was *not* a full moon, but four days before the new moon, and the waning crescent Moon hung low in the eastern sky before sunrise on the solstice. What else was in the sky on that morning? The answer is remarkable.

At 3:00 a.m., an hour before the Sun rose at 4:08 a.m., the Moon's thin crescent was 19° above the eastern horizon. Jupiter shone about 3° below the Moon, and Venus was 2½° below Jupiter or about 13° above the horizon. The two brightest planets alone should have caught the eye of anyone watching the morning sky in the days preceding the Sun Dance, but there was more to the spectacle. Saturn was 7° to the south of the Moon, and Mars, farther west along the ecliptic, was 13½° from the Moon. In other words, *all* of the naked-eye planets except for Mercury (seen by very few people), were visible in the predawn sky near the waning Moon! Could this Sun Dance have been timed to coincide with the solstice and this remarkable display of the Morning Star with the other naked-eye planets? Did this conjunction take precedence over the full moon? The Lakota could have known the precise date of the solstice due to the availability of modern calendars in 1881.

Bourke's diary provides a vivid and thorough account of this Sun Dance. He spares no detail. First of all, when Bourke reached Fort Robinson on 4 June, he "learned with great regret that" the date of the Sun Dance had been postponed from "the full of the moon, June 11th, 1881 until the 20th of the same month." He notes the Sun Dance is normally held "in the Full of the Moon of Leaves . . . the middle of June."[60] His travels took him back to Omaha, where he met with General Sheridan and former president Grant. After returning to Fort Robinson, Bourke journeyed to Pine Ridge, arriving on the morning of 20 June. Bourke also reveals that sign language expert Lt. William Clark was present at this Sun Dance.[61]

Given the detail Bourke includes in his diaries, one would expect him to include some reference to the appearance of the predawn sky on June 22. Unfortunately, what he says is disappointing to an astronomer who always hopes for clear, weather-friendly skies. On 20 June he notes that a "severe thunder storm, suddenly arriving, interrupted the ceremony for 15 or 20 minutes." Later in the day he reports a "driving rain-storm" and that the "sun came out at a quarter past three." That evening the sky was clear, and the morning of 21 June "opened fine and almost cloudless." Bourke notes the Sun Dance structure was completed by 2 o'clock in the afternoon, and eight thousand Lakota were in attendance. However, "at sundown, we had a brief but severe storm of rain, thunder and lightning." What would the morning of the solstice sunrise bring?

Bourke does not say at what hour he arose, nor does he indicate when he went to bed the previous night. He does, however, solve the mystery of why there is no comment about the morning sky in any of the accounts of this Sun Dance: "A cloudy day without indication of storm." It seems as though nature conspired to conceal the celestial display from the diarist as well as the assembled Lakota.

Nowhere in Bourke's diary does he reveal why the Sun Dance was postponed until later in June. Could it have been due to the timing of the solstice? Might the appearance in the sky of the four planets and the Moon have influenced the decision? Could it have been the appearance of the Moon near Venus, the Morning Star? The answer may never be known.

Edgar Beecher Bronson observed this Sun Dance as well.[62] Agent McGillycuddy invited Bronson, a nearby Nebraska rancher, to attend the Sun Dance. Bronson said the Sun Dance was "held but once a year— always in the full of a spring moon, usually in June, when the green grass was well up and the ponies fat and strong and ready for whatever desperate foray the excitement of the dance might inspire." Bronson noted the presence of "Major Bourke."[63] Bronson wrote that he didn't remember exactly whether this Sun Dance was in 1880 or 1881, but the presence of Bourke certainly makes it 1881. He also says it took place about two miles south of the agency along White Clay Creek at a place he calls "Sun Dance Flat," a bit farther south than Bourke's estimate of a few thousand yards south of the agency, which is probably more accurate. Bronson claims the teepees of the assembled multitude were arranged in an elliptical shape parallel to the course of the creek, with the opening to the ellipse at the *north* end. Given the Lakota penchant to face east, this may be a lapse in Bronson's memory, or simply a secondary entrance he saw. In any case, the twelve thousand Oglala and Brulé made a lasting impression on Bronson.

The dancers were housed in a very large teepee due east of the Sun Dance pole and took part in a succession of sweat baths prior to the actual Sun Dance. Although Bronson does not mention the number of poles supporting the Sun Dance lodge roof, he does state the lodge was circular and notes an entrance to the lodge was on the east side.

On the day of the Sun Dance, the dance began "just as the sun rose above the horizon." His observation of the sunrise disagrees with Bourke's comments about the weather. He may be referring to sunrise on a different day of this Sun Dance or simply may have embellished his account, written years after the actual event. The degree to which he was amazed by what was happening in the dance, as opposed to the sky, is evidenced in his lack of comment about the Moon *not* being full.

Location and Orientation of the Sun Dance Lodge

Could astronomy have something to do with the selection of a Sun Dance site? Probable locations are known for the 1875 Chadron and 1881 Pine Ridge Sun Dances, and published accounts can be checked for any reference to how the dance lodge or Sun Dance tree was erected with respect to the horizon.

The 1881 Sun Dance at Pine Ridge took place south of Pine Ridge along the banks of White Clay Creek, most likely in what is now Nebraska.[64] It also is possible this event actually occurred in South Dakota, just south of the current Pine Ridge rodeo grounds, the location of present-day large-scale gatherings.[65] The actual site of the 1881 Sun Dance may now be underwater because a small dam has been built on White Clay Creek about one-third mile north of the South Dakota–Nebraska border. A small undeveloped campground, Three Moccasin Park, is located less than a mile north of the border. All of these locations are relatively flat and accessible.

Regardless of the exact site, the terrain along White Clay Creek would have allowed for a gathering of a large number of Oglala. The rise of hills to the west of the creek might have served as a location for the type of crier witnessed by Schwatka in 1875. The land gradually slopes upward about five hundred feet in seven miles ($< 1°$) in the direction of the sunrise. The relatively featureless eastern horizon in 1881 would have provided a good view of the planetary conjunction.

Likewise, Schwatka's 1875 Sun Dance at the site of the present-day Chadron Airport obviously presented a large, flat area to accommodate the huge gathering. The ceremony was held along the banks of the White

River on a large, flat plain. The terrain in the direction of the sunrise gradually rises only about two hundred feet in seven miles. In neither this case nor that of the 1881 dance are there any dramatic horizon markers that could have been used for Sun watching prior to the Sun Dance.

Even though these specific Sun Dance sites show no astronomical alignment or positioning, the Sun Dance lodge is astronomically aligned.[66] Sign language expert Clark notes, "The tepees were formed in a circle, with an open space towards the east."[67] Black Elk faced the Sun Dance lodge entrance to the east. He also stated that twenty-eight additional poles are used to form the sides and roof of the Sun Dance lodge. This is in keeping with his idea of the sacredness of this number. Twenty-eight is not only the number of days in the lunar synodic month when the moon is visible, but it is also four times seven, recalling the four cardinal directions and the seven council fires of the Lakota.[68]

Black Elk's statement, coupled with Clark's 1877 observation and Hill's observation at Fort Sully in 1875, makes it seem clear that the alignment of the Sun Dance lodge entrance facing east is intentional and a persistent feature of the Sun Dance. It also is consistent with arranging the entrance to a tipi, camp circle, ceremonial altar, or sweat lodge so it faces east, although the eastward orientation of these structures is not a rigid requirement.[69]

The Sun Dance tree likewise shows an alignment with the Sun. A fork in the tree was aligned so a north-south line passed through the fork. Michael Melody notes, "Thus, symbolically the sun passes through the fork of the pole. At noon, the sun is directly above the pole. It could thus be viewed as a resting place for the sun."[70]

The Sun Dance lodge with its entrance facing east; twenty-eight poles supporting the sides of the shelter; and the symbols of the Sun, Moon, and stars as adornments on both the lodge and the dancers is yet another image of the sky brought down to earth. Archaeoastronomer Ray Williamson referred to Casa Rinconada at Chaco Canyon in New Mexico as a metaphor in wood and stone for the cosmos.[71] The Sun Dance and its lodge is yet another Native American metaphor for the heavens. The dance allows the participants to connect themselves to the energy from the Sun, which stands highest in the sky at the summer solstice.[72] The Sun Dance is an attempt to participate in the harmony of the heavens. Arthur Amiotte noted that in the Sun Dance, the dancer realizes "the wholeness and unity of all things. The spiritual, the temporal, the gross, the profane, the common all come together at one time."[73] The ceremonial conjunction of the Spirit and the Sky can be added to his list.

10

CONTEMPORARY LAKOTA ASTRONOMY

In many respects, Comet Halley heralded a new age in 1910. Physics and astronomy underwent incredible paradigm shifts in the early twentieth century, and scientists adapted to new ways of looking at the physical world. The Lakota, now confined to reservations and relegated to a very different way of life, also adapted. Lakota astronomy did not end but followed new paths. Astronomy continues to be a part of Lakota culture even into the twenty-first century. A Lakota holy man and a contemporary book reflect this continuity.

Archie Fire Lame Deer and the Sweat Lodge

Archie Fire Lame Deer (1935–2001), the son of John Fire Lame Deer (d. 1976) and a resident of the Rosebud Reservation, was a twentieth-century Lakota holy man whose thought demonstrates an integration of contemporary concepts with an older tradition. His book *Gift of Power*, coauthored with Richard Erdoes, discusses sixteen Great Mysteries as embodied in the design of the Lakota sweat lodge. Precise interpretation can be challenging.

Lame Deer and Erdoes illustrate the mysteries with a sweat lodge diagram they call a Lakota cosmology, claiming Lame Deer learned these mysteries from his grandfather. In its modern use *cosmology* refers to the structure and evolution of the universe. A cosmologist is concerned with understanding the origin of the universe, the relationship between its components, and its ultimate evolutionary fate. In their usage, however, *cosmology* represents the relationships among sixteen Great Mysteries.

Eight poles hold up the roof of the sweat lodge. These poles have sixteen ends, and the ends are said to represent the sixteen Great Mysteries.

The extent to which these sixteen concepts reflect nineteenth-century Lakota beliefs is unknown. Four concentric circular roof supports complete the structure, holding up the hide roof of the sweat lodge. The second circular support from the center intersects a pair of poles in eight places. These eight intersections are labeled with the names of the planets known in the last half of the twentieth century, but not in astronomical order. Starting with Mercury, which is to the left of the west-facing door, the order is Mercury, Saturn, Venus, Neptune, Mars, Pluto, Uranus, and Jupiter.[1]

Three planetary objects—Uranus, Neptune, and Pluto—appearing on this sweat lodge scheme, suggest the cosmology is from the very late nineteenth century or most likely the early twentieth century. Very faint Uranus was discovered in 1781 by the German-born English astronomer and church musician William Herschel, who used a telescope to make his discovery. There are reports of naked-eye observations of Uranus, but they are extremely rare. A person with excellent eyesight might be able to see Uranus if he or she knew exactly where to look.

Deviations in the orbit of Uranus led to predictions of an eighth planet by the French astronomer Urbain Jean Joseph LeVerrier and the English mathematician John Couch Adams. German astronomer Johann Gottfried Galle subsequently discovered Neptune telescopically in 1846. Neptune is fainter than the limit of naked-eye seeing and cannot be seen without a telescope.[2]

Clyde Tombaugh discovered Pluto photographically in 1930. Pluto would have been totally unknown to the nineteenth-century Lakota, and most likely to Archie Fire Lame Deer's grandfather. Hence any reference to Pluto is post-1930. In 2007 Pluto was declassified as a planet and given the status of a trans-Neptunian dwarf planet. Should Pluto be removed to update the diagram? What would replace Pluto to maintain the symmetry? It is possible the Lakota first learned of Uranus and Neptune in the boarding schools of the late nineteenth century. What is certain, however, is that Pluto was *not* known to the late nineteenth-century Lakota. The sweat lodge scheme described by Archie Fire Lame Dear reflects a definite twentieth-century influence.

Further complicating the issue of what is traditional knowledge and what is innovation or borrowing is the uncertain role of Erdoes as co-author of *Gift of Power*. Previously, Erdoes coauthored another book with Archie Fire Lame Deer's father, John Fire Lame Deer, *Lame Deer: Seeker of Visions*. Some material in the earlier book was gleaned by Erdoes from published anthropological sources, including writings of James Walker. It seems possible—even likely—that Erdoes introduced planetary references into the sweat lodge and attributed the information to Archie Fire Lame Deer.[3] Early descriptions of the sweat lodge do not include this cosmology.[4] The best conclusion is that Erdoes (and perhaps the younger Archie Fire Lame Deer) modified the sweat lodge description to include modern astronomical concepts. What is certain, and important for this discussion, is that astronomy continued to be a part of Lakota culture in the twentieth century.

Lakota Star Knowledge

In the late 1980s the Lakota Studies Department at Sinte Gleska University on the Rosebud Reservation undertook an oral history project to document what late twentieth-century Lakota elders believed about the stars. Lakota who contributed to this effort also associated constellations with specific locations in the Black Hills. These associations and other aspects of what they call "star knowledge" are the basis of Ronald Goodman's *Lakota Star Knowledge: Studies in Lakota Stellar Theology*.[5] Although the book does not directly bear Goodman's name and was a collective effort of sixty-one Lakota acknowledged in the book, he is apparently the author of the uncredited first-person accounts in the book. The Sinte Gleska University website summarized the Lakota Star Knowledge Project Collection and also indicated Goodman died in 2001.

These records were generated by an ethnoastronomy project conducted by SGU Instructor Ronald Goodman (1932–2001.) The project was designed to document star knowledge existing in the memory of Lakota elders. Included are audiotaped interviews with tribal elders, handwritten notes about other interviews, correspondence, news clippings, and drafts for articles. Goodman published the results of his study in Lakota Star Knowledge: Studies in Lakota Stellar Theology. Access to the Star Knowledge Project materials (except secondary articles collected by Goodman while doing his research) is subject to approval by the Chairperson of the Sinte Gleska University Lakota Studies Department. Contact Archives Staff for information on restrictions.[6]

The names for stars or constellations in the booklet are mostly from Buechel's dictionary or his ethnographic notes and generally follow Buechel's orthography. Presumably the names not in the Buechel dictionary are terms used in the late twentieth century or from the project's consultants. This cataloging of the contemporary names is an important contribution to ethnoastronomy.

In addition to general information on stars and constellations, the book also has several contemporary interpretations of Lakota culture, including "The After-Death Journey among the Stars" and "Lakota Midwives and the Stars." Goodman's essay on "The Hand" constellation is included as well.[7] The Fallen Star story also is paraphrased and interpreted.[8]

In an appendix Lakota Star Knowledge lists eleven constellations on the ecliptic and three circumpolar constellations. Some of these have already been tabulated in table 4.[9] The number eleven in itself is not troubling, given that the delineation of a constellation is arbitrary. What is troublesome, at least to astronomy, is that the sixth "constellation" is Venus as the Morning Star. Although Venus is always near the ecliptic, it is not always the Morning Star, and its location along the ecliptic, unlike a constellation, is constantly changing. Moreover, Venus is never visible for several hours each night due to its solar system location as an inferior planet. The only real correlation with traditional ecliptic constellations of the zodiac is Mathóthipila (part of Gemini) and Heȟáka (part of Pisces). This suggests the ecliptic of Lakota Star Knowledge is not the ecliptic of traditional astronomy.

The Milky Way is also listed as an ecliptic "constellation." The plane of our Milky Way galaxy is not aligned in any direct sense with the celestial sphere and in particular not with the ecliptic. Although the Milky

TABLE 11. *Lakota Star Knowledge* ecliptic constellations

LAKOTA NAME	TRANSLATION	COMMON STARS/ CONSTELLATION
Chaŋšáša Ipúsye	Dried Willow	Triangulum, Alpha and Beta Arietis
Wichíŋcala Šakówiŋ	Seven Little Girls	Pleiades
Thayámni	First born of the three relations	Pleiades, Orion's belt, Betelguese, Rigel, Sirius
Ki Inyanka Ki'íŋyaŋka Ocháŋku	The Race Track	Castor, Pollux, Procyon, Sirius, Rigel, Pleiades, Capella, and Beta Aurigae
Mathóthipila	Bear's Lodge	8 of the 12 stars in Gemini
Áŋpo Wicháȟpi	Morning Star	Venus
Itkób ú	Going Toward	Alpha Böotes
Wanáǧi Thacháŋku	The Road of the Spirits	Milky Way
Napé	The Hand	Orion's Belt, Orion's Sword, Rigel, and Beta Eridani
Zuzéca	The Snake	(No correlation given)
Heȟáa	The Elk	Five stars in Pisces

Way crosses the ecliptic in Sagittarius in the summer sky and passes through Gemini and Taurus in the winter sky, it is not a constellation in the traditional sense, and indeed only a small part of it encounters the ecliptic. The importance of the Milky Way as the *Wanáǧi Thacháŋku*, the Spirits' Road, may account for including the Milky Way with the ecliptic constellations. This departure from traditional astronomy suggests *Lakota Star Knowledge* uses different definitions of *ecliptic* and *constellation*. These definitions may be more conceptual than geometrical; that is, they relate cultural concepts as opposed to spatial relationships.

Another example illustrates this departure from astronomy. At the Northern Plains Indian Art Market in Sioux Falls in 2009, a speaker from the Star Knowledge Project discussed the ideas the project had documented. At times he used thirteen constellations on the ecliptic and at other times only twelve, but not the eleven cited in the book. Precession of the equinox was discussed, but the physical explanation of the cause was incorrect and added to the inconsistency.

Lakota Star Knowledge also lists three circumpolar constellations: *Wicháȟpi Owáŋžila*, "star which stands in one place" (Polaris); *Wakíŋyaŋ*, the Thunderbird (thirteen stars of Draco plus two stars from Ursa Major); and *Wichákiyuhapi*, the dipper (seven stars of the Big Dipper asterism). Polaris, of course, is not a constellation, and its minute circumpolar path can be detected only with precise measurements. The Big and Little Dippers and Draco are the most prominent circumpolar constellations from the latitude of Rosebud, South Dakota. However, the omission of other prominent circumpolar constellations such as Cassiopeia is curious, and hence the list is incomplete.

The delineation of eighty-eight constellations by the International Astronomical Union is a modern definition. (And the precise definition of *ecliptic* is the apparent path of the Sun through the background of stars.) The traditional thirteen ecliptic constellations of astronomy are deeply rooted in the fact that 12.4 lunar months fit into the solar year. Although the very first Western calendars were based in astronomy, they served a cultural purpose, namely the regulation of civil and religious affairs.

While from the perspective of modern astronomy the project has taken great liberty with the use of *constellation* and *ecliptic*, the reason for the difficulties with the Star Knowledge Project's list of constellations actually may be in forcing the modern astronomical definitions of *constellation* and *ecliptic* onto celestial phenomena the Lakota actually saw: the appearance of the brightest planet, the movement of the planets or Sun among the stars, and the fuzzy plane of the galaxy. Embedded in the book is an effort to relate the patterns seen in the sky to patterns on earth, and this is a cultural construct. The result is a complex linkage between earth and sky.

The Star Knowledge Project identifies star groups that lie on "The Race Track," a circular path that they say is mirrored by geographical features in the Black Hills. Two maps, one celestial and one terrestrial, drawn on hides,

TABLE 12. Some stars on the Race Track

CELESTIAL STAR GROUPING	TERRESTRIAL ASSOCIATION	CEREMONY
Chaŋšáša Ipúsye (Big Dipper)	The winter camps	Vernal Equinox and Pipe Ceremony
Wichíŋcala Šakówiŋ (Pleiades)	Harney Peak	Welcoming back the thunders
Thayámni (Betelgeuse; Rigel, ribs; Orion's belt, backbone, Aldebaran and Pleiades, head; Sirius, tail)	An animal	
Center of *Ki'íŋyaŋka Ocháŋku* (The Race Track)	Pe Sla, a bare hill in the Black Hills now called Slate Prairie	Welcoming back all life in peace
Mathó Thípila (The Bear Lodge)	Devils Tower	Summer Solstice and Sun Dance

and interviews with Lakota elders were the source of their information. One of the hides was lost following the 1973 Wounded Knee occupation, and presumably consultants to the project would have recalled it from memory. Although the book includes a hand-drawn replica of the other hide, the author does not reproduce a photograph but indicates the source was a hide belonging to Amos Bad Heart Bull. *Lakota Star Knowledge* does not mention that the hide was buried with Bad Heart Bull's daughter.

The drawing of the original Bad Heart Bull hide was taken from a pictographic history created by Amos Bad Heart Bull and turned into a book edited by Helen Blish.[10] Bad Heart Bull's history relates games, customs, battles, treaties, and dealings with the white culture and contains little of religious or astronomical significance. The author of *Lakota Star Knowledge* relied on drawing no. 198 in *A Pictographic History of the Oglala Sioux*.[11] Some of the star groupings on the Race Track are drawn as astronomers customarily depict them. *Thayámni*, specific to the Lakota, combines six stars, constellations, or asterisms.

The terrestrial associations on the Race Track encircle the Black Hills. Essentially, modern I-90 from Rapid City to the Wyoming border traces the northeastern quadrant of the circle. Besides the Race Track itself, nine other geographic features are identified in the drawing: Bear Lodge Butte (i.e., Devils Tower, northwest of the Black Hills), Slim Buttes (north of the Black Hills), Black Butte (northwestern Black Hills), Old Baldy (north central Black Hills), Ghost Butte (western Black Hills), Bear Butte (northern Black Hills), Hot Springs (southern Black Hills), Buffalo Gap (southeastern Black Hills), and Thunder Butte (northeast of the Black Hills).

A geographer may be troubled by the inclusion of Bear Lodge Butte, or Devils Tower, *within* the mountainous Black Hills instead of on the prairies to the northwest of the Hills. Although our nation's first national monument lies outside the Black Hills proper, most tourist guidebooks include it with the Black Hills, and indeed many visitors to the region see Devils Tower as a part of their Black Hills vacation. The author of *Lakota Star Knowledge* recognized this discrepancy and noted that the Black Hills are a "sacred enclosure," and with that "theological meaning" Bad Heart Bull included Bear Lodge Butte inside the "Sacred Circle."[12]

This statement gives an insight into the interpretation of the maps. In terms of contemporary Lakota sacred geography, Bear Lodge Butte (Devils Tower) is very much a part of the Black Hills. The Bad Heart Bull map is a conceptual, almost idealized, image of the Black Hills rather than a literal topography. It shows relationships between the earthly and the sacred ceremonies, between the sky and the sacred ceremonies, between the earth and the sky.

The Race Track is only one part of the Star Knowledge Project. The project also made reference to "sticks" used for "telling time," but it is not clear whether these are calendar sticks used to mark the passage of time. Crossed sticks, ×, resembling equilateral triangles represent a vortex in which the sky and earth meet. The project gives examples of Lakota art in which this mandala is used. A symbol with two equilateral triangles touching at their vertices suggests a mirroring of what is in the sky on the earth, specifically the Black Hills.

Lakota Star Knowledge, while an important contribution to contemporary ethnoastronomy, runs into difficulty with its interpretation of material the project collected. For example, using precession of the equinox, the project dates Lakota occupation of the Black Hills much earlier (perhaps two thousand years earlier) than most historical accounts allow. To his credit, Goodman apparently consulted with three reputable astronomers: Ray Williamson, the now-deceased John Eddy, and Von Del Chamberlain. While there is no problem with the calculations themselves, the interpretation of the precession is questionable. One can show an alignment of just about *any* structure or geographical feature on earth with some point in the sky at some time in the past, present, or future. The alignment itself has little meaning, but the culture finds and defines the meaning in the alignment.

Another difficulty is found in the subtitle, *Studies in Lakota Stellar Theology*. The Fallen Star story is referred to as sacred literature, and the story is placed into a larger cultural context by Goodman.

> The stories of the Lakota Oral Tradition are sacred literature. Therefore, they must like other scriptures, be understood on four levels of consciousness. These levels correspond, the Lakota say, to our physical, emotional, intellectual and spiritual natures and these are related to the unfolding of the four stages of life; childhood, youth, adulthood, and old age. The first three levels of understanding can come eventually to any earnest seeker, as he or she grows and matures. But the spirits alone can give us the last and highest comprehension.[13]

In a footnote, the author adds: "Similar levels when reading Jewish and Christian scriptures have traditionally been called: (1) literal, (2) allegorical, (3) moral/philosophical, and (4) anagogical."[14] While the four stages of childhood, youth, adulthood, and old age fit with the Lakota culture, the "emotional" and "intellectual" categories of "consciousness" seem foreign to a traditional Lakota worldview.

Part of the difficulty lies in the use of the word *theology*. A more precise, although wordy, subtitle might be "Studies in Lakota Spiritual Connections with the Stars" because that is what the book attempts to do: relate spiritual aspects of Lakota culture with the sky.

These are the same questions encountered with Black Elk: What is traditional and what is contemporary? What is traditional and what has a Christian twist to it? There is a new challenge: New Age culture. Unfortunately, *Lakota Star Knowledge* has itself become sacred scripture for adherents of New Age religions, UFO believers, and those who have met extraterrestrial visitors to Earth.[15]

In Kelley and Milone's encyclopedic work on archaeoastronomy, the limited discussion of Lakota ethnoastronomy is based mostly on the *Lakota Star Knowledge* book. They make an important observation: "A great deal of the material is a reconstruction, often based on combining materials from several informants. The end result is often convincing, but it should be borne in mind that the goals are far from the search for balanced alternatives so dear to conventional scholarship."[16] Williamson and Farrer make a similar observation in their preface to Goodman's article on "The Hand": "His [Goodman's] sensitivity to the Native view and his adherence to their requests cause him to summarize where others have been able to quote directly."[17]

Lakota Star Knowledge may represent a Lakota reinterpretation of their traditional spiritual relationship to the land. In that respect the book connects with the AIM occupation of specific sites in the 1970s. Philip Arnold observed that "the ongoing oral history project directed by the Lakota Studies Department at Rosebud Reservation's Sinte Gleska University . . . has developed a clearer picture of an indigenous worldview that could serve as a way of understanding Black Elk's religion." Arnold further notes, "By challenging anthropological claims and locating Lakota people in the Black Hills 2000 years earlier, these scholars are actively defending an aboriginal title to the Black Hills. Similar to *Black Elk Speaks* and AIM, the Oral History Project is explicitly addressing legal and political issues by documenting through creative methods a Lakota religious connection to the land."[18] In other words, the astronomy of *Lakota Star Knowledge* is very definitely cultural astronomy.

Cheyenne and Kiowa peoples predate the Lakota in the Black Hills. As the Lakota came into geographical and cultural proximity, they could have adopted the astronomical traditions and beliefs of the Cheyenne and Kiowa.[19] Linea Sundstrom has written extensively about the Black Hills. She examines traditions about the Black Hills and astronomy. In her discussion of sacred geography, she clearly summarizes the connection between earth and sky.

In conclusion, ethnographic traditions referring to the Black Hills suggest that certain points in the landscape were central to the religious traditions of its occupants for at least the last few centuries. As one group replaced another over the last several centuries, these locations continued to be recognized as sacred locales and to operate within a system of ethnoastronomical and mythological beliefs.

Transference of such traditions took place between groups that differed in language, religion, economic focus and area of origin. It is worth noting that this belief system appears to have originated among the Kiowas and Kiowa-Apaches or earlier occupants of the Black Hills, none of whom practiced even incipient horticulture. This demands re-examination of the traditional association between astronomy and agriculture in anthropological thought.

As groups entered new territories they gradually adapted their belief systems to their new physical environments. This often involved adopting many of the traditions of earlier occupants of the area. The development of a sacred landscape thus was a process of transferring old mythic locales to new points on the landscape and incorporating new beliefs borrowed from groups with whom they were coming into contact. Shades of very old belief systems are retained even today by the various Native American groups who once occupied the Black Hills. One example is the residual reference to bear taboos, clearly an expression of a very old Kiowa and Kiowa-Apache belief system, still seen in the Lakota names for and traditions about Devils Tower (Bear Lodge) and Bear Butte. Similarly, an ancient connection between the geography of the Black Hills and constellations is expressed in Kiowa and Kiowa-Apache traditions about Devil's Tower, which are remembered and retold today, nearly 200 years since the Kiowas last occupied the Black Hills.[20]

It is quite possible that the nineteenth-century Lakota noticed prominent constellations at specific times of the year as they migrated to sacred sites in the Black Hills. They may have then associated the constellations with a terrestrial location and the season of the year. This association became legendary and continued into the twentieth century. The distribution of stars in the sky is random, although some of the brighter stars form discernible patterns. We can discern a mirror pattern in the sky for any object or pattern on earth, whether an animal, a water dipper, or a geographical feature. The culture determines the meaning of the patterns.

In his preface to the story of Fallen Star, James LaPointe makes an interesting observation: "The ancient wise men said that all heavenly bodies exert influences upon life on earth, and the destinies of individual life are at all times under the spell of the sun, the moon, and the stars."[21] This statement describes astrology, the ancient Babylonian religion that claims celestial bodies assert an influence on human destiny. Alignments on the day one was born have consequences in the future. For the Lakota, looking at the stars will tell you where to make camp next month. Patterns in the sky determine patterns on earth.

Whatever the limitations or agenda of *Lakota Star Knowledge*, its ultimate importance is that it represents the ongoing Lakota quest to understand the relationship between the earth and the spirit, between the earth and the sky, and between the sky and the spirit. *Lakota Star Knowledge* is a three-way intersection of earth, sky, and spirit. *Lakota Star Knowledge* is an example of DeMallie's characterization of the Lakota pursuit to understand the nature of the sacred or *wakháŋ*. The quest, like Lakota culture itself, has evolved and changed to meet new threats or challenges and to incorporate new ideas. Land ownership, a developing issue in the nineteenth century, became even more critical in the late twentieth century and beyond. *Lakota Star Knowledge* also places the Lakota squarely in the larger context of Great Plains ethnoastronomy by showing a connection to the Cheyenne and Kiowa.

Astronomy did not end in the Lakota world with the passage of Comet Halley in 1910. Using older concepts and meanings, twentieth-century Lakota found new ways to adapt astronomy to new cultural contexts. They found new ways to relate earth and sky, to connect the spirit to the sky.

11

THE SPIRIT AND THE SKY

The nineteenth-century Lakota gave names to the stars and constellations. They drew pictographs in winter counts depicting meteors, meteor showers, comets, and eclipses. They used the motions of the Sun, Moon, and stars to tell time. They told stories about the stars. Ethnoastronomy, in any century, serves a cultural purpose as well as a scientific one.

Native science shares some of the goals of modern science. The origins of science are in the necessity to relate to the natural environment because of the need for survival. A desire to understand the cycles of the heavens prompted astronomy's early development. For thousands of years much of astronomy's importance in culture was the regulation and timing of human rituals. It is not surprising that Julius Caesar and Pope Gregory XIII consulted astronomers to devise calendars. Humans became curious about the cosmos. As science evolved and began to understand the physics of the universe, questions about how the universe works became important. Western astronomy and Lakota astronomy share this goal: making sense of the world. However, they have different approaches and present different kinds of "knowledge."

Native Americans and Science

Native views and the perspective of modern science have much in common, although in slightly different ways than we might expect.[1] For example, consider the important task of understanding the how the world works. In physics and astronomy we use the symbols of mathematics to construct models that explain how the world works. No one has ever actually seen an electron, neutron, or proton, but the model of the hydrogen atom consisting of those elementary particles makes sense, and hydrogen's role in fusion explains how stars work.

In the Lakota culture stories, myths, and symbols are ways to express the "truth" about the world. These stories, myths, and symbols help make sense of the world. Early non-Native observers sometimes dismissed Lakota celestial mythology as meaningless. However, there is a discernible parallel between Indigenous mythology and physical science's dependence on mathematics. As Gregory Cajete explains,

> Ancient Indigenous peoples had very sophisticated understandings of how things work, how things move, and how things happen in the universe. They used the coded form of mythology to try and convey their understanding, because in some ways it is understanding beyond words. Incidentally, this is why physics is heavily dependent on mathematics. There are certain things that cannot be explained in words, and the relationship is not transparent unless you quantify it into some symbolic form. Indigenous people are doing the same thing in another form by coding their knowledge, understanding, and insights into the rituals that they perform, the mythologies they have created, and the stories that they pass down.[2]

In physics, knowledge, understanding, and insights are coded into mathematical models that explain and predict the world. Likewise, Native rituals and mythologies create understanding and meaning, and both Native science and modern astronomy are concerned with understanding the nature of the universe and the place of humans in it. The Lakota and modern astronomy both are interested in the *sky*, but for the Lakota the *spirit* is also a part of their vision of the cosmos.[3] However, modern astronomy with its emphasis on empiricism stands aloof from culture and hence from the spiritual dimension.

Native Americans and Astronomy

Nineteenth-century Lakota astronomy adds other dimensions to the reality about the cosmos, just as modern cosmology has extended the number of dimensions of the physical universe for astronomers. Newtonian astronomy and physics, with an emphasis on order, predictability, and quantification, were reluctant to allow for chance to intervene. However, with the birth of quantum mechanics and chaos theory, as Stephen Hawking has suggested, not only does God throw dice with the universe, but sometimes God throws dice where we can't see them.[4] Native science seems more open to the possibility of chance and to the inclusion of a spiritual dimension.[5]

Although many prominent scientists have been Christians, Jews, Muslims, Hindus, Buddhists (and atheists), matters of faith or spirituality generally have been left outside the laboratory door in the interest of objectivity. On the other hand many well-meaning people of faith have ignored well-established scientific data and theories because the data or theories conflicted with strongly held beliefs.[6]

In Native American astronomy there is a connection between astronomy and *spirituality*, not between astronomy and religion. Religion tends to propose dogmatic, doctrinal answers. Spirituality looks inward, seeks meaning, and stands in awe of the universe. Spirituality can tolerate ambiguity. This perspective makes ambiguity tolerable in Lakota ethnoastronomy and distinguishes it from Western science.[7] This spiritual dimension also suggests that knowledge in Lakota ethnoastronomy is different from knowledge in Western science.

The Native spiritual foci also see connections between parts of the universe. Compared to a three-dimensional Newtonian-Cartesian existence, Native peoples "perceived multiple realities."[8] These realities rely on connections. There is no better statement of this idea than the Lakota phrase *mitákuye oyás'iŋ*, "all my relatives." Much of the Lakota language focuses on relationships, and the language of relationships focuses on kinship—how members of an extended family relate to one another and to those outside the *thiyóšpaye*, the community.[9] This relationship extends beyond humans. It includes the created world as well. As Albert White Hat states, "The Lakota rituals remind us of our Creation story. We all come from one source. *Mitákuye oyás'iŋ*, 'we are all related.' This concept is the foundation for the *thiyóšpaye*."[10]

When my Lakota friend and I were at the summit of Bear Butte, he offered a prayer in Lakota. It was a sevenfold prayer: first to the compass directions west, north, east, south; then up for the sky and down for mother earth; and finally a circular motion to unify all into one. The final circle incorporates human beings into the unity of the universe's *thiyóšpaye*. It brings harmony between humans and the universe.

The idea of harmony can be illustrated by a physical phenomenon. Resonance occurs when two systems are literally in tune with one another. The sound box of a guitar reverberates at the frequency of the vibrating strings. The system of strings and sound box is linked and functions in an interrelated manner. In Native American cultures humans are not separate from the earth or the sky, but an integral part of it. Humans and the cosmos are interrelated in a resonant harmony that transcends the physical. According to Cajete,

> Native astronomies helped to make sense of life and relationships and reaffirm the belief in the interrelationship and interdependence of all things in an animate and living universe. Like the Earth, plants, and animals, celestial bodies are traditionally viewed by Native cultures as living beings with a creative life force that relates to and affects human beings physically and spiritually.[11]

Pulitzer Prize–winning English professor N. Scott Momaday, a Kiowa, says Native Americans have a "comprehensive" view of the world. While non-Indians divide the world into astronomy, botany, and zoology, the traditional Native view is more holistic.

> When the Native American looks at nature, it isn't with the idea of training a glass upon it, or pushing it away so that he can focus upon it from a distance. In his mind, nature is not something apart from him. He conceives of it, rather, as an element in which he exists. He has existence within that element, much in the same way we think of having existence within the element of air. It would be unimaginable for him to think of it in the way the nineteenth century "nature poets" thought of looking at nature and writing about it. They employed a kind of "esthetic distance," as it is sometimes called. This idea would be alien to the Indian.[12]

Focusing on nature from an "esthetic distance" is seen in the A to Z fragmentation of science into the specific disciplines of today: Astronomy has its cosmologists, astrophysicists, and planetologists. Biological science has microbiologists, ecologists, and zoologists, to name a few. Even physics, which focuses on the quest for a grand unified theory of everything, is fragmented into fields like high-energy particle physics, low-temperature physics, and nuclear physics.

The traditional Lakota dwelling demonstrates the inclusion of nature in the Lakota culture. The design and orientation of the tipi is a model of the cosmos. Norbert Running from Rosebud Reservation explains:

> When they build a tipi, those three poles come first. That three pole triangle is a star. . . . Then seven more poles, that's the directions, west, north, east, south, above, below, and center. Fire [is] at the center. That makes ten poles. Those ten are the laws of this whole world and for the Lakota people.[13]

The tipi poles link the sky to the Earth and transmit powers from the heavens down into the dwelling. Power from the heavens can be brought into modern dwellings. Stellar processes create energy from the nuclei of atoms, and that energy courses through the universe in the form of heat and light. The Sun provides energy to the Earth, where human-made machines transform it. The electrical power grid ultimately brings that energy into homes, thus connecting modern dwellings to the heavens. Likewise, for the Lakota and for all Native Americans, what one does, and experiences, on earth does connect to what happens in the heavens.[14]

One of the most imaginative and creative intersections of traditional modern science and a Native American perspective is a first-person "conversation" between a geologist and an Ojibwe named Earth Walks. Earth Walk's poetic view of the connection between planet Earth and the night sky reflects a holistic, integrated approach to science and Native American culture.

> I think that not only are you [the geologist] and I [the Ojibwe], science and the Native American holistic view of this land and planet,

compatible, but each is actually necessary to ensure the health and well-being of the other. To know that continents move, that Mount Everest is so high because India is colliding with Asia, that there are strange life-forms down in the dark, on the bottom of the sea floor, that thrive without sunlight, to be able to understand earthquakes, predict and witness volcanic eruptions, decipher glacial deposits, watch hummingbirds dance, see a wolf pack encircle a starving moose, watch an Indian sit on the ground listening to Mother Earth, dance in a powwow, see sun rise on the winter [solstice] or spring equinox, or be like a laughing child and run into a meadow full of wild flowers and vanish from reality for a short while—goosebumps, elation, humility, reverence, respect, and imagination. This is part spirit, part science—a moving, never-ending circle of stars, animals, geology, land, and us, all connected and all beginning and ending with planet earth.[15]

We tend to think of compatibility as sameness, but it may be that the compatibility between modern astronomy and a Native view, the "elation, humility, reverence, respect, and imagination" common to each, is actually due to the *differences* between the two. Modern astronomy and Native views tolerate each other because they each seek to understand the heavens, albeit from very different perspectives and by asking very different questions.[16]

The "never-ending circle of stars" is indeed part spirit and part science. In the astronomy of the Lakota, the spirit and the sky come together in a marvelous constellation linking the planet Earth beneath their feet with the sky over their heads. It is clear that the nineteenth-century Lakota had a deep interest in the celestial realm, but their interest was different from that of modern astronomy. Why did they focus so much on the night sky? What did it mean to them?[17] Cajete explores this question.

Why did Native cultures place so much emphasis, spend such time, and expend such thought in taking measures to align themselves and their societies with what they perceived was the cosmic order? Native astronomers were driven not only by their own awe and curiosity, but were also serving the innermost needs of their societies—to resonate with the cosmos and to be the power brokers of their worlds. Observations of the sun, moon, and stars formed the basis for the ceremonial calendars designed to time essential life activities such as hunting, gathering, planting, and fishing. These observations also formed the foundation for attempts to predict celestial events; set ceremonial events; mark the time of festivals and war; and legitimize political and religious authority. Indeed, Native cultures recognized no clear dividing lines between nature and the cosmos on the one hand, and human spirituality and affairs on the other.[18]

Although there was a utilitarian need to set the times of ceremonies, there was a deeper quest for harmony. This harmony between the earth and the sky, a connection between the spirit and the sky, is woven into the very fabric of the Lakota culture, and the threads of this fabric remain strong even today.

Wakháŋ and the Stars

Visiting places like Bear Butte, the Black Hills, or the Wyoming Medicine Wheel brings an awareness of the rock underneath and the stars above. On a clear night on the Great Plains with the only light coming from the stars, one cannot help but gaze skyward. Existing intimately with their environment, the Lakota in the nineteenth century were aware of the subtle yet obvious voice of the world around them.

Much of the astronomy in nineteenth-century Lakota culture involved the recurring nature of celestial phenomena. Their quest was to bring the harmonious order in the universe down to Earth. The phases of the Moon, the motions of the Sun, and the changing positions of the constellations represented the order and harmony in the universe. The daily progression of the Sun gave the time of day. Naming the months and correlating them with nature gave a calendar.[19] The sudden appearance of meteors, comets, or the aurora borealis presented the unexpected and extraordinary to the Lakota. A spectacular meteor shower became the mnemonic for a year. The appearance of the aurora marked the death of a Lakota holy man. A natural tension between the repeatable, harmonious cosmos and the unexpected, spectacular universe emerged. This tension is a key feature of Lakota astronomy. This tension may be the result of the Lakota drive to understand and live within the incomprehensible nature of the universe.

The traditional preferential timing of the Sun Dance to coincide with the summer solstice linked the Sun Dance on earth with the sky above. The orientation and shape of the Lakota Sun Dance lodge on earth are a metaphor for the sky above. The balance and harmony of the sky extended down to earth in the Sun Dance, and the Sun Dance combined ritual, belief, community, and the sky. Although astronomy can give insights into the timing of the Sun Dance and the orientation of the dance lodge, it is Lakota culture that gives meaning to the ceremony.

The message of ethnoastronomy is that astronomy is a part of culture, not apart from culture. Everything the Lakota did or said in relationship to the stars was done within their cultural context, and their astronomy reflects the culture. It is worth repeating a key idea from DeMallie:

> In the nineteenth-century Lakota system of belief, the unity of *Wakan Tanka* embraced all time and space, together with the entirety of being, in a universe where the place of human beings was minor but well-defined. Because this universe was most fundamentally characterized by incomprehensibility, it was beyond humanity's power ever to know it fully, and perhaps it was this futility that made the quest for understanding of the *wakan* the driving force in Lakota culture.[20]

More than anything else, the Lakota quest to understand the *wakháŋ* is seen throughout Lakota ethnoastronomy. However futile, this quest to understand the *wakháŋ* made the Lakota reach for the stars. There is a hint of this futility in a conversation between James Walker and Ringing Shield from May 1903, in which the stars are said to be *wakháŋ*.

> A wise man said this. The stars are *wakan*. They do not care for the earth or anything on it. They have nothing to do with mankind. Sometimes they come to the world and sometimes the Lakotas go to

them. There are many stories told of these things. No medicine can be made to the stars. They have nothing to do with anything that moves and breathes. A holy man knows about them. This must not be told to the people. If the people knew these things, they would pull the stars from above. There is one star for the evening and one for the morning. One star never moves and it is *wakan*. Other stars move in a circle about it. They are dancing in the dance circle.

There are seven stars [Big Dipper]. This is why there are seven council fires among the Lakotas. Sometimes there are many stars and sometimes there are not so many. When there are not so many, the others are asleep. The spirit way [Milky Way, *wanáǧi thacháŋku*] is among the stars. This moves about so that bad spirits can not find it. *Wakan Tanka* keeps the bad spirits away from the spirit way. The spirit way begins at the edge of the world. No man can find it. *Taku Skanskan* is there and he tells the good spirits where to go to find it. The winds will show a good spirit where to go to find the beginning of this trail. The bad spirits must wander always on the trail of the winds. The stars hide from the sun. They must fear him. So mankind should not try to learn about them. It is not good to talk about them. It is not good to fight by the light of the stars. They must be evil for they fear the sun.[21]

Ringing Shield's discourse on Lakota celestial understanding is filled with explanations *and* contradictions. Consider the North Star: *Wicháȟpi Owáŋžila*, the "Star that always stands in one place." What is especially interesting about Ringing Shield's words is that the pole star is *wakháŋ* because it does *not* move. This suggests Polaris is *wakháŋ* compared to the other stars because it is different. It is the status of being different and extraordinary that makes Polaris *wakháŋ*.

Moreover, the *tákuškaŋškaŋ*, the force that causes all things to move, tells the good spirits where to go to find the beginning of the spirit way (i.e., the Milky Way, *Wanáǧi Thacháŋku*). Although Ringing Shield probably knew nothing about Newtonian physics, he inadvertently alluded to Newton's second law. This fundamental principle of physics states that a force causes a change in motion. Even more interesting is the idea that an object in motion has *energy*. Kinetic energy is the energy of motion, and all objects in motion have kinetic energy. Continuing the analogy even further, the nightly motion of the stars is *wakháŋ* because they are in motion and have the energy that comes from the *tákuškaŋškaŋ*.

These ideas about the stars seem to be in conflict with the statement that "mankind should not try to learn about them [the stars]. It is not good to talk about them." Ringing Shield says, in essence, "Don't even think about the stars," yet he, and nineteenth-century Lakota as a whole, gave names to the stars and told legends about the stars. In a similar discussion Little Wound said, "The stars are *Wakan Tanka*, but they have nothing to do with the people on earth. Mankind need pay no attention to the stars."[22] Yet, celestial events were recorded on hides, motions of the Sun and Moon determined the timing of important events, stories about the stars were retold. Paying no attention to the stars while telling stories about them appears to be a contradiction or ambiguity about the Lakota's interest in the stars.[23] The Sun, the Moon, and the stars permeate Lakota thought and culture. Why? Ringing Shield and Little Wound were telling us that the stars and their motions, or nonmotions, are a part of the "great incomprehensibility." They are an integral part of the energy of the universe. They are *wakháŋ*, and this is why the contradiction surfaces. Humans cannot fully understand the stars or their meanings because of their *wakháŋ* nature.

The ultimate reason the Lakota took such a strong interest in the sky was for the sake of their cosmology: how do we relate to the world around us? When the Lakota connected the sacred natures of the earth and the sky, they essentially were doing cosmology. It is because meteors, comets, the aurora, the Sun, the Moon, and the stars are *wakháŋ* that they were noted, recorded, and relived in stories and ritual. The stars are worthy of wonder, they are mysterious, they are incomprehensible. As fruitless as it may seem, grasping for the stars brings the great mystery a little closer to the earth beneath our feet. For the Lakota the earth, the spirit, and the sky are in a symbiotic relationship: *mitákuye oyás'iŋ*. We can visualize the relationship among the earth, the spirit,

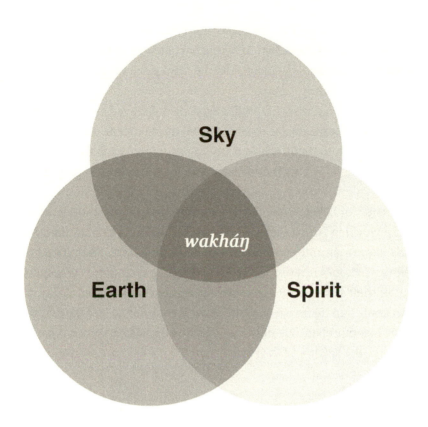

FIG. 24. Earth, Spirit, Sky and *Wakháŋ*. Earth, spirit, and sky come together in Lakota astronomy, now and in the past. The intersection of all three is *wakháŋ*, the incomprehensible. Bringing the sky down to earth and incorporating it into art and ritual is yet another attempt to understand the nature of what is *wakháŋ* for the Lakota. Drawing by Mark Hollabaugh.

and the sky with three overlapping circles. At the center, where all three coincide, is *wakháŋ*, the unifying concept.[24]

This three-part connection is seen in a more traditional manner in Lakota celestial art, an integral part of Lakota culture. Although the meteor, comet, and eclipse images preserved on winter count hides and in ledger books are mnemonics for an event, the image also serves to capture the event and make the apparitions more comprehensible. Suns, moons, and stars on clothing serve an ornamentation function, but they also connect to the belief and ritual of the Lakota. The ornamentation makes the celestial objects participants in the ritual and in a sense makes the Sun, the Moon, and the stars members of the *thiyóšpaye*, the extended family.

Archaeoastronomer Ray Williamson has observed that "traditional Native American men and women weave their perceptions of the celestial patterns into their lives in order to participate directly in the ways of the universe."[25] This is especially true for the Lakota in any century.

The center of Lakota belief is the incomprehensibility, and sacredness, of the world in which they live. The stars, although extraordinary and *wakháŋ*, are an integral part of this holistic world. The nineteenth-century Lakota's interest in the Sun, Moon, and stars was an essential part of their never-ending quest to understand the *wakháŋ*. Today their astronomy and their visions of the cosmos continue to be a participation in the incomprehensible universe. Lakota ethnoastronomy is a meeting place for the spirit and the sky.

APPENDIX

List of Museums

Several lesser-known museums have significant collections of Lakota artifacts and contemporary art as well as general material related to the American West. In most cases, a visitor should either phone or check the museum's website for schedules. These museums usually have reduced hours from Labor Day through Memorial Day. Most of these museums also have archives of value to scholars. Contact information is correct as of summer 2014.

Akta Lakota Museum & Cultural Center
St. Joseph's Indian School
P.O. Box 89
Chamberlain SD 57325
800-798-3452
aktalakota@stjo.org
www.aktalakota.org

Aktá Lakhóta means "to honor the people" in Lakota. The Akta Lakota Museum & Cultural Center not only honors Native American people and culture but also is an educational center as well. The museum is a continuing monument to the Lakota people and their culture.

Buechel Memorial Lakota Museum (BMLM)
350 Oak Street
P.O. Box 499
St. Francis SD 57572-0499
605-747-2745
www.sfmission.org/museum/

The Buechel Memorial Lakota Museum demonstrates the St. Francis Mission's enduring respect for the traditions, culture, and history of the Lakota of the Rosebud Reservation. The museum contains many unique artifacts, images, and documents that can be viewed by the public, groups, and scholars during regular hours or by special arrangement. The museum houses the artifacts collected by Father Eugene Buechel, S.J. The winter counts on display clearly show the 1833 Leonid meteor shower. The Buechel Memorial Lakota Museum is open to visitors between Memorial Day and Labor Day, Monday–Friday: 8:00 a.m. until 5:00 p.m. Visitors may browse the exhibit and purchase Lakota articles and art. From Labor Day through Memorial Day the museum is open by appointment only.

Center for Western Studies (CWS)
Augustana University
2121 S. Summit Avenue
Sioux Falls SD 57197
800-727-2844
cws@augie.edu
www.augie.edu/cws/

The mission of the Center for Western Studies at Augustana University is preserving and interpreting the history and cultures of the Northern Plains. The center serves as a repository for over 500 substantive collections and maintains a library in excess of 36,000 volumes on the American West. In addition, the center holds an extensive art and artifact collection.

Crazy Horse Memorial
Crazy Horse SD 57730-8900
605-673-4681
www.crazyhorsememorial.org

Sculptor Korczak Ziolkowski and Lakota Chief Henry Standing Bear
officially started Crazy Horse Memorial 3 June 1948. The memorial's
mission is to honor the culture, tradition, and living heritage of North
American Indians. The Indian Museum of North America is home to
an extraordinary collection of art and artifacts reflecting the diverse
histories and cultures of the American Indian people.

Fort Robinson Museum
P.O. Box 304
Crawford NE 69339-0304
308-665-2919
http://www.nebraskahistory.org/sites/fortrob/

Fort Robinson was host to visitors ranging from Crazy Horse to the U.S.
cavalry to the K-9 Corps. The museum at Fort Robinson is located in the
1905 post headquarters building. Museum exhibits trace the history from
the post's role guarding the Red Cloud Agency (1874–77) through the
housing of World War II German POWs (1943–46). The museum's exhibits
include nineteenth-century Sioux objects related to the Red Cloud Agency. The museum also houses several artifacts and documents pertaining to
John G. Bourke, who observed the 1881 Sun Dance at Pine Ridge.

Heritage Center of Red Cloud Indian School
Red Cloud Indian School
100 Mission Drive
Pine Ridge SD 57770
605-867-8257
heritagecenter@redcloudschool.org
http://www.redcloudschool.org/museum/

The Heritage Center of Red Cloud Indian School opened as a museum in 1982. It offers to the public—local, national, and international—an outstanding collection of Native American fine arts and Lakota tribal arts. The Heritage Center's fine arts collection includes over two thousand paintings, drawings, and sculptures representing a large number of different Native American tribal traditions. Its tribal arts collection concentrates on traditional Lakota arts and history. One of the early successful museums located on an Indian reservation, the Heritage Center serves as an extremely valuable cultural resource not only for the students of Red Cloud Indian School but also for students of the other reservation schools and for all the Lakota people of the Pine Ridge Indian Reservation.

Journey Museum & Learning Center (Sioux Indian Museum)
222 New York Street
Rapid City SD 57701
605-394-6923
http://www.journeymuseum.org

The Journey Museum & Learning Center takes you on an incredible trek through time, from the violent upheaval that formed the mystical Black Hills over 2.5 billion years ago to the continuing saga of the western frontier. It brings together four major prehistoric and historic collections to tell the complete story of the western Great Plains—from the perspective of the Lakota people and the pioneers who shaped its past to the scientists who now study it. The Battiste Good and Big Missouri Winter Counts are on display in the Lakota section of the museum.

Museum of the Fur Trade
6321 Hwy 20
Chadron NE 69337
308-432-3843
http://www.furtrade.org

The Museum of the Fur Trade combines an outstanding collection and scholarship to interpret the story of the fur trade. The nonprofit museum's exhibits discuss the fur trade from early colonial days to the present century. The exhibits trace the everyday lives of British, French, and Spanish traders, voyageurs, mountain men, professional buffalo hunters, and typical Plains and Woodland Indians. Exhibits include the entire range of trade goods, including munitions, cutlery, axes, firearms, textiles, costumes, paints, and beads.

State Historical Society of North Dakota Heritage Center
612 East Boulevard Avenue
Bismarck ND 58505
701-328-2666
histsoc@nd.gov
http://history.nd.gov

Archeological investigations have documented the presence of big game hunting cultures after the retreat of the glaciers and later settlements of hunting and gathering, and farming peoples. The Heritage Center features objects from 10,000 BCE to the eighteenth century, including a reproduction of the oldest house ever excavated in North Dakota, 550–410 BCE.

South Dakota State Historical Society
900 Governors Dr.
Pierre SD 57501-2217
605-773-3458
http://history.sd.gov/Museum/

In the language of *Ochéthi Šakówiŋ*, the "Seven Council Fires," *Oyáte Thawíchohʼaŋ* means "The Ways of the People." The historical society exhibit focuses on the importance of kinship obligations, which determine an individual's place in the tribe and the universe, and the values of courage, wisdom, generosity, and fortitude as prescriptions for daily living.

NOTES

Preface and Acknowledgments
1. Eddy, "Astronomical Alignment."
2. Walker, *Lakota Belief and Ritual*, 114.
3. Hollabaugh, "Celestial Imagery."
4. Burke, "Collecting Lakota Histories," 82.
5. Research like this uncovers interesting material that is peripheral to the primary discussion. For example, when reading about the Lakota language, I learned the names of Lakota code talkers from World War II and realized I knew family members of one code talker. See Hunhoff, "Last Lakota Code Talker"; Melmer, "Politics Surrounds Code Talkers"; Martin Brokenleg, personal communication with the author. Although information like this is interesting, it was omitted from the book. I have included a few personal experiences, reflections, or opinions in the endnotes of the chapters.
6. Readers may also notice apparent inconsistencies in capitalization. Astronomers use uppercase for *Sun, Earth,* and *Moon* when referring to our star, our planet, or the satellite of Earth. However, when referring to the land on which the people walk, lowercase *earth* is used. Likewise, the phases of the Moon are *not* uppercase, e.g., *full moon, waxing crescent moon,* etc.

1. The Lakota People
1. For a creative treatment of this idea, see Morton and Gawboy, *Talking Rocks*. They discuss the role of lakes and woodlands in shaping Ojibwe culture.
2. Calloway, *One Vast Winter Count*, 3.
3. Raymond DeMallie ("Sioux until 1850," 719) notes that "Archaeology adds nothing to the question of Sioux origins."
4. A petroglyph is a carved or pecked pattern in stone, whereas a pictograph is a painted or drawn image. A petroglyph may also be painted to emphasize the relief image.

5. Sundstrom, *Rock Art*, 88–119.

6. Hughes, "Investigations in Western South Dakota," 277.

7. Sheldon, "Ancient Indian Fireplaces," 44–48.

8. T. H. Lewis, "Stone Monuments," 159–66. However, one type of stone structure, the Medicine Wheel, is discussed in chapter 2.

9. DeMallie, "Sioux until 1850," 718–19.

10. DeMallie, "Sioux until 1850," 718.

11. Buechel and Manhart, *Lakota Dictionary*, 95. The Lakota word for the Ojibwe is *Ȟaȟáthuŋwan*, "village by the falls," and most likely refers to the waterfalls on the St. Mary's River at Sault Ste. Marie. Like many Native words that are transliterated into English, there are alternate spellings, and in this case *Ahnisnabae* is also used.

12. I have heard Dakota and Lakota people referring to themselves as Sioux. The proper legal names of the two major Lakota tribal groups are the Oglala Sioux Tribe and the Rosebud Sioux Tribe.

13. Buechel and Manhart, *Lakota Dictionary*, 188.

14. DeMallie, "Sioux until 1850," 736–49. DeMallie gives detailed names of the smaller bands within each subgroup.

15. For a detailed retelling of the story see Ostler, *Plains Sioux;* Ostler, *Lakotas;* Utley, *Indian Frontier.*

16. Prucha, *Documents*, 84–85.

17. Prucha, *Documents*, 110.

18. Prucha, *Documents*, 112.

19. In Lakota, the adjective follows the noun; the Black Hills are called *Phahá Sápa*, literally "hills black."

20. See Ostler, *Lakotas*, for a thorough history of what he appropriately calls "the struggle for sacred ground."

21. DeMallie, "'These Have No Ears,'" 516–17.

22. Ostler, *Plains Sioux*, 134.

23. Ostler, *Plains Sioux*, 174–76.

24. Utley, *Lance and the Shield*, 183–98.

25. Ostler, *Plains Sioux*, 13.

26. Ostler, *Plains Sioux*, 188.

27. For an in-depth discussion see Fritz, *Movement for Indian Assimilation.*

28. Ostler, *Plains Sioux*, 243–88. For a thorough discussion of the Ghost Dance see Mooney, *Ghost-Dance Religion.* Many museums have examples of these shirts, including the Buechel Memorial Lakota Museum (BMLM), item 439. See figures 9 and 10.

29. Utley, *Indian Frontier*, 255–59; Ostler, *Plains Sioux*, 338–60.
30. Johnson, "To Some Sioux." Doris Leader Charge was a Lakota language instructor at the Sinte Gleska University on the Rosebud Reservation. She also was a Lakota language consultant and played the role of Pretty Shield, the wife of Ten Bears, in the film *Dances with Wolves*. She and the late Floyd Red Crow Westerman (Ten Bears) were a very natural pairing in *Dances with Wolves*—she essentially played herself. Doris died in 2001.
31. Giago, "Black Hills."
32. United States v. Sioux Nation of Indians, 448 U.S. 371 (1980).
33. *Sioux Nation of Indians*.
34. *Starry Night* is available from Simulation Curriculum Corp., 11900 Wayzata Blvd, Suite 126, Minnetonka, MN 55305, http://www.starrynighteducation .com/products.html.
35. Accessible at Naval Oceanography Portal, http://www.usno.navy.mil/usno.
36. Accessible at NASA Eclipse Web Site, http://eclipse.gsfc.nasa.gov/eclipse .html.
37. Carver, *Travels through the Interior;* Carver, *Journals of Jonathan Carver*.
38. DeMallie, "'These Have No Ears,'" 515.
39. DeMallie, "'These Have No Ears,'" 516.
40. DeMallie, "'These Have No Ears,'" 518.
41. Walker, *Lakota Belief and Ritual*; Walker, *Lakota Myth*; Walker, *Lakota Society*.
42. Walker, *Sun Dance and Other Ceremonies*.
43. Walker, *Lakota Belief and Ritual*, 75.
44. E. Deloria, "Sun Dance."
45. Jahner, "Transitional Narratives," 149.
46. Parks and DeMallie, "Plains Indian Native Literatures," 121–31.
47. Ostler, *Plains Sioux*, 47. In 1849 the office responsible for Indian affairs was transferred from the War Department to the newly created Department of the Interior, where Indian Affairs resides today.
48. For an assessment of Wissler, who produced some major studies on the Lakota, see Freed and Freed, "Clark Wissler."
49. Mallery, *Picture-Writing*.
50. This biographical summary of Black Elk is largely based on DeMallie's biography in the introduction to *The Sixth Grandfather*.
51. See chapter 7 for a detailed description and discussion of this aurora.
52. Neihardt, *Black Elk Speaks*.
53. It is common even in the twenty-first century to see *Black Elk Speaks* and *The Sacred Pipe* on the reading list for college religion or Native American

studies courses. As William Powers has observed, "When Black Elk speaks, everyone listens" (Powers, "When Black Elk Speaks").

54. William Powers (Review of *The Sixth Grandfather*, 122) gave this assessment: "It is a wonder, given the verbal gymnastics of the translation process, that we know anything at all about what Black Elk really said. Just envision the old man speaking in Lakota to his son [Ben Black Elk], who translates his father's words into English to Neihardt's daughter [Hilda], who takes down the translation in shorthand, and later transcribes it into typescript (frequently deleting what she judges to be redundancies), and then hands it over to her father, who shapes the words into the perfect literary imagery comprehensible to a white readership." Likewise, Julian Rice (*Black Elk's Story*, x) gave a succinct summary of the problem: "Black Elk must be cleanly disentangled from Neihardt."

55. J. Brown, *Sacred Pipe*.

56. DeMallie, *Sixth Grandfather*, 71.

57. Mails, *Sundancing*.

58. Mails, *Fools Crow*.

59. Mails, *Fools Crow: Wisdom and Power*.

60. George Tinker, a member of the Osage Nation and a professor at Iliff School of Theology, Denver, wrote that *Wisdom and Power* is "appealing and even irresistible to New Age aficionados and Lakota wannabes" (Tinker, Review of *Fools Crow: Wisdom and Power*, 393). Much to my dismay, my own initial work on Lakota celestial imagery found its way to a New Age conference on Native spirituality that included everything from sweat lodges to unidentified flying objects (UFOs) and alien abductions. See note 15 in chapter 10.

2. The Sky

1. Discussions of the goals and methods of archaeoastronomy and ethnoastronomy began over forty years ago (Baity et al., "Archaeoastronomy and Ethnoastronomy"). My archaeology colleagues often use the older term *astroarchaeology* instead of archaeoastronomy. Anthony Aveni, one of the leading authorities in the United States on archaeoastronomy, points out that "Astroarchaeology . . . is the now obsolete name given to a field methodology for retrieving astronomical information from the study of alignments associated with ancient architecture and the landscape." (Aveni, "Archaeoastronomy," 150)

2. Aveni, *Skywatchers of Ancient Mexico*.

3. Williamson, *Living the Sky*; Malville and Putnam, *Prehistoric Astronomy*;

Zeilik, "Ethnoastronomy, I"; Zeilik, "Sun Shrines and Symbols"; Zeilik, "Fajada Butte Solar Marker"; Zeilik, "Sun Watching"; Zeilik, "Ethnoastronomy, II." My introduction to the wider archaeoastronomy and ethnoastronomy community came at the Fifth Oxford International Conference in Santa Fe in 1996, where I met Von Del Chamberlain, McKim Malville, and John Carlson. Several years earlier, when I was at Hovenweep National Monument to observe the summer solstice sunrise, I serendipitously met Ray Williamson, whose book I had reviewed.

4. Provenance refers to the origin and authenticity of an artifact or object of art. In the best of all possible worlds, a complete provenance, much like a pedigree, helps establish authenticity.

5. See Porter, *Paper Medicine Man*, for a complete biography of Bourke.

6. Zeilik, "Ethnoastronomy, I"; Zeilik, "Sun Watching." In the southwestern United States *historic* refers to postconquest cultures, and *ancient* refers to preconquest cultures.

7. Lankford, *Reachable Stars*. The concept of proximity is used here from a latitude perspective. It is related to the idea of *diffusion*, an idea proposed by anthropologists in the nineteenth century. Clark Wissler, who studied the Lakota in great detail, used diffusion as a model for cultural areas of the Native Americans in an effort to understand how cultural ideas and practices spread (Wissler, "Diffusion of Horse Culture"; Wissler, "Distribution and Functions"; Wissler, "Psychological and Historical Interpretations"). An idea in a culture had a point of origin and then diffused outward to other cultural areas. In the 1920s through 1930s, anthropologists mostly abandoned this idea and criticized Wissler's ideas (see Goldenweiser, "Diffusionism"; Woods, "Criticism"; Freed and Freed, "Clark Wissler"). Even so, the ethnographic material Wissler compiled is still useful, regardless of how he understood it.

8. Even after two thousand years, the jury is still unable to reach a verdict about this apparition. Was it a conjunction of planets; a supernova; or a post-event reference to a comet seen in the year 66? See Jenkins, "Star of Bethlehem"; Coates, "Linguist's Angle"; Kelley and Milone, *Exploring Ancient Skies*, 482–86.

9. A light year is the distance light travels in one year, about 9.5 million million kilometers.

10. The Moon's slight deviation from the ecliptic is due to the inclination, or angle, of the Moon's orbital plane around the Earth.

11. The Sun Dance is discussed in detail in chapter 9.

12. The Moon also rotates on its axis within a period of 27.33 days, which is

why we only see one side of the lunar surface. This is an example of synchronous motion.

13. A simple calculation helps to illustrate this point. The Earth rotates 360° in about 24 hours and hence rotates 15° in one hour (360/24 = 15). Time zones are 15° of longitude in width. For every degree of longitude you move west, the Sun will cross your meridian four minutes later (60 min/15° = 4 minutes per degree of longitude).

14. Astronomers use the term *transit* to refer to any object's crossing of the meridian.

15. Some close allies of the Lakota referred to George A. Custer as "Son of the Morning Star," hence the title of Evan S. Connell's biography of Custer (Connell, *Son of the Morning Star*). The Lakota referred to Custer as "Long Hair."

16. 365/29.5 = 12.37 lunar synodic months per solar year.

17. If you have trouble visualizing this, ask an astronomy professor to demonstrate it with a celestial sphere.

18. The Gregorian fix to the calendar decreed only the century years divisible evenly by 400 would be leap years. The year 1900 was not a leap year, but 2000 was.

19. Precession was the idea behind the phrase "this is the dawning of the Age of Aquarius" from a song in the popular late 1960s rock musical *Hair*.

20. Buechel and Manhart, *Lakota Dictionary*, 378. Buechel's source was Tom Little Bull.

21. Freedman and Kaufman, *Universe*, 50–56.

22. Fr. Raymond Bucko commented to me, "The Jesuits endeared themselves to the Chinese with this knowledge!"

23. Perihelion is the point in the orbit of a comet, or planet, when it is closest to the Sun. Comets are named for their discoverer and may bear up to three names.

24. I easily saw Hale–Bopp in March 1997 from Colorado Springs with no optical aids. A diffuse tail was noticeable. Halley was not as spectacular in 1986.

25. Freedman and Kaufman, *Universe*, 396.

26. Winter counts are discussed in chapter 6.

27. For a basic introduction to descriptive astronomy, see Neil Comins's excellent textbook, *Discovering the Universe* (current ed., Comin and Kaufmann). For a more mathematical and in-depth introduction to astronomy, read *Universe* by Roger Freedman (current ed., Freedman, Geller, and Kaufmann).

28. See Carlson ("America's Ancient Skywatchers") and Williamson (*Living the Sky*) for a detailed discussion of these sites.

29. McKim Malville has done extensive archaeoastronomy research in the Four Corners area of Colorado (Malville and Putnam, *Prehistoric Astronomy*).

30. A series of photos showing the lunar standstill sunrise of 26 December 2004 is available at the Chimney Rock National Monument web site: http://www .chimneyrockco.org/.

31. Eddy, "Astronomical Alignment." Another article Eddy wrote on the Medicine Wheel for *National Geographic* was the genesis of my own interest in the archaeoastronomy and ethnoastronomy of the Native Americans. John Eddy died in 2009 at age seventy-eight. He was a founder of the Historical Astronomy Division of the American Astronomical Society and is also considered a founder of archaeoastronomy in North America.

32. I have visited the site in June to observe the solstice sunset, and even then the hike required a difficult and cautious passage across steep, icy snow fields.

33. Doll, *Vision Quest*, 10–11.

34. Hollabaugh, "Blue Mound Stone Wall."

35. Chamberlain, "North American"; Chamberlin, *When Stars Came Down to Earth*.

36. Williamson, *Living the Sky*; Monroe and Williamson, *They Dance*; Williamson and Farrar, *Earth & Sky*.

37. Goodman, *Lakota Star Knowledge*.

38. Goodman, "On the Necessity."

3. Lakota Culture

1. DeMallie, "These Have No Ears," 533. Rewriting one sentence of his statement directly shows this connection: "To attempt an understanding of [Lakota ethnoastronomy] it is essential to come to an understanding of Sioux culture, which provides the context."

2. For a complete discussion of diversity of beliefs see Lankford, *Reachable Stars*. See also Hollabaugh, Review of *Reachable Stars*.

3. DeMallie, "Lakota Belief and Ritual," 43.

4. Mails, *Fools Crow: Wisdom and Power*, 51.

5. The use of these colors can be seen on the Sinte Gleska University emblem on the university home page, http://www.sintegleska.edu/.

6. Hassrick, *Sioux*, 32–54.

7. Hassrick, *Sioux*, 34.

8. Doll and Alinder, *Crying for a Vision*. This photo essay lacks page numbers.

9. Powers, *Sacred Language*, 128.

10. Walker, *Sun Dance and Other Ceremonies*, 159–60. Walker is relating information from Thomas Tyon.
11. J. Brown, *Sacred Pipe*, 80.
12. Sundstrom, "Mirror of Heaven."
13. Black often symbolizes mourning in Western cultures. In the Christian church, white is used on Christmas and Easter, red on Pentecost.
14. Howard, *Canadian Sioux*, 102–3. Howard's sources are Robert Good Voice and Sam Buffalo.
15. Walker, *Lakota Society*, 105.
16. An interesting question for Lakota historians is "why?" Is the use of the colors in modern times the result of the Lakota's involvement in the American Indian Movement and events of the early 1970s at Pine Ridge? For further discussion see Lincoln, "Lakota Sun Dance."
17. Powers, *Sacred Language*, 138–43.
18. Mails, *Fools Crow*.
19. Howard, *Canadian Sioux*, 102.
20. Walker, *Sun Dance and Other Ceremonies*, 85.
21. Not only is the preference to sit in a circle, but also to move clockwise about the circle. As one approaches the Wyoming Medicine Wheel, a small sign reads "Walk left," directing the visitor to circle the wheel in a clockwise manner.
22. Walker, *Sun Dance and Other Ceremonies*, 160. Walker is relating information from Thomas Tyon.
23. Mails, *Fools Crow*, 48.
24. DeMallie, *Sixth Grandfather*, 80.
25. I have used Joseph Brown's Lakota names for the rites as he heard them from Benjamin Black Elk, Black Elk's son, who translated for Brown (see J. Brown, *Sacred Pipe*). The Lakota phrase for the Keeping of the Spirit and Releasing of the Spirit, however, is from Charlotte Black Elk (Doll, *Vision Quest*, 156–57).
26. For a thorough discussion of the Sweat, see Bucko, *Lakota Ritual*.
27. Buechel, *Lakota-English Dictionary*, 525. Interestingly, the revised, 2002 edition adds the word *holy* to the definition (Buechel and Manhart, *Lakota Dictionary*, 333).
28. *Dakota Legend of Creation*. The American Indian Culture Research Center materials formerly at Blue Cloud Abbey are now housed at the Center for Western Studies (CWS), Augustana University, Sioux Falls.
29. Although the Pleiades are known as the *Seven* Sisters, the seventh brightest star, Pleione (magnitude 5.09), is about 60 percent fainter than the sixth

brightest star, near the limit of naked-eye seeing, and may have been difficult to see particularly if Good Seat's vision was less than perfect. This may be the reason he mentions six stars.

30. Walker, *Lakota Belief and Ritual*, 70–72.
31. White Hat, *Reading and Writing*, 98.
32. Walker, *Lakota Belief and Ritual*, 72–74.
33. Walker, *Lakota Belief and Ritual*, 70.
34. DeMallie, "Lakota Belief and Ritual," 43.
35. DeMallie, "Lakota Belief and Ritual," 32. DeMallie's idea that "the quest for understanding of the *wakan* [is] the driving force in Lakota culture" is the single most important idea that has shaped my research, my thinking, and this book.

4. The Stars and Constellations

1. Astronomers use *seeing* to describe the clarity and stability of the night air. Cooler, drier air generally is better for viewing, hence the location of observatories on mountain tops in the West. See http://mysite.du.edu/~rstencel/MtEvans/ for information on the University of Denver observatory on Mt. Evans and the perils of high-altitude observing.
2. Springer, "Journal." Although Springer's journal was published in 1971, I read a typed copy of his original journal at the Denver Public Library.
3. *Cynthia* is another name for the Moon.
4. Bourke, *Diaries*, 1:231–32. Although many microfilm copies of Bourke's journals are available, the originals are in the archives at the U.S. Military Academy. I have not corrected or altered Bourke's nineteenth-century spellings and punctuation.
5. The appearance of the sky on a given night can be re-created using Starry Night.
6. It usually confuses astronomy students when they learn blue is a "hot" color and red is a "cool" color, just the opposite of what they learned in an art class.
7. Zitkala-Ša, *Old Indian Legends*, 113.
8. Walker, *Lakota Myth*, 212. Only Walker uses *Škáŋ* as a noun. This is a part of Walker's "Literary Cycle" and contains numerous references to the significance of colors.
9. By "Bannacks" Clark probably means the Bannock. Clark, *Indian Sign Language*, 358.
10. C. Eastman, *Wigwam Evenings*, 205–9. Stories of earth women marrying star

men are common in Lakota cosmology. Many stories are similar. Helping your relatives is an important part of Lakota culture.

11. Beckwith, "Mythology of the Oglala," 342.

12. Wallis, "Beliefs and Tales," 45.

13. Goodman, *Lakota Star Knowledge*.

14. Goodman, *Lakota Star Knowledge*, 56–57 (I have not altered his orthography); Buechel MS (1915), *Digital Archive*, BMLM; Buechel and Manhart, *Lakota Dictionary*.

15. Walker, *Lakota Belief and Ritual*, 114–15. This quote from Ringing Shield is the spark that ignited my thoughts that resulted in this book.

16. LaPointe, *Legends of the Lakota*, 29–34.

17. Kohl, *Kitchi-Gami*, 118. Kohl traveled extensively in the Lake Superior region in 1855, and his detailed descriptions of Ojibwe life are an important source. The translation as "star of the north" may reflect a French influence and may have influenced the Minnesota leadership to choose *Etole du Nord*, Star of the North, for the state motto when Minnesota became a state in 1858.

18. An asterism is a grouping of stars that are not a constellation. For example, the Big Dipper asterism is actually the body and tail of the Great Bear, Ursa Major. Other Northern Hemisphere examples include the Keystone of Hercules and the Northern Cross, an asterism of the brightest stars in Cygnus.

19. LaPointe, *Legends of the Lakota*, 29.

20. Wallis, "Beliefs and Tales," 44. A modern Lakota spelling is *wichákhiyuhapi* (Buechel and Manhart, *Lakota Dictionary*, 372). For the a comparison to the Skidi Pawnee concept of the Dipper see Chamberlain, *When Stars Came Down to Earth*, 106–12.

21. Buechel and Manhart, *Lakota Dictionary*, 53.

22. Not only do the stars of the Pleiades appear to be close together, but they are gravitationally bound in what astronomers call an open star cluster. Although there are a thousand stars in this cluster, only six or seven of the brightest dozen or so stars are visible to the naked eye.

23. Goodman, *Lakota Star Knowledge*, 56.

24. Walker, *Lakota Belief and Ritual*, 114–15.

25. Another good example of a true star cluster is Messier 13, a globular cluster of 400,000 gravitationally bound stars, 25,000 light years from our solar system, and seen in the Keystone of Hercules. M-13 is not discernible to the naked eye.

26. LaPointe, *Legends of the Lakota*, 30. *Pa yamini pa* is a variant of *Thayámnipha* recorded both by Buechel and Goodman.

27. Wallis, "Beliefs and Tales," 44.

28. Although the Lakota saw the bright stars of Sagittarius outlining a sweat lodge, many astronomers, amateur and professional, see the shape as a teapot.

29. Monroe and Williamson, *They Dance*, 117.

30. Wallis, "Beliefs and Tales," 40. Wallis addressed several concepts related to what he calls *Cosmology*. When anthropologists and folklorists like Wallis use the word *cosmology*, they are usually referring to astronomy in general. In modern astronomy, *cosmology* refers to the structure and evolution of the universe as a whole.

31. Wallis, "Beliefs and Tales," 44. *Bdóza* is the loon in the Eastern Dakota dialect.

32. LaPointe, *Legends of the Lakota*, 31. It is not clear to what object "faint nebula" refers. The most likely nebula is the North American Nebula in Cygnus, which has a magnitude of 4.0. There are naked eye nebulae in Sagittarius, but they are not "high in the heavens."

33. LaPointe, *Legends of the Lakota*, 29–34.

34. Buechel and Manhart, *Lakota Tales & Text*, 53–63.

35. This may be a subtle allusion to the Roman Catholic Two Roads Map catechetical aid, which depicted the Black Road or Golden Road that humankind could follow. A Two Roads "Pictorial Catechism" on display at the Buechel Memorial Lakota Museum on the Rosebud Reservation shows a black road and a golden or yellow road. (Some versions showed a black road and a red road.) The chart, twenty-six inches wide and forty inches long, is in English and French and was produced by C. O. Beauchemin & Fils., Montreal, Canada. Branches lead between the two roads. At one branch Martin Luther is depicted as leaving the golden road and heading toward the dark side.

36. Buechel and Manhart, *Lakota Tales & Text*, 232–33.

5. The Sun and Moon

1. Astronomers use angular size to measure how large an object appears in the sky. Although the Moon is physically much smaller than the more distant Sun, its closeness to the Earth results in the same apparent or angular size as the Sun (see Freedman and Kaufman, *Universe*, 9–10).

2. For example, the biblical Priestly creation story in Gen. 1:1 to 2:4a, especially Gen. 1:14–19.

3. Walker, *Lakota Belief and Ritual*, 99.

4. C. Eastman, "Sioux Mythology," 222.

5. C. Eastman, *Wigwam Evenings*, 214–19.

6. See Morton and Gawboy, *Talking Rocks*.

7. Wallis, "Beliefs and Tales," 40. *Aŋpétuwi* 'sun'; *haŋyétuwi* 'moon'.

8. Buechel and Manhart, *Lakota Dictionary*. Mooney ("Myths of the Cherokees," 105) recorded a variation in the genders in his collection of Cherokee myths. Note the reference to the *seven* young men, a possible allusion to the Pleiades. "The earth is a flat surface, and the sky is an arch of solid rock suspended above it. This arch rises and falls continually, so that the space at the point of juncture is constantly opening and closing, like a pair of scissors. The sun is a man (some say a woman), so bright that no one can look at him long enough to see his exact shape, who comes through the eastern opening every morning, travels across the heavens, and disappears through the western opening, returning by night to the starting-point. This was discovered by seven young men who started out to find where the sun rises. They succeeded in passing through the eastern opening, but on their return one was crushed by the descending rock, and only six got back alive to tell the story. Mr. J. Owen Dorsey has found the same theory of the sun and horizon among the Omahas and Ponkas."

9. Wallis, "Beliefs and Tales," 41–44.

10. Dorsey, "Study of Siouan Cults," 449, quoting Riggs.

11. Clark, *Indian Sign Language*, 260.

12. C. Eastman, "Sioux Mythology," 222.

13. American Indian Culture Research Center Collection, cws.

14. Coleson, *Among the Sioux Indians*, 24–25. Although much of the dialogue is most likely fictional and the details of her experience greatly embellished, the general description of her experiences is plausible.

15. Walker, *Lakota Society*, 99.

16. Crazy Horse was killed in 1877. Father Buechel obtained the shirt at Holy Rosary Mission in 1915.

17. Wissler, "Some Protective Designs," 23.

18. Schmittou and Logan, "Fluidity of Meaning."

19. Wissler, "Some Protective Designs," 23–26.

20. Wissler, "Some Protective Designs," 23–26.

21. *Ógle wakháŋ* literally means "*wakháŋ* shirt." There is also an obvious chronological problem with this particular collection note. If the shirt was sixty years old in 1915, it would predate the Ghost Dance, which reached the Lakota in 1889 (Ostler, *Plains Sioux*). It may be that Father Buechel wrote the note later in his life when the shirt would have been about sixty years old, and the 1915 date refers to when he received the shirt. Buechel himself noted, "Is it really a ghost shirt?"

22. Marie Kills in Sight, conversation with author, St. Francis SD, 20 August 2009. Wissler ("Some Protective Designs," 32) includes a sketch of a shirt resplendent with dragonflies and an upturned crescent moon.
23. Walker, *Lakota Belief and Ritual*, 277.

6. Telling Time

1. Due to the tilt of the Earth's axis with respect to the ecliptic, as well as the elliptical orbit of the Earth, the Sun can be fast or slow in crossing the meridian. The figure-eight-shaped analemma seen on some globes of the Earth is a graphical representation of the correction to sundial time.
2. Walker, *Lakota Myth*, 65.
3. Walker, *Lakota Society*, 122–23.
4. Ricker, "Ricker Tablet" 25:127.
5. Carver, *Journals of Jonathan Carver*, 250–51.
6. Beckwith, "Mythology of the Oglala," 404.
7. Buechel MS (1915), *Digital Archive*, BMLM, 100.
8. Or *thaŋíŋšni wí*, "lost moon."
9. Walker, *Lakota Society*, 122–23.
10. Walker, *Lakota Society*; Riggs, *Dakota-English Dictionary*; Neihardt, *Black Elk Speaks*; Hassrick, *Sioux*; Belden, *Belden, the White Chief*, 289–90; Herman, "Primitive Sioux Calendar."
11. Clark, *Indian Sign Language*, 260–61. Clark omits July, and there is no entry for October.
12. The Lieutenant Scott to whom Clark refers is not identified, but it is possible he is the Hugh Lenox Scott who observed a partial eclipse on 29 July 1878.
13. Walker (*Lakota Society*) and Hassrick (*Sioux*) use this name for September.
14. The problems with intertwining a solar and a lunar calendar persist today. The editors of the *Minnesota SkyWatch Calendar* sought my advice on the inclusion of the Dakota names for each moon on their 2006 calendar. But there was a problem with December 2005, when there was a new moon on 1 December and another new moon on 30 December. What should they call the second new moon in December? More importantly, what about the new moon late in January 2006? It was not possible to include a thirteenth "discernible-not moon" in a twelve-month Gregorian-based calendar. My recommendation in situations like this would be to call the 30 December new moon the "discernible-not moon" or "lost moon" and, taking advantage of a teachable moment, to include an explanatory note. This problem of calendar synchronization was not unique to the Lakota. Kohl noted the

occasional inclusion of a thirteenth month by the Ojibwe and commented, "I grant that all the Indians cannot divide the months with equal correctness; and it is often comical to listen to the old men disputing as to what moon they are in" (Kohl, *Kitchi-Gami*, 120).

15. Alexander Marshack made an extensive study of calendar sticks. The abstract of his article is worth quoting: "The microscopic and sequential analysis of an early nineteenth-century American Indian calendar stick documents the notation of a precise, non-arithmetic, observational lunar year of twelve months with the evidence for added, subsidiary months suggesting the use of a thirteenth intercalary month every three years to bring the calendar into phase with the solar tropical year. The calendar stick is the most complex astronomical-calendric, problem-solving device known from the Americas outside of the high Mesoamerican and Andean Civilizations, but it is not derived from these late traditions. The analysis suggests the presence of an underlying observational conceptual base that may have come into the Americas from Asia." Marshack, "Lunar-Solar Year Calendar," 27.

16. Smithsonian Institution Catalog #218,134.

17. It is possible to see the day-old moon, but you need a very clear sky and an unobstructed view of the western horizon. Thus, each lunar month the moon is not seen for one to three days.

18. Hassrick, *Sioux*, 11.

19. Pond, *Dakota Life*, 84. The Ojibwe also used long calendar sticks for marking the passage of time. A large notch was cut every new moon, and smaller notches were cut for each successive day. Densmore, "Sun Dance."

20. DeMallie and Parks, "Tribal Traditions and Records," 1070; also in DeMallie, "Dissonant Voices," and Calloway, *One Vast Winter Count*.

21. In 1988, due to Bourke's report of calendar sticks among the southwest pueblo people and Mike Zeilik's curiosity, I examined several archaeological collections in Santa Fe and Albuquerque in search of the elusive sticks from the Anasazi culture. Although the collections contained many wood sticks, I found none that bore the distinctive marks of a calendar stick.

22. DeMallie, *Lakota Winter Counts*.

23. Howard, "Dakota Winter Counts," 339.

24. DeMallie, *Lakota Winter Counts*. See also DeMallie and Parks, "Tribal Traditions and Record."

25. Burke, "Collecting Lakota Histories."

26. Cheney, *Big Missouri Winter Count*; Powers, *A Winter Count*; Feraca, *Wounded Bear Winter Count*; Finster, *Hardin Winter Count*; Higginbotham, "Wind-

Roan Bear"; Thornton, "Rosebud Reservation Winter Count"; Greene and Thornton, *Year the Stars Fell.*

27. Amiotte, "Winter Count"; Beckwith, "Mythology of the Oglala"; Bettelyoun, *Lone Dog's Winter Count*; Waggoner, "Oglala Sioux Winter Count." Susan Bordeaux Bettelyoun was the daughter of French American fur trader James Bordeaux and his Brulé Lakota wife. Much of the Bordeaux history is preserved at the trading post that is now the Museum of the Fur Trade located east of Chadron NE. Numerous Bordeaux descendants live today on the Lakota reservations, and Louis Bordeaux is memorialized on a window in the mission church at St. Francis SD. A note on the Bettelyoun manuscript reads "Corrected and approved by Mrs. Waggoner 4/18/36." Waggoner was also the daughter of a white father and a Lakota mother. She and Bettelyoun met at the Old Soldiers Home in Hot Springs SD, and Waggoner frequently interviewed Bettelyoun, becoming very interested in Lakota oral history. Their collaboration is recorded in Bettelyoun and Waggoner, *With My Own Eyes.*

28. Greene and Thornton's *The Year the Stars Fell* catalogs the seventeen most extensive Lakota winter counts at the Smithsonian. Winter counts continue in the present time. Smithsonian Lakota curator Emil Her Many Horses provided a contemporary winter count that begins in 1999 and goes through 2005, the year his count was submitted to the book's authors. His count chronicles his extended family and contains extensive explanatory notes. See also Hollabaugh, "Review of *The Year the Stars Fell.*"

29. Cheney, *Big Missouri Winter Count.*

30. Mallery, *Picture-Writing.* John Wesley Powell, in his preface to Mallery's monumental report, gives glowing praise for Mallery's work. See Woodbury and Woodbury, "Rise and Fall."

31. Quoted in Maurer, *Visions of the People,* 286.

32. Some contemporary artists have adopted the winter count as a form of artistic expression. A copy by the late Lakota artist Melvin Miner of the Big Missouri Winter Count, the best-known count on a hide, is displayed at the Journey Museum in Rapid City SD. Miner produced replicas of the Big Missouri and other winter counts utilizing traditional materials and processes. I met Melvin at the 2009 Northern Plains Indian Art Market in Sioux Falls. He described to me in detail the process of preparing the hide and drawing the winter count on it. Melvin Miner (*Maka Sitomni Iyanke*—He Who Runs Around the World) died on 15 December 2010 from a heart attack.

33. Burke, "Collecting Lakota Histories"; Granger, "Garnier Oglala Winter Count"; Henning, "Western Dakota Winter Count"; Higginbotham, "Wind-Roan Bear";

Howard, "Dakota Winter Counts"; Howard, "Yaktonai Ethnohistory." Although there is some disagreement about the methodology, winter count analysis remains a viable tool (Thurman, "Plains Indian"; DeMallie, "Teton Dakota Time Concepts"). For example, winter counts have been used to tabulate epidemics that devastated the Indigenous people of the Great Plains (Sundstrom, "Smallpox Used Them Up"). The pictographs became a visual text (Risch, "Grammar of Time"). Problems of interpretation aside, winter counts are valuable tools for historians, particularly when combined with actual historical records (DeMallie and Parks, "Tribal Traditions and Record").

34. Howard, "Dakota Winter Counts," 340.
35. Chamberlain, "North American."
36. C. Eastman, *Wigwam Evenings*, 214–19. Another Star Boy story, "The Girl Who Married a Star" (205–9), is discussed in chapter 4. A young woman decides to marry a twinkling star. Their child is Star Boy, who "grew to be a handsome young man and had many adventures. His guides by night through the pathless woods were the star children of his mother's sister, his cousins in the sky."
37. Walker, *Lakota Myth*, 52–89, 369.
38. *Yata* is Walker's shortened form of *Wazíyata* 'North'.
39. DeMallie, "Teton Dakota Time Concepts," 7.
40. DeMallie, "Lakota Belief and Ritual," 31.
41. DeMallie and Parks, "Tribal Traditions and Records," 1072.
42. Hassrick, *Sioux*, 11.

7. Eclipses and the Aurora Borealis

1. Although today we can predict eclipse events far into the future, and daily monitoring of the Sun's activity permits alerts to intense solar flare activity that can cause aurora, these celestial phenomena still catch the modern public's attention.
2. The NASA Eclipse Web Site (eclipse.gsfc.nasa.gov/eclipse.html), managed by Fred Espenak, gives complete data for all the eclipses referenced in this book. In addition to the NASA website, the eclipse data from Chamberlain ("North American"), Greene and Thornton (*Year the Stars Fell*), and the *Starry Night* program were used in this study.
3. I have prepared an astronomy lab exercise using *Starry Night* to examine some of the eclipses visible to the nineteenth-century Lakota.
4. For a complete list, see Chamberlain , "North American."
5. The Moon can also appear orange-red when near the horizon or when there

is smoke in the atmosphere. This is due to blue light being scattered more than red light. Lightning-caused forest fires could also contribute to a reddish Moon or Sun.

6. Walker, *Lakota Society*, 151.
7. Beede, *Beede's Interpretation*.
8. Howard, "Dakota Winter Counts," 402. It should be noted the Swift Dog and High Dog counts *should* closely agree because they are thought to have been made by the same person.
9. See http://eclipse.gsfc.nasa.gov/SEsearch/SEsearchmap.php?Ecl=18890101 for a map showing the eclipse path. The eclipse timing for Williston was obtained from *Starry Night*.
10. The *"Rocky"* provided news of Colorado and the West for 150 years and ceased operations in 2009.
11. *Rocky Mountain News*, "Great Eclipse," 1. The *Rocky* reveled in the number of telescopes and spectrometers deployed to view the spectacle. A spectrometer uses a prism or diffraction grating to spread out light so that individual colors (wavelengths) can be seen and recorded in a spectrograph. The science of astronomical spectroscopy began in 1817, when the German scientist Joseph Fraunhofer attached a spectrometer to a telescope. Because each chemical element emits a particular set of wavelengths of light, a spectrometer allows an astronomer to identify the elements present in the gas surrounding the nucleus of a comet or in the atmosphere of a star like the Sun. You can mimic the use of a diffraction grating by reflecting the light from a street light off the recorded side of a CD-ROM or DVD.
12. Espenak, NASA Eclipse Web Site.
13. Technically speaking, today much of the region west of the Missouri River is in the mountain time zone except the Rosebud Reservation.
14. Mallery, *Picture-Writing*, 286. See Mooney, "In Memoriam," for a thorough biography of Washington Matthews, a physician-turned-anthropologist.
15. Poole, *Among the Sioux*, 76–77.
16. Chamberlain, "North American," S40.
17. Greene and Thornton, *Year the Stars Fell*, 265.
18. *Rocky Mountain News*, "Denver Eclipse," 1. The headline heralded, "The Great Event of the Century in Colorado." Apparently the *Rocky* functioned as a surrogate scientific journal for the astronomically literate on the waning frontier, including technical details on the solar spectrum that would be too advanced for the average newspaper reader today. Similar to today's eclipse cruises, the Pennsylvania Railroad offered half-priced fares to westward-bound astrono-

mers, and several notable scientists accepted the offer. Thirty-one-year-old Thomas Edison journeyed to Rawlins, Wyoming, taking with him a device to measure the Sun's heat energy (Eddy, "Great Eclipse of 1878").

19. Espenak, NASA Eclipse Web Site.
20. Scott, *Some Memories*, 90. Scott was a cadet at West Point from 1871 to 1876. Rising to the rank of major general, he later served as the academy's superintendent from 1906 to 1910 and U.S. Army chief of staff from 1914 to 1917.
21. Ostler, *Plains Sioux*.
22. Cheney, *Sioux Winter Count*, 34.
23. Wallis, "Beliefs and Tales," 40.
24. In space weather, the *Kp* index indicates the probability one will see an aurora. Generally, in order to see aurora at the latitude of Minneapolis and St. Paul, the index must be greater than 6, but in Duluth, the number drops to 4, and by the time one reaches the Minnesota-Ontario border, it is 3. Hence many campers returning from the Boundary Waters Canoe Area Wilderness tell stories of brilliant displays of the northern lights. During the solar minimum the index rarely exceeds 3 or 4. Even so I have frequently observed a glowing night sky to the north from my cabin near Grand Marais, Minnesota. During solar maximum we can expect to see spectacular shimmering sheets of light virtually every night. In the South Dakota Badlands, the index must approach 7 before aurora are visible. This would be an intense geomagnetic storm level. The NOAA Space Weather Prediction Center website (http://www.swpc.noaa.gov) provides daily data on the *Kp* index. There also are many "apps" for smart phones that give space weather predictions.
25. I had not given much thought to the Lakota's observing the northern lights until I saw aurora while camping one summer in the Badlands National Park.
26. The *New Lakota Dictionary* (797) gives several alternate Lakota words for the aurora borealis, including *wanáǧi tȟawáčhipi* and *Hóhe tȟamáȟpiya*.
27. Buechel and Manhart, *Lakota Dictionary*, 193.
28. Riggs, *Dakota-English Dictionary*, 305.
29. Clark, *Indian Sign Language*, 55.
30. The Dakota form of the word *Wazíya* appears today in the name Wayzata, a western suburb of Minneapolis.
31. Walker, *Lakota Belief and Ritual*, 125.
32. Walker, *Lakota Belief and Ritual*, 104.
33. M. Eastman, *Dahcotah*.
34. Walker, *Lakota Belief and Ritual*, 204.
35. Steltenkamp, *Black Elk*, 131.

36. Steltenkamp, *Black Elk*, 131–32. The original letter is in the archives of Marquette University.

37. Certainly part of the motivation for the International Geophysical Year in 1957–1958 was the need to further understand the effect of the aurora on communications with strategic forces. See http://www.nas.edu/history/igy/.

38. *New York Times*, "News from Korea."

39. Deloris Knipp, email communication with author, 12 September 2009.

8. Meteors and Comets

1. Clark, *Indian Sign Language*, 255.

2. Hyde, *Red Cloud's Folk*, 316–317. This connection is doubtful.

3. Mallery, *Picture-Writing*, 723. The figure captions are from Mallery.

4. Greene and Thornton, *Year the Stars Fell*, 169–71.

5. Chamberlain ("North American," S30–33) concluded the event on the winter counts and Snelling's observation were *not* the same meteor.

6. Keating, *Narrative of an Expedition*, 317.

7. Keating probably means syenite, a granite-like intrusive igneous rock.

8. Keating, *Narrative of an Expedition*, 315–16. William Hypolitus Keating (1799–1840) accompanied Stephen H. Long (the namesake of Longs Peak in Rocky Mountain National Park) on his journey of discovery.

9. M. Eastman, *Dahcotah*, 26.

10. Doane Robinson relates a similar legend that he titles "Bribing the Meteor" He most likely summarized the story from Eastman's book. Robinson is uncomplimentary about the nature of such legends and also comments, "The folklore of the Sioux is simple, childish and usually pointless. Apparently there is little of it common to all of the bands but each principal band seems to have preserved certain stories for a long period." Robinson, "Tales of the Dakota," 485–537.

11. Wallis, "Beliefs and Tales," 44.

12. Rao, "Leonids," 24–31.

13. Hyde, *Spotted Tail's Folk*, 29.

14. Mallery, *Picture-Writing*, 723.

15. Schmittou and Logan, "Fluidity of Meaning."

16. The figure captions include Mallery's notations from *Picture-Writing of the American Indians*.

17. Thornton, "Rosebud Reservation Winter Count."

18. Hirschfelder and Molin, *Encyclopedia*.

19. Walker, *Lakota Myth*, 9.

20. Buechel and Manhart, *Lakota Dictionary*, 386.

21. Marie Kills in Sight, conversation with the author, 20 August 2009, St. Francis SD. Marie subsequently told me that after we had talked, she mentioned our conversation to a coworker, who said she had heard the same story from *her* grandmother.

22. The comet was named posthumously for Edmond Halley (1656–1742), who predicted its return visit in 1759.

23. Of course, the cyanogen dispersed into space and never made it to the Earth's surface!

24. Howard, "Dakota Winter Counts," 409. See also Maurer, *Visions of the People*; Chamberlain, "North American." Howard suggests, "The Swift Dog and High Dog counts are nearly identical, and in my opinion were both made by the same man, Swift Dog." He also suggests the High Dog count may not be accurate. "It was procured by the Reverend Mr. Beede [an Episcopal missionary among the Lakota], who writes 'High Dog copied this for me from one which he had (about new).' With the count is an interpretation of the count in Dakota, apparently written by an Indian. This text is rather garbled. It is accompanied by what purports to be a translation and interpretation of this Dakota text and the count pictographs by Beede. Much of Beede's material seems to be merely conjectural, and, where the translation of the Dakota is possible, is often shown to be highly erroneous. . . . The count apparently pertains to the Hunkpapa and Sihasapa bands of the Teton Dakota and to the Yanktonai." Howard, "Dakota Winter Counts, 344.

25. Beede, *Beede's Interpretation*. See also Maurer, *Visions of the People*, 275.

26. Wallis, "Beliefs and Tales," 45.

9. The Sun Dance

1. Clements, "Plains Indian Tribal Correlations."

2. E. Deloria, "Sun Dance"; Densmore, "Sun Dance"; Fletcher, "Sun Dance"; Fletcher, "Lakota Ceremonies"; Walker, *Sun Dance and Other Ceremonies*; Wallis, *Sundance*.

3. White Hat, *Reading and Writing*, 15. White Hat also interprets this phrase as "we are all related" by virtue of coming "from one source" (29).

4. For example, Schwatka, "Sundance of the Sioux"; Welsh, *Report and Supplementary Report*; Larned, Papers, 1921–1922.

5. Mails, *Sundancing*.

6. E. Deloria, "Sun Dance," 354.

7. Walker, *Sun Dance and Other Ceremonies*, 60–121.

8. J. Brown, *Sacred Pipe*, 67–100.
9. Amiotte, "Lakota Sun Dance," 84.
10. Hill, *Sundance of the Sioux*.
11. Paige, "George W. Hill's Account." Paige notes there are two versions of Hill's paper, one incorporating revisions by Hill's son. The typed version in the State Historical Society of North Dakota archives that I read bears this notation: "This is a true and unedited copy of a typewritten manuscript (the handwritten original of which is missing) written by Capt. George William Hill, and found amongst his papers."
12. Clark, *Indian Sign Language*, 361–63.
13. This would not contradict the idea that one does not do the Sun Dance for "his own glory or prestige" if the supernatural aid was used to benefit the community.
14. Hassrick, *Sioux*, 280–88.
15. Amiotte, "Lakota Sun Dance," 86–87.
16. For a detailed discussion of the Sweat Lodge, see Bucko, *Lakota Ritual*.
17. Walker tends to use *shaman* to mean *wicháša wakháŋ*, "holy man."
18. Walker, *Sun Dance and Other Ceremonies*, 142.
19. Walker may have meant *Áŋpao*, "dawn."
20. Walker, *Sun Dance and Other Ceremonies*, 142.
21. Clark, *Indian Sign Language*, 361.
22. Welsh, *Report and Supplementary Report*, 14.
23. Walker, *Sun Dance and Other Ceremonies*, 81–82.
24. Walker, *Lakota Society*, 99.
25. J. Brown, *Sacred Pipe*, 71.
26. Clark, *Indian Sign Language*, 363.
27. Fletcher, "Sun Dance."
28. Thomas Lewis, "Oglala (Teton Dakota)"; Herman, "Primitive Sioux Calendar."
29. Froiland, *Natural History*, 92–96.
30. J. Brown, *Sacred Pipe*, 67.
31. Walker, *Sun Dance and Other Ceremonies*, 61.
32. Clark, *Indian Sign Language*, 361.
33. Hill, *Sundance of the Sioux*; Hassrick, *Sioux*.
34. Amiotte, "Lakota Sun Dance," 77.
35. Amiotte, "Lakota Sun Dance," 78.
36. Zeilik, "Ethnoastronomy, I."
37. Arthur Amiotte, conversation with author, Sioux Falls SD, 28 September 1996.
38. J. Brown, *Sacred Pipe*, 85, 129.

39. 8 × 365 days = 5 × 584 days = 2920 days, a time interval determined by the Maya.

40. Buechel MS (1915), *Digital Archive*, BMLM, 28. Buechel does not necessarily mean Venus in this comment, and he may refer to the last star visible in the sky before dawn. According to Buechel, the *šiyóthaŋka* is a small whistle perhaps made from the leg bone of a grouse, and the *wíŋyaŋ wicháglata* refers to a rattle mounted on a long stick and decorated with feathers.

41. Mails, *Sundancing*. The Sun Dances occurred in 1974 and 1975.

42. Lincoln, "Lakota Sun Dance." The timing of the Sun Dance today seems to be less influenced by the budding of plants, time of the solstice, or the phase of the moon and more by the demands of modern society, the availability of a three-day weekend, and the scheduling of other Sun Dances.

43. Hedren, *Traveler's Guide*, 56.

44. DeMallie, "'These Have No Ears,'" 516.

45. James Hanson, email communication with author, 7 October 2002. Hanson's complete email is worth including for its historical details: "The site of Spotted Tail Agency in 1875 was several miles south of the mouth of Beaver Creek, about halfway between the mouth and the town of Hay Springs. It's a well-known spot and has been marked by the Sheridan County Historical Society. The site of the big sun dance Schwatka observed is, I believe, where the Chadron airport is located. At least it was pointed out to me 48 years ago [1954] by Professor E. P. Wilson, who interviewed many old Indians and visited various area sites with them, and by my father, who was good friends with Hudson Meade, an early surveyor and recorder of presettlement history. In about 1967, the same site was pointed out to me by Willy Running Hawk, descendant of Man Afraid of His Horses and son-in-law of John Bissonette, who was himself the son of an early fur trader. I don't know of any real forks on Chadron Creek—what Schwatka may have been referring to as a fork is the White River."

46. Schwatka, "Sundance of the Sioux," 754.

47. Schwatka, "Sundance of the Sioux," 759.

48. Schwatka, "Sundance of the Sioux," 754.

49. Joseph Porter observed a Crow Sun Dance in 1990 and noted a crier wakening everyone and then greeting the sun (email communication with author, 24 January 2002). The Curtis photo (portfolio 3, plate 109) is available at the Library of Congress and online at http://hdl.loc.gov/loc.award/iencurt.cp03034.

50. Hill, *Sundance of the Sioux*.

51. Walker places the announcement of the sun before the capture of the tree. Walker, *Sun Dance and Other Ceremonies*.
52. Thomas Lewis, "Oglala (Teton Dakota)."
53. Porter, *Paper Medicine Man*; Bourke, *Diaries*.
54. Porter, *Paper Medicine Man*. Bourke led a group of Shoshoni warriors in battle against the Lakota. He rescued fallen bugler Elmer A. Snow from certain death. From Bourke we know Lt. Charles Schwatka was a participant in the Bighorn and Yellowstone campaigns with Crook and was present at the Battle of the Rosebud. Bourke's diary entry for 29 May 1876 lists Lt. Schwatka as an officer with Company "M," Third Cavalry. Bourke, *Diaries*.
55. The government's and military's interest in the culture of Native Americans was not due to scientific curiosity or a desire to preserve the culture, but rather to facilitate bringing the Indian peoples into white society, i.e., assimilation. From reading his diaries, one gets the impression that Bourke was the ideal person to send into the field to observe Native American tribes, and he carried out his task with enthusiasm and a sense of scholarly curiosity.
56. It is from Bourke's visits to the pueblos that we know about the use of calendar sticks and horizon sun watching among the historic pueblos, and presumably among their pre-Columbian ancestors.
57. Sutherland, "Diaries of John Gregory Bourke." Sutherland, like Bourke, was a soldier-scholar. A 1936 U.S. Military Academy graduate, he was present at the D-Day invasion, rose to the rank of brigadier general, and taught in the English Department at West Point. His complete obituary is available at http://www.nytimes.com/1997/01/17/world/edwin-sutherland-82-soldier-and-scholar-is-dead.html.
58. The original Bourke diaries are in the archives at the U.S. Military Academy, West Point. Microfilm copies are available, and historian Charles Robinson has transcribed and published Bourke's diaries. The Fort Robinson State Park Museum houses many artifacts relating to Bourke and his time with General Crook.
59. Porter, *Paper Medicine Man*.
60. Sutherland, "Diaries of John Gregory Bourke."
61. Sutherland, "Diaries of John Gregory Bourke."
62. Hanson, "Oglala Sioux Sun Dance"; Bronson, *Reminiscences of a Ranchman*.
63. Bourke ultimately achieved the rank of major, and Bronson wrote this account many years after the Sun Dance.
64. Bourke, *Diaries*; Bronson, *Reminiscences of a Ranchman*; DeMallie, conversation with author, 15 March 2007, St. Olaf College, Northfield MN.

65. Brother C. M. Simon, conversation with author, Heritage Center, Pine Ridge SD, August 2002; Thomas Lewis, "Oglala (Teton Dakota)." Brother Simon died suddenly on 14 July 2006. He was sixty-nine years old, had been a Jesuit brother for forty-seven years, and had served the Lakota people on the Pine Ridge Reservation for forty-two years.

66. At a 1975 Plains Cree Sweetwater Sun Dance in Saskatchewan the Sun Dance lodge entrance was aligned with the sunrise direction. It is likely this orientation was intentional. Kehoe and Kehoe, "Stones, Solstices."

67. Clark, *Indian Sign Language*, 361.

68. J. Brown, *Sacred Pipe*.

69. There is a great deal of variation in Lakota practice, and Bucko (*Lakota Ritual*, 113–15) notes this variation and a pragmatic approach to the entrance to the sweat lodge, which is not always east. When I attended a Sunday morning outdoor Episcopal Eucharist led by the late Fr. Noah Brokenleg on the Rosebud Reservation, the congregants, celebrant, and a temporary altar table faced east. A Pendleton blanket was a temporary but beautiful altar covering.

70. Melody, "Lakota Sun Dance." Note that "directly overhead" poetically refers to the passage of the Sun across the meridian. An observer must be between latitudes 23.5 N and 23.5 S for the Sun to be directly overhead, so the Sun would never be directly overhead in the latitudes of the Great Plains.

71. Williamson, *Living the Sky*, 138.

72. Lincoln, "Lakota Sun Dance."

73. Amiotte, "Lakota Sun Dance," 78.

10. Contemporary Lakota Astronomy

1. Lame Deer and Erdoes, *Gift of Power*, 252.

2. Freedman and Kaufmann, *Universe*, 355–56.

3. Rice, "Ventriloquy of Anthros," 169.

4. For a complete discussion of the Lakota sweat lodge ceremony, see Bucko, *Lakota Ritual*.

5. Goodman, *Lakota Star Knowledge*.

6. *Lakota Star Knowledge Project Collection*.

7. Goodman, "On the Necessity."

8. For a discussion of Fallen Star, see the section on the Milky Way in chapter 4.

9. I have not used their orthographic markings.

10. Bad Heart Bull and Blish, *Pictographic History*, drawing no. 198.

11. DeMallie and Parks, "Tribal Traditions and Record," 1072.

12. Goodman, *Lakota Star Knowledge*, 9.

13. Goodman, *Lakota Star Knowledge*, 3.
14. These four categories are reminiscent of the church father Origen.
15. A "Star Knowledge Conference" was held on the Yankton Sioux Reservation, Marty SD, 12–16 June 1996. Speakers with unimpressive ethnoastronomical credentials (such as the "former Acting Finnish Surgeon-general" and several retired military personnel) participated. Visits from extraterrestrials—Star People—were discussed in depth. Although the original motivation, a revitalization of Lakota spirituality, was admirable, the outcome fueled UFO aficionados, Indian "wannabes," and proponents of alien abductions. (An online copy of Richard Boylan's report is available at http://www.v-j-enterprises.com/skcrichb.html, accessed 4 January 2012.). A similar gathering, the "Star Visions Conference," was held in Fort Collins CO, 7–11 November 1996. (Report by Boylan available at http://www.padrak.com/ufo/WORLDS.html.) Postulating that extraterrestrials brought "star knowledge" to Native Americans has always struck me as condescending because such a view presupposes the Lakota and other Native peoples weren't smart enough to figure it out without extraterrestrial alien help.
16. Kelley and Milone, *Exploring Ancient Skies*, 425.
17. Williamson and Farrer, *Earth & Sky*, 215. Goodman's article in *Earth & Sky* is almost identical to chapter 6 in his *Lakota Star Knowledge*.
18. Arnold, "Black Elk," 99.
19. See note 7, chapter 2, on *diffusion*. Lankford (*Reachable Stars*) develops the proximity idea, using an analysis of folklore.
20. Sundstrom, "Mirror of Heaven,"187–88. For an excellent narrative discussion of the celestial connection with the need for a sacred Black Hills see Ostler, *Lakotas*, 12–22.
21. LaPointe, *Legends of the Lakota*, 30.

11. The Spirit and the Sky

1. There is not one "Native view." There is diversity among different tribal cultures and even within a tribal group.
2. Cajete, *Native Science*, 234. Much of this discussion draws on ideas from Cajete, a Tewa from the Santa Clara Pueblo in New Mexico, who has been on the education faculty at the University of New Mexico as well as the Institute of American Indian Arts in Santa Fe. Although the relation to the physical world of plants, animals, and the land occupies a large portion of his book, he devotes one chapter to Native astronomy, drawing on the work of several prominent archaeoastronomers and ethnoastronomers. The Lakota are well represented in his discussion.

3. Cajete, *Native Science*; Cajete, "Philosophy of Native Science." Cajete proposes twenty-two methodological elements and tools of Native science. Some of his categories relate more directly to modern science; others are more closely allied to Native spirituality. The categories provide a useful paradigm for understanding how the ethnoastronomy of the Lakota relates to larger Native cultures and how it is similar to and different from modern science. His categories also provide a connection between Native science and modern astronomy.

4. Hawking's comments on Einstein's statement that "God does not play dice" can be found in a lecture on his website: "Does God Play Dice?" http://www .hawking.org.uk/does-god-play-dice.html.

5. A key book in my own development of the idea of chance was *Chance and Providence* by William Pollard, a physicist at Oak Ridge National Laboratory who was also an Episcopal clergyman.

6. My article on evolution and faith that appeared in the *Lutheran* (December 2006) angered some readers yet pleased many others, including my former science and theology professors. Some of the best sermons I've heard came from my college physics, mathematics, chemistry, and biology professors in chapel talks at St. Olaf College. Some of the best statements of the role of science in our world came from my professors at Luther Theological Seminary.

7. This is not to imply modern scientists are not in awe of the universe. In fact, one of the great privileges of being an astronomer is to be aware of the "awesome" nature of the cosmos. While Native spirituality may be able to coexist with the ambiguities, modern scientists, from my perspective, work to resolve the ambiguities and answer the questions.

8. Cajete, *Native Science*, 178.

9. Kinship and the "making of relatives" are fundamental to Lakota culture. See DeMallie, "Sioux until 1850," 734–35.

10. White Hat, *Reading and Writing*, 29. Kinship is a unifying motif in White Hat's book.

11. Cajete, *Native Science*, 216. Note that Cajete uses "astronomies." Within the unity of a Native viewpoint there is diversity, which is also the point made by Lankford (*Reachable Stars*).

12. Momaday, "Native American Attitudes," 10. It is interesting that Momaday refers to the nineteenth-century nature poets. Many well-intentioned New Englanders were at the forefront of the nineteenth-century movements to "save" the Indian. Perhaps a differing view of nature was one reason for the ultimate clash of cultures.

13. Bol, "Nature as a Model," 240, citing Joseph Epes Brown.
14. For an excellent discussion of how the Navajo incorporate the cosmos into not just dwellings but also their beautiful sand paintings, see *Earth Is My Mother, Sky Is My Father* by the late Trudy Griffin-Pierce.
15. Morton and Gawboy, *Talking Rocks*, 199. The "conversation" in *Talking Rocks: Geology and 10,000 years of Native American Tradition in the Lake Superior Region* is between Ron Morton, a professor of geology at the University of Minnesota–Duluth, and Carl Gawboy, a retired professor of American Indian studies at the College of St. Scholastica, also in Duluth. Gawboy has had a longtime interest in Native American ethnoastronomy. He also sees many connections between what geologists have learned about the history of the Lake Superior region and Native American, especially Ojibwe, legends. Gawboy's view of the connection between planet Earth and the night sky is one of the best statements I have read of this holistic, integrated approach to science and Native American culture. Gawboy is also an artist and contributed artwork to the visitor's center at the Grand Portage National Monument in Minnesota.
16. Sebastian Braun, personal communication with author, 26 September 2014.
17. In academic circles this is what is known as the "research question."
18. Cajete, *Native Science*, 217–18.
19. Just like the scientist who modifies a theory based on new data, the Lakota modified their lunar calendar with the thirteenth moon about every three years in order to keep the calendar in step with the seasons; i.e., the theory supports the data.
20. DeMallie, "Lakota Belief and Ritual," 32.
21. Walker, *Lakota Belief and Ritual*, 114–15.
22. Walker, *Lakota Belief and Ritual*, 70. An interesting hypothesis is that because the stars are *wakháŋ*, only the *wicháša wakháŋ*, not ordinary people, i.e., humans, should talk about the stars.
23. En route to the Fifth Oxford International Conference in 1996, I stopped in Denver and gave a seminar for the Department of Physics and Astronomy at the University of Denver, where I had completed an M.S. in astronomy. Astronomer Bob Stencel commented on the contradiction.
24. This is a Venn diagram, which shows connections between ideas. The Venn diagram dates back to 1880 and has been used in a wide variety of contexts to convey conceptual relationships.
25. Williamson, *Living the Sky*, 319. For more than twenty-five years, I used this quotation to end my classroom lectures on Native American astronomy.

BIBLIOGRAPHY

Albers, Patricia C. "Santee." In DeMallie, *Handbook of North American Indians* 13, 761–76.

Amiotte, Arthur. "The Lakota Sun Dance: Historical and Contemporary Perspectives." In *Sioux Indian Religion*, edited by Raymond J. DeMallie and Douglas R. Parks, 75–89. Norman: University of Oklahoma Press, 1987.

———. "Winter Count in ledger book belonging to George H. Mesthith, Manderson, SD." In the Arthur Amiotte Collection, Center for Western Studies, Augustana University, Sioux Falls SD.

Arnold, Philip P. "Black Elk and Book Culture." *Journal of the American Academy of Religion* 67, no. 1 (1999): 85–111.

Aveni, Anthony. "Archaeoastronomy in the Ancient Americas." *Journal of Archaeological Research* 11, no. 2 (2003): 149–91.

———. *Skywatchers of Ancient Mexico*. Austin: University of Texas Press, 1983.

Bad Heart Bull, Amos, and Helen Blish. *A Pictographic History of the Oglala Sioux*. Lincoln: University of Nebraska Press, 1967.

Baity, Elizabeth Chesley, Anthony F. Aveni, Rainer Berger, David A. Bretternitz, Geoffrey A. Clark, James W. Dow, P.-R. Giot, David H. Kelley, Leo S. Klejn, H. H. E. Loops, Rolf Muller, Richard Pittioni, Emilie Pleslova-Stikova, Zenon S. Pohorecky, Jonathan E. Reyman, S. B. Roy, Charles H. Smiley, Dean R. Snow, James L. Swauger, and P. M. Vermeersch. "Archaeoastronomy and Ethnoastronomy So Far." *Current Anthropology* 14, no. 4(1973): 389–449.

Beckwith, Martha Warren. "Mythology of the Oglala Dakota." *Journal of American Folklore* 43, no. 170 (1930.): 339–442.

Beede, Aaron. *Beede's Interpretation of High Dogs' Winter Count*. State Historical Society of North Dakota. Accessed 19 April 2016. http://history.nd.gov/textbook/unit3_1_beede.html.

Belden, George P. *Belden, The White Chief*. Athens: Ohio University Press, n.d. (Copy in the collection of the Colorado historical society, History Colorado, Denver.)

Bettelyoun, Susan Bordeaux. *Lone Dog's Winter Count.* Typed manuscript (1936). South Dakota Historical Society archives, Pierre.

Bettelyoun, Susan Bordeaux, and Josephine Waggoner. *With My Own Eyes: A Lakota Woman Tells Her People's History.* Edited by Emily Levine. Lincoln: University of Nebraska Press, 1998.

Bol, Marsha C. "Nature as a Model of American Indian Societies: An Overview." In *Stars Above, Earth Below,* edited by Marsha C. Bol. Niwot CO: Roberts Rinehart, 1998.

Bourke, John G. *The Diaries of John Gregory Bourke.* Edited and annotated by Charles M. Robinson III. Denton: University of North Texas, 2003.

Brackett, Col. Albert G. "The Sioux or Dakota Indians." In *Smithsonian Institution, Annual Report for 1886.* Washington DC: Smithsonian Institution, 1887.

Bronson, Edgar Beecher. *Reminiscences of a Ranchman.* Chicago: A. C. McClurg, 1910.

Brown, Dee. *Bury My Heart at Wounded Knee.* New York: Henry Holt, 1970.

———. *The Fetterman Massacre.* Lincoln: University of Nebraska Press, 1962.

Brown, Joseph Epes, ed. *The Sacred Pipe: Black Elk's Account of the Seven Rites of the Oglala Sioux.* Norman: University of Oklahoma Press, 1989.

———. *The Spiritual Legacy of the American Indian.* Bloomington IN: World Wisdom, 2007.

Bucko, Raymond A., S.J. *The Lakota Ritual of the Sweat Lodge.* Lincoln: University of Nebraska Press, 1998.

Buechel, Eugene, S.J. *Digital Archive: Fr. Eugene Buechel, S.J. Lakota Material Culture Collection and Associated Notes.* Edited by Raymond Bucko, S.J., and Mike Marshall. St. Francis SD: St. Francis Mission, 2003. Buechel Memorial Lakota Museum (BMLM).

———. *Lakota-English Dictionary.* Edited by Paul Manhart. Pine Ridge SD: Red Cloud Indian School, Holy Rosary Mission, 1983.

Buechel, Eugene, S.J., and Paul Manhart, S.J. *Lakota Dictionary.* Rev. ed. Lincoln: University of Nebraska Press, 2002.

———. *Lakota Tales & Text.* Chamberlain SD: Tipi Press, 1998.

Burke, Cristina E. "Collecting Lakota Histories: Winter Count Pictographs and Texts in the National Anthropological Archives." *American Indian Art Magazine* 26, no. 1 (2000): 82–103.

Cajete, Gregory. *Native Science: Natural Laws of Interdependence.* Santa Fe: Clear Light, 2002.

———. "Philosophy of Native Science." In *American Indian Thought: Philosophical Essays,* edited by Anne Waters. Malden MA: Blackwell, 2004.

Calloway, Colin. *One Vast Winter Count*. Lincoln: University of Nebraska Press, 2003.

Carlson, John B. "America's Ancient Skywatchers." *National Geographic* 177, no. 3 (March 1990): 76–107.

Carver, Jonathan. *The Journals of Jonathan Carver and Related Documents, 1766–1770*. Edited by John Parker. St. Paul: Minnesota Historical Society Press, 1976.

———. *Travels through the Interior Parts of North America in the Years 1766, 1767, and 1768*. Minneapolis: Ross & Haines, 1956.

Chamberlain, Von Del. "North American Plains Indian Calendars." *Archaeoastronomy: Supplement to Journal for the History of Astronomy* 15, no. 6 (1984): S1-S54.

———. *When Stars Came Down to Earth: Cosmology of the Skidi Pawnee Indians of North America*. Ballena Press Anthropological Papers, 26. Los Altos CA: Ballena Press; College Park MD: Center for Archeoastronomy, 1982.

Cheney, Roberta Carkeek. *The Big Missouri Winter Count*. Happy Camp CA: Naturegraph, 1979.

———. *Sioux Winter Count*. Happy Camp CA: Naturegraph, 1998.

Chomsky, Carol. "The United States–Dakota War Trials: A Study in Military Injustice." *Stanford Law Review* 43, no. 1 (1999): 13–98.

Clark, W. P. *The Indian Sign Language*. New York: L. R. Hamersly, 1885. Reprint, Lincoln: University of Nebraska Press, 1982.

Clements, F. "Plains Indian Tribal Correlations with Sun Dance Data." *American Anthropologist* 33, no. 2 (1931): 216–27.

Coates, Richard. "A Linguist's Angle on the Star of Bethlehem." *Astronomy & Geophysics* 49 (2008): 5.27–5.32.

Coleson, Ann. *Among the Sioux Indians*. Philadelphia: Barclay, 1864. (Copy in the South Dakota Historical Society archives, Pierre.)

Comins, Neil F., and William J. Kaufmann. *Discovering the Universe*. 10th ed. New York: W. H. Freeman, 2014.

Connell, Evan S. *Son of the Morning Star*. New York: HarperCollins, 1991.

A Dakota Legend of Creation. American Indian Culture Research Center Collection, Center for Western Studies, Augustana University, Sioux Falls SD.

Deloria, Ella C. "Sun Dance of the Oglala Sioux." *Journal of American Folklore* 42 (1929): 354–413.

Deloria, Vine, Jr. "Commentary: Research, Redskins, and Reality." *American Indian Quarterly* 15, no. 4 (Fall 1991): 457–68.

———. *Custer Died for Your Sins*. New York: Macmillan, 1969.

———. "Indians, Archaeologists, and the Future." *American Antiquity* 57, no. 4 (1992): 595–98.

———. "Sundancing and Stargazing." *Archaeoastronomy* 5, no. 3 (1982): 33–35.

DeMallie, Raymond J. "Dissonant Voices: Anthropologists, Historians, and the Lakota People." Paper presented at the conference "Crosscurrents of Culture, 1492–1992," New York University, 4 April 1992.

———, ed. *Handbook of North American Indians*, vol. 13: *Plains*, pts. 1 and 2. Washington DC: Smithsonian Institution, 2001.

———. "Lakota Belief and Ritual in the Nineteenth Century." In *Sioux Indian Religion*, edited by Raymond J. DeMallie and Douglas R. Parks, 25–44. Norman: University of Oklahoma Press, 1987.

———. "Lakota Winter Counts." Phi Beta Kappa lecture presented at St. Olaf College, Northfield MN, 15 March 2007.

———. Review of *Black Elk's Religion: The Sun Dance and Lakota Catholicism*, by Clyde Holler. *Journal of American History* 84, no. 1 (1997): 245.

———. "Sioux until 1850." In DeMallie, *Handbook of North American Indians* 13, 718–60.

———. *The Sixth Grandfather: Black Elk's Teachings Given to John G. Neihardt*. Lincoln: University of Nebraska Press, 1984.

———. "Teton Dakota Time Concepts: Methodological Foundations for the Writing of Ethnohistory." *Folklore Forum* 9, *Bibliographic and Special Series* 5 (1976): 7–17.

———. "'These Have No Ears:' Narrative and the Ethnohistorical Method." *Ethnohistory* 40, no. 4 (1993): 515–38.

DeMallie, Raymond J., and Douglas R. Parks. "Tribal Traditions and Records." In DeMallie, *Handbook of North American Indians* 13, pt. 2, 1062–73.

Densmore, Frances. *Chippewa Customs*. St. Paul: Minnesota Historical Society Press, 1979. (Originally published as Bulletin 86 of the Bureau of American Ethnology, 1929.)

———. "The Sun Dance of the Teton Sioux." *Nature* 104 (1920): 437–40.

———. *Teton Sioux Music and Culture*. Lincoln: University of Nebraska Press, 1992.

Doll, Don, S.J. *Vision Quest: Men, Women, and Sacred Sites of the Sioux Nation*. New York: Crown, 1994.

Doll, Don, S.J., and Jim Alinder, eds. *Crying for a Vision: A Rosebud Sioux Trilogy, 1886–1976*. Dobbs Ferry NY: Morgan & Morgan, 1976.

Dorsey, James O. "A Study of Siouan Cults." In *Bureau of American Ethnology Annual Report* 14. Washington DC: Government Printing Office, 1894.

———. "Teton Folk-Lore." *American Anthropologist* 2, no. 2 (April 1889):143–58.

Eastman, Charles A. "Sioux Mythology." In *International Folklore Congress of the World's Columbian Exposition*, 221–26. Chicago: Charles Sergel, 1898.

———. *Wigwam Evenings: Sioux Folk Tales Retold.* Lincoln: University of Nebraska Press, 1990.

Eastman, Mary. *Dahcotah, or, Life and Legends of the Sioux around Fort Snelling.* New York: John Wiley, 1849. Reprint, Afton MN: Afton Historical Society Press, 1995.

Eddy, John. "Astronomical Alignment of the Big Horn Medicine Wheel." *Science* 184, no. 4141 (1974): 1035–43.

———. "The Great Eclipse of 1878." *Sky & Telescope*, June 1973, 340.

Emery, Steven C. Review of *Black Elk: Holy Man of the Oglala*, by Michael F. Steltenkamp. *Journal of American History* 81, no. 4 (1995): 1753.

Espenak, Fred. NASA Eclipse Web Site, NASA/Goddard Space Flight Center. http://eclipse.gsfc.nasa.gov/eclipse.html.

Fenlon, James V. Review of *The Plains Sioux and U. S. Colonialism from Lewis and Clark to Wounded Knee*, by Jeffrey Ostler. *Wicazo Sa Review* 21, no. 2 (Fall 2006): 184–92.

Feraca, Stephen. *The Wounded Bear Winter Count.* Kendall Park NJ: Lakota Books, 1994.

Finster, David. *The Hardin Winter Count.* Kendall Park NJ: Lakota Books, 1995.

Fletcher, Alice C. "Lakota Ceremonies." *Archaeology and Ethnology* 3, nos. 3 and 4 (1884): 260–307.

———. "Sun Dance of the Oglala Sioux." *Proceedings of the American Association for the Advancement of Science* 31, pt. 2 (1882): 580–84.

Freed, Stanley A., and Ruth S. Freed. "Clark Wissler and the Development of Anthropology in the United States." *American Anthropologist* 85, no. 4 (1983): 800–825.

Freedman, Roger, Robert M. Geller, and William J. Kaufmann. *Universe.* 10th ed. New York: W. H. Freeman, 2014.

Fritz, Henry E. *The Movement for Indian Assimilation, 1860–1890.* Philadelphia: University of Pennsylvania Press, 1963.

Froiland, Sven G. *Natural History of the Black Hills and Badlands.* Sioux Falls SD: Center for Western Studies, Augustana College, 1990.

Gawboy, Carl, and Ron Morton. *Talking Sky: Ojibwe Constellations as a Reflection of Life on the Land.* Duluth MN: Rockflower Press, 2014.

Giago, Tim. "The Black Hills: A Case of Dishonest Dealings." *Huffington Post,*

3 June 2007. http://www.huffingtonpost.com/tim-giago/the-black-hills-a
-case-of_b_50480.html.

Goldenweiser, Alexander. "Diffusionism and the American School of Historical Ethnology." *American Journal of Sociology* 31, no. 1 (1925): 19–38.

Goodman, Ronald. *Lakota Star Knowledge: Studies in Lakota Stellar Theology.* Rosebud SD: Sinte Gleska University, 1992.

———. "On the Necessity of Sacrifice in Lakota Stellar Theology as Seen in 'The Hand' Constellation and the Story of 'The Chief Who Lost His Arm.'" In *Earth & Sky: Visions of the Cosmos in Native American Folklore,* edited by Ray A. Williamson and Claire R. Farrer. Albuquerque: University of New Mexico Press, 1992.

Granger, Roger T. "The Garnier Oglala Winter Count." *Plains Anthropologist* 8, no. 20 (1963): 74–79.

Greene, Candace S., and Russell Thornton. *The Year the Stars Fell: Lakota Winter Counts at the Smithsonian.* Lincoln: University of Nebraska Press; Washington DC: Smithsonian Institution, 2007.

Griffin-Pierce, Trudy. *Earth Is My Mother, Sky Is My Father.* Albuquerque: University of New Mexico Press, 1992.

Grinnell, George Byrd. *The Cheyenne Indians.* New Haven CT: Yale University Press, 1923.

Grobsmith, Elizabeth S. *Lakota of the Rosebud.* New York: Harcourt Brace, 1981.

Hanson, James. "The Oglala Sioux Sun Dance." *Museum of the Fur Trade Quarterly* 1, no. 3 (1965): 3–5.

Hassrick, Royal B. *The Sioux.* Norman: University of Oklahoma Press, 1964.

Hedren, Paul L. *Traveler's Guide to the Great Sioux War.* Helena: Montana Historical Society Press, 1996.

Henne, Richard B. Review of *Reading and Writing the Lakota Language,* by Albert White Hat Sr., edited by Jael Kampfe. *International Journal of American Linguistics* 67, no. 3 (2001): 359–61.

Henning, Elizabeth R. P. "Western Dakota Winter Count: An Analysis of the Effects of Westward Migration and Culture Change." *Plains Anthropologist* 27, no. 95 (1982): 57–65.

Herman, Jake. "Primitive Sioux Calendar." Unpublished manuscript. Western History Collection, Denver Public Library. (Transcribed sometime before 1966.)

Higginbotham, N. A. "The Wind-Roan Bear Winter Count." *Plains Anthropologist* 26, no. 91 (1981): 1–42.

Hill, George W. *Sundance of the Sioux.* Papers, MS 10607 (1875). State Historical Society of North Dakota, Bismarck.

Hirschfelder, Arlene, and Paulette Molin. *The Encyclopedia of Native American Religions*. New York: Facts on File, 1992.

Hollabaugh, Mark. "The Blue Mound Stone Wall: A Minnesota Stonehenge?" Unpublished manuscript, 2002. (Copy available from the author on request.)

——. "Celestial Imagery in Lakota Culture." In *Current Studies in Archaeoastronomy: Selected Papers from the Fifth Oxford International Conference*. Durham NC: Carolina Academic Press, 1996.

——. Review of *Reachable Stars: Patterns in the Ethnoastronomy of Eastern North America*, by George E. Lankford. *American Ethnologist* 35, no. 2 (2008): 2066–68. doi:10.1111/j.1548–1425.2008.00065.x.

——. Review of *The Year the Stars Fell: Lakota Winter Counts at the Smithsonian*, edited by Candace S. Greene and Russell Thornton. *Archaeoastronomy* 21 (2008), 109–10.

Howard, James H. *The Canadian Sioux*. Lincoln: University of Nebraska Press, 1984.

——. "Dakota Winter Counts as a Source of Plains History." *Anthropological Papers*, no. 61 (1960): 335–416. Smithsonian Institution, Bureau of American Ethnology Bulletin 173.

——. "Yaktonai Ethnohistory and the John K. Bear Winter Count." *Plains Anthropologist* 21, no. 73 (1976): 1–64.

Hughes, Jack T. "Investigations in Western South Dakota and Northeastern Wyoming: Archaeological Researches in the Missouri Basin by the Smithsonian River Basin Surveys and Cooperating Agencies, Society for American Archaeology." *American Antiquity* 14, no. 4 (1949): 266–77.

Hunhoff, Bernie. "The Last Lakota Code Talker." *South Dakota Magazine*, May–June 2007. http://www.southdakotamagazine.com/clarence-wolf-guts.

Hyde, George E. *Red Cloud's Folk*. Norman: University of Oklahoma Press, 1975.

——. *A Sioux Chronicle*. Norman: University of Oklahoma Press, 1993.

——. *Spotted Tail's Folk*. Norman: University of Oklahoma Press, 1961.

Jahner, Elaine A. "Transitional Narratives and Cultural Continuity." In "1492–1992: American Indian Persistence and Resurgence," special issue of *boundary 2* 19, no. 3 (1992): 148–79.

Jenkins, R. M. "The Star of Bethlehem and the Comet of AD 66." *Journal of the British Astronomical Association* 114, no. 6 (2004): 336–42.

Johnson, Dirk. "To Some Sioux, Costner Now Dances with Devil." *New York Times*, 24 February 1995, A:12.

Karol, Joseph S. *Everyday Lakota*. St. Francis SD: Rosebud Educational Society, 1974.

Keating, William Hypolitus. *Narrative of an Expedition to the Sources of St. Peter's*

River, Lake Winnepeek, Lake of the Woods, Etc. Performed in the Year 1823, by Order of J. C. Calhoun, Secretary of War, under the Command of Stephen H. Long, Major U.S.T.E. Minneapolis: Ross & Haines, 1959.

Kehoe, Thomas, and Alice Kehoe. "Stones, Solstices and Sun Dance Structures." *Plains Anthropologist* 22, no. 76 (1977): 85–95.

Kelley, David H., and Eugene F. Milone. *Exploring Ancient Skies: An Encyclopedic Survey of Archaeoastronomy.* New York: Springer, 2011.

Kohl, Johann Georg. *Kitchi-Gami: Life among the Lake Superior Ojibway.* London: Chapman and Hall, 1860. Reprint, St. Paul: Minnesota Historical Society Press, 1985.

Lakota Star Knowledge Project Collection. Sinte Gleska University, Sicangu Heritage Center, Rosebud SD. http://www.sintegleska.edu/heritage_cntr/Collections/star.htm (site discontinued).

Lame Deer, Archie Fire, and Richard Erdoes. *Gift of Power: The Life and Teachings of a Lakota Medicine Man.* Santa Fe: Bear, 1992.

Lankford, George E. *Reachable Stars: Patterns in the Ethnoastronomy of Eastern North America.* Tuscaloosa: University of Alabama Press, 2007.

LaPointe, James. *Legends of the Lakota.* San Francisco: Indian Historian Press, 1976.

Larned, Horatio H. Papers, MS 20152 (1921–1922). State Historical Society of North Dakota, Bismarck.

Lewis, T. H. "Stone Monuments in Southern Dakota." *American Anthropologist* 2, no. 2 (1889): 159–66.

Lewis, Thomas. "Oglala (Teton Dakota) Sun Dance." *Plains Anthropologist* 17, no. 55 (1972): 44–49.

Lincoln, Bruce. "A Lakota Sun Dance and the Problematics of Sociocosmic Reunion." *History of Religions* 34, no. 1 (1994): 1–14.

Mails, Thomas E. *Fools Crow.* New York: Doubleday, 1979. Reprint, Lincoln: University of Nebraska Press, 1991.

———. *Fools Crow: Wisdom and Power.* Tulsa OK: Council Oaks Books, 1991.

———. *Sundancing at Rosebud and Pine Ridge.* Sioux Falls SD: Center for Western Studies, Augustana College, 1978.

Mallery, Garrick. *Picture-Writing of the American Indians.* New York: Dover, 1972. (Originally published in the *Tenth Annual Report of the Bureau of Ethnology, 1888–1889.* Washington DC: Smithsonian Institution, Bureau of American Ethnology, 1893.)

Malville, J. McKim, and Claudia Putnam. *Prehistoric Astronomy in the Southwest.* Boulder CO: Johnson Books, 1989.

Marshack, Alexander. "A Lunar-Solar Year Calendar Stick from North America." *American Antiquity* 50, no. 1 (1985): 27–51.

Maurer, Evan M. *Visions of the People: A Pictorial History of Plains Indian Life.* Minneapolis: Minneapolis Institute of Arts, 1992.

Melmer, David. "Politics Surrounds Code Talkers." *Indian Country Today*, 9 July 2002. http://indiancountrytodaymedianetwork.com/2002/07/09 /politics-surrounds-code-talkers-87880.

Melody, Michael. "Lakota Sun Dance: A Composite Review and Analysis." *South Dakota History* 6, no. 4 (1976): 433–55.

Miller, David Reed. Review of *Black Elk: Holy Man of the Oglala*, by Michael F. Steltenkamp. *Ethnohistory* 42, no. 3 (1995): 536–37.

Momaday, N. Scott. "Native American Attitudes to the Environment." In *Stars Above, Earth Below*, edited by Marsha C. Bol. Niwot CO: Roberts Rinehart, 1998.

Monroe, Jean G., and Ray A. Williamson. *They Dance in the Sky: Native American Sky Myths*. New York: Houghton Mifflin, 1987.

Mooney, James. *The Ghost-Dance Religion and the Sioux Outbreak of 1890*. Lincoln: University of Nebraska Press, 1991. (Originally published as part 2 of the *Fourteenth Annual Report of the Bureau of Ethnology, 1892–1893*. Washington DC: Smithsonian Institution, Bureau of American Ethnology, 1896.)

———. "In Memoriam: Washington Matthews." *American Anthropologist* 7, no. 3 (1905): 514–23. Accessed 28 April 2016. doi:10.1525/aa.1905.7.3.02a00060.

———. "Myths of the Cherokees." *Journal of American Folklore* 1, no. 2 (1888): 97–108.

Morton, Ron, and Carl Gawboy. *Talking Rocks: Geology and 10,000 Years of Native American Tradition in the Lake Superior Region*. Minneapolis: University of Minnesota Press, 2003.

Neihardt, John G. *Black Elk Speaks*. Lincoln: University of Nebraska Press, 1961.

New Lakota Dictionary. Bloomington IN: Lakota Language Consortium, 2008.

New York Times. "News from Korea Cut Off for Hours." 20 August 1950, 5.

Ostler, Jeffrey. *The Lakotas and the Black Hills: The Struggle for Sacred Ground*. New York: Viking Penguin, 2010.

———. *The Plains Sioux and U.S. Colonialism from Lewis and Clark to Wounded Knee*. New York: Cambridge University Press, 2004.

Paige, Darcy. "George W. Hill's Account of the Sioux Sun Dance of 1866." *Plains Anthropologist* 24 (1979): 99–112.

Parks, Douglas R., and Raymond J. DeMallie. "Plains Indian Native Literatures." In "1492–1992: American Indian Persistence and Resurgence," special issue of *boundary 2* 19, no. 3 (1992): 105–47.

Pond, Samuel W. *Dakota Life in the Upper Midwest*. St. Paul: Minnesota Historical Society, 2002.

Poole, D. C. *Among the Sioux of Dakota*. New York: Van Nostrand, 1881. (Copy in the collection of the Colorado Historical Society, Denver.)

Porter, Joseph C. *Paper Medicine Man*. Norman: University of Oklahoma Press, 1986.

Powers, William K. Review of *Black Elk: Holy Man of the Oglala*, by Michael F. Steltenkamp. *Journal of Religion* 75, no. 2 (1995): 304–6.

———. Review of *Black Elk's Religion: The Sun Dance and Lakota Catholicism*, by Clyde Holler. *American Anthropologist* 98, no. 3 (1996): 651–53.

———. Review of *The Sixth Grandfather: Black Elk's Teaching Given to John G. Neihardt*, by Raymond J. DeMallie. *Ethnohistory* 33, no. 1 (1986): 121–23.

———. *Sacred Language: The Nature of Supernatural Discourse in Lakota*. Lincoln: University of Nebraska Press, 1986.

———. "When Black Elk Speaks, Everybody Listens." *Social Text* 24 (1990): 43–56.

———. *A Winter Count of the Oglala*. Kendall Park NJ: Lakota Books, 1994.

Powers, William K., James Garrett, and Kathleen J. Martin. "Lakota Religious Traditions." *Encyclopedia of Religion*, ed. Lindsay Jones, 2nd ed., vol. 8, 5295–98. Detroit: Macmillan Reference USA, 2005.

Prucha, Francis Paul. *Documents of United States Indian Policy*. 3rd ed. Lincoln: University of Nebraska Press, 2000.

Rao, Joe. "The Leonids: King of the Meteor Showers." *Sky & Telescope* 90, no. 5 (1995): 24–31.

Rice, Julian. *Black Elk's Story*. Albuquerque: University of New Mexico Press, 1991.

———. "A Ventriloquy of Anthros: Densmore, Dorsey, Lame Deer and Erdoes." *American Indian Quarterly* 18, no. 2 (1994): 169.

Ricker, Eli. "Ricker Tablet" 25. Microfilm copy. Minnesota Historical Society, St. Paul.

Riggs, Stephen Return. *A Dakota-English Dictionary*. St. Paul: Minnesota Historical Society Press, 1992.

Risch, Barbara. "A Grammar of Time: Lakota Winter Counts, 1700–1900." *American Indian Culture and Research Journal* 24, no. 2 (2000): 23–48.

Robinson, Doane. "Tales of the Dakota: One Hundred Anecdotes Illustrative of Sioux Life and Thinking." *Collections of the State Historical Society of South Dakota*, vol. 14: 485–537. Pierre: State Historical Society of South Dakota, 1928.

Rocky Mountain News. "Denver Eclipse: The Great Event of the Century in

Colorado." 30 July 1878, 1. (Microfilm in the Western History Collection, Denver Public Library.)

————. "The Great Eclipse." 13 August 1869, 1. (Microfilm in the Western History Collection, Denver Public Library.)

Rudin, Catherine. Review of *Reading and Writing the Lakota Language*, by Albert White Hat Sr., edited by Jael Kampfe. *Language* 76, no. 2(2000): 470–71.

Schmittou, Douglas A., and Michael H. Logan. "Fluidity of Meaning: Flag Imagery in Plains Indian Art." *American Indian Quarterly* 26, no. 4 (2002): 559–605.

Schwatka, Frederick. "Sundance of the Sioux." *Century Magazine*, March 1890, 753–59.

Scott, Hugh Lenox. *Some Memories of a Soldier*. New York: Century, 1928.

Sheldon, A. E., "Ancient Indian Fireplaces in South Dakota Bad-Lands." *American Anthropologist*, n.s., 7, no. 1 (1905): 44–48.

Springer, Charles H. "Journal." Typescript copy in Western History Department, Denver Public Library. Published as *Soldiering in Sioux Country: 1865*. San Diego: Frontier Heritage Press, 1971.

Steltenkamp, Michael, S.J. *Black Elk: Holy Man of the Oglala*. Norman: University of Oklahoma Press, 1993.

Smith, Denny. Review of *The Plains Sioux and U. S. Colonialism from Lewis and Clark to Wounded Knee*, by Jeffrey Ostler. *History: Review of New Books* 33, no. 2 (Winter 2005): 64–65.

Stover, Dale. "Eurocentrism and Native Americans." Review of *Black Elk's Religion: The Sun Dance and Lakota Catholicism*, by Clyde Holler. *CrossCurrents* 47, no. 3 (1997): 390–97.

Sundstrom, Linea. "Mirror of Heaven: Cross-Cultural Transference of the Sacred Geography of the Black Hills." *World Archaeology* 28, no. 2 (1996): 177–89.

————. *Rock Art of Western South Dakota: The North Cave Hills and the Southern Black Hills*. Section 2, "The Southern Black Hills." Sioux Falls: South Dakota Archaeological Society, 1984.

————. "Smallpox Used Them Up: References to Epidemic Disease in Northern Plains Winter Counts." *Ethnohistory* 44, no. 2 (1997): 305–43.

Sutherland, Edwin Van Valkenburg. "The Diaries of John Gregory Bourke: Their Anthropological and Folklore Content." PhD diss., Graduate School of Arts and Sciences, University of Pennsylvania, 1964.

Thornton, Russell. "A Rosebud Reservation Winter Count." *Ethnohistory* 49, no. 4 (2002): 723–41.

Thurman, Melburn D. "Plains Indian Winter Counts and the New Ethnohistory."
　　Plains Anthropologist 27, no. 96 (1982): 173–75.
Tinker, George E. Review of *Fools Crow: Wisdom and Power,* by Thomas Mails.
　　American Indian Quarterly 17, no. 3 (1993): 393–95.
United States v. Sioux Nation of Indians, 448 U.S. 371 (1980).
Utley, Robert M. *The Indian Frontier of the American West, 1846–1890.* Albuquer-
　　que: University of New Mexico Press, 1984.
―――. *The Lance and the Shield: The Life and Times of Sitting Bull.* New York:
　　Henry Holt, 1993.
―――. *The Last Days of the Sioux Nation.* 2nd ed. New Haven CT: Yale Uni-
　　versity Press, 2004.
Waggoner, J. F. "Oglala Sioux Winter Count." *Museum of the Fur Trade Quarterly*
　　24, no. 4 (1988): 11–14.
Walker, James R. *Lakota Belief and Ritual.* Edited by Raymond J. DeMallie and
　　Elaine A. Jahner. Lincoln: University of Nebraska Press, 1991.
―――. *Lakota Myth.* Edited by Elaine A. Jahner. Lincoln: University of Ne-
　　braska Press, 1983.
―――. *Lakota Society.* Edited by Raymond J. DeMallie. Lincoln: University of
　　Nebraska Press, 1982.
―――. *The Sun Dance and Other Ceremonies of the Oglala Division of the Teton
　　Dakota.* Kendall Park NJ: Lakota Books. (Originally published in *Anthropo-
　　logical Papers of the American Museum of Natural History* 16, pt. 2 [1917].)
Wallis, Wilson D. "Beliefs and Tales of the Canadian Dakota." *Journal of American
　　Folklore* 36, no. 139 (1923): 36–101.
―――. *Sundance of the Canadian Dakota.* 1919. Reprint, Kendall NJ: Lakota
　　Books, 1993.
Welsh, William. *Report and Supplementary Report of a Visit to Spotted Tail's
　　Tribe of Brulé Sioux Indians, the Yankton and Santee Sioux, Ponkas and the
　　Chippewas of Minnesota, October, 1870.* Philadelphia: M'Calla & Stavely, 1870.
　　(Copy in the Western History Department, Denver Public Library.)
White Hat, Albert, Sr. *Reading and Writing the Lakota Language: Lakota Iyapi
　　uŋ Wowapi nahaŋ Yawapi.* Edited by Jael Kampfe. Salt Lake City: University
　　of Utah Press, 1999.
Williamson, Ray A. *Living the Sky.* New York: Houghton Mifflin, 1984.
Williamson, Ray A., and Claire R. Farrer, eds. *Earth & Sky: Visions of the Cos-
　　mos in Native American Folklore.* Albuquerque: University of New Mexico
　　Press, 1992.
Wissler, Clark. "The Diffusion of Horse Culture among the North American

Indians." *Proceedings of the National Academy of Sciences of the United States of America* 1, no. 4 (1915): 254–56.

———. "The Distribution and Functions of Tribal Societies among the Plains Indians: A Preliminary Report." *Proceedings of the National Academy of Sciences of the United States of America* 1, no. 7 (1915): 401–3.

———. "Psychological and Historical Interpretations for Culture." *Science*, n.s., 43, no. 1102 (1916): 193–20.

———. *Some Protective Designs of the Dakota*. Kendall NJ: Lakota Books, 1998. (Originally published in *Anthropological Papers of the American Museum of Natural History* 1, pt. 2 [1907]: 19–53.)

Woodbury, Richard B., and Nathalie F. S. Woodbury. "The Rise and Fall of the Bureau of American Ethnology." *Journal of the Southwest* 41, no. 3 (1999): 283.

Woods, Carter A. "A Criticism of Wissler's North American Culture Areas." *American Anthropologist*, n.s., 36, no. 4 (1934): 517–23.

Zeilik, Michael. "The Ethnoastronomy of the Historic Pueblos, I: Calendrical Sun Watching." In "Archaeoastronomy," supplement, *Journal for the History of Astronomy* 8 (1985): S1–S24.

———. "The Ethnoastronomy of the Historic Pueblos, II: Moon Watching." In "Archaeoastronomy," supplement, *Journal for the History of Astronomy* 10 (1986): S1–S22.

———. "The Fajada Butte Solar Marker: A Reevaluation." *Science* 228 (1985): 1311–13.

———. "Sun Shrines and Symbols in the U.S. Southwest." "Archaeoastronomy," supplement, *Journal for the History of Astronomy* 9 (1985): S86–S96.

———. "Sun Watching: Prehistoric Astronomy in New Mexico." *New Mexico Magazine*, March 1985, 48–55.

Zitkala-Ša (Gertrude Bonnin). *Old Indian Legends*. Lincoln: University of Nebraska Press, 1985.

INDEX

Page numbers in italic indicate illustrations.

ogy of, 2; Arthur Amiotte in, 138; autumn in, 88; and constellations, 161; description of, 4–5, 8, 192n19; Lakota territory in, 4–7, 167–70; as landmark, 61, 166; Last Bear in, 79; maps of, 164–65; and Native American astronomy, 8, 164–66, 169; sacred sites in, 46, 51, 53–54

Black Moon, 108

Blackmun, Harry, 7

Blish, Helen, 165

blue, 42, 46, 47, 60, 79, *80 fig. 10*, 144, 199n6

Blue Mound State Park stone wall, 38

Blunt Horn, John, 116

boarding schools, 6, 160

Böotes, 60

Bordeaux family, 205n27

Boundary Waters Canoe Area Wilderness, 33, 208n24

Bourke, John Gregory: on calendar sticks, 92, 204n21, 213n56; diaries of, 213n58; on night sky, 58–60, 199n4; observations of Lakota by, 12; on puebloan astronomy, 18, 152, 213n56; at 1881 Pine Ridge Sun Dance, 151–54, 213n54, 213n63

Bozeman Trail, 4

Bradley, James, 93

Brave Bear (Southern Cheyenne), 10–11

bravery, 43, 47

Brokenleg, Father Noah, 44, 214n69

Bronson, Edgar Beecher, 154–55

Brown, Joseph Epes, 14, 15, 198n25

Brulé Sioux, 3, 149, 154

Bucko, Father Raymond, 196n22, 214n69

Buechel, Father Eugene: on aurora borealis, 115; collection of, 78, 79, *80*, 202n16; on comets, 133; and Milky Way stories, 71–72; on Moon's appearance, 85; observations of Lakota by, 12–13; on star names, 64, 67–68, 162; on Sun Dance, 147, 212n40; on *wakháŋ*, 51

Buechel Memorial Lakota Museum, 13, 78, 95, *96*, 130, 133, 201n35

buffalo, 3–4, 6, 13, 45–46, 53, 101, 142, 143, 145

Buffalo, Sam, 48

Buffalo Bill. *See* Cody, William F. (Buffalo Bill)

Buffalo Dance, 142

Buffalo Gap, 166

buffalo hide, 93, 95, 98–99, *110*, 205n32

Bureau of American Ethnology, 98

Burke, Christina, xii

Cajete, Gregory, 174, *176*, 178–79, 215n2, 216n3, 216n11

calendar day, 83. *See also* days

calendars: availability to Lakota of modern, 153; and Big Dipper, 65; in ethnoastronomy, 38; imprecision of Native American, 88–89, 92–93, 99, 103, 130, 134, 147, 203–4n14; influence of, on Native beliefs, 46; of Mayans, 17; purpose of, 164, 179, 217n19; types of, 25–28, 73, 85–86, 137. *See also* Gregorian calendar; time; winter counts

calendar sticks, 89–93, 146, 166, 204n15, 204n21, 213n56

Calloway, Colin, 1

camp circles, 50, 154, 156. *See also* tipis

Canada, 6, 21, 33, 46–47, 63, 69, 85, 214n66

Cancer constellation, 22

Canis Major, 60

Cannon Ball River, 3

Capricornus constellation, 22, 109

Carlisle Indian School, 6, 11

Carlson, John, 194–95n3

Carver, Jonathan, 9, 84

Casa Rinconada, 36, 156

Cassiopeia, 164

Castor, 22, 109

Catholic Church, 15, 16, 46, 55, 72, 201n35. *See also* religion

celestial equator, 19, 23–24, 27

celestial events: Native Americans' attitudes toward, 78–81, 93, 99, *100–101*, 103, 105, 106, 109–22, *110*, 126–35, *131*, 179–83; predictability of, 73–74, 76, 102, 105, 121, 179–80, 206n1; rituals coordinated with, 137, 140, 145, 147

celestial poles, 19, 27, 33

celestial sphere: alignment of structures with, 17, 36–38, 137, 156, 167, 194n1, 214n66; description of, 19–22

Centennial Trail, *52*

Central America, 21, 27

Century Magazine, 150

Cepheus constellation, 69

Chaco Canyon NM, 2, 17, 35–36, 156

Chadron NE, 149–51, 155–56, 205n27, 212n45

Chamberlain, Von Del, xv, 38, 99, 112, 167, 194–95n3

Cheney, Roberta Carkeek, 113–14

Cherokee Indians, 202n8

Cheyenne Indians: astronomy of, 21, 168–70; and 1878 eclipse, 113; on Little Bighorn, 10–11; months according to, 87–88; and road after death, 70; sacred sites of, 51–52, *52*, 113; Sun Dances of, 137, 141–42; and U.S. troops, 5

Chief Eagle, Dallas (Lakota), 16

"Chief Who Lost His Arms" story, 39

childbearing, 43

Chimney Rock CO, 17, *36*, 36–37, 197n30

China, 31

Chippewa Indians. *See* Ojibwe Indians

chokecherries, 144–45

Christianity: belief system of, 42; calendar of, 26, 28, 137; color white in, 198n13; concept of heaven in, 48; conversions to, 6, 13–14, 16, 139; influence of, on Black Elk, 55, 144, 168; and science, 175; scriptures of, 167; and Sun Dance, 142; and whites' translations, 12, 55. *See also* religion; *and specific denominations*

Christmas, 26, 198n13

circle, 48–50, 141, 144, 154, 160, 164–66, 176, 181, 198n21

Clark, William P.: on meteors and comets, 121; on month names, 87, 88; sign language dictionary of, 61, 77, 87, 106, 115; and Sun Dances, 139–40, 142, 144, 145, 153, 156

Clear Fork, 58, 59

clockwise motion, 48–49, 198n21

clothing, 78–81, 202n21

DeMallie, Raymond J.: on circular shape, 50; on Lakota astronomy, 41, 56, 180, 197n1; orthography of, xiv, xvi; on timekeeping, 102–3; on *wakháŋ*, 170; and whites' translations, 10–11, 14, 15

Denver CO, 113. See also *Rocky Mountain News*

Des Moines IA, 109

Devil's Tower. *See* Bear Lodge Butte

diffusion, 169, 195n7, 215n19

directions, cardinal: colors of, 48; and comets, 134; Lakota beliefs about, 43–48, *49*, 100–101, 176, 177; structures aligned with, 36, 156. *See also* east (direction); north (direction); west (direction)

discernible-not moon, 88

diseases, 3, 11, 98, 128, 205–6n33. *See also* health

Dorsey, James O., 76, 202n8

Draco, 164

dragonflies, 79, *80 fig. 9*

Dubhe, 68

Eagle Hawk (Oglala Lakota), 84

Earth: and aurora borealis, 115, 117; and celestial sphere, 19, 20; as center of universe, 17, 57; and connection to sky, 70–72, 79–81, 103, 117, 128, 135, 140, 145, 147, 156, 164–66, 169–71, 174, 176–84, *183*, 217n15; in eclipses, 30–32; magnetic field of, 33; motions of, 21–27, 31, 49, 83, 89, 196n13, 203n1; passage of, through comet tail, 133; and relationship to Sun and Moon, 28, 29, *29*, 73–81, 143,

201n1; Lakota beliefs about, 45, 49, 73–75, 144, 176

earth lodges, 99

Earth Walks (Ojibwe), 177–78

east (direction), 21, 141–42, 147, 154, 156, 214n69. *See also* directions, cardinal

Easter, 26, 28, 137, 198n13

Eastman, Charles, 62, 74, 77–78, 100–101

Eastman, Mary, 116, 127–28, 209n10

eclipse, 1869 solar, 109–112

eclipse, 1878 solar, 112–114

eclipses: description of, 29–32, *30*, 73, 196n22; documentation of, 106–14, *107*, *108*, *110*, 207n11; and Ghost Dance, 6; Lakota references to, xi–xii, 120; perceptions of, 105–14, 206n1; resources on, 8–9, 106, 206n2; timekeeping by, 99, 100, 103. *See also* solar eclipses

ecliptic, 23, 85, 162–64, *163*, 203n1

Eddy, John, xi, 37–38, 167, 197n31

Edison, Thomas, 207–8n18

education. *See* boarding schools

Elk Head (keeper of sacred pipe), 15

England, 13

English language, 11–12, 14, 192n11, 194n54, 201n35

Episcopal Church, 11, 13–14, 16, 55, 210n24, 214n69. *See also* religion

equinoxes: at Medicine Wheel, 38; rituals during, 137; structures aligned with, 36, 38; timing of, 21, 23–27, *67*, 89, 100, 145–46, 167

Erdoes, Richard, 159, 161

Espenak, Fred, 206n2

ethics. *See* virtues

Moon (*continued*)
195n10, 194–95n12, 197n30; phases of, 28–29, *29*, 77, 85–86, *86*, 103, 179, 212n42; in pictographs, 12, *108*, 109, *131 fig. 20*; and relationship to Sun, 73–76, 81, 201n1, 202n8; resources on, 8–9; rock art of, 2; sacredness of, 52–54, 73, 143–44, 156; shape of, 49; Sioux references to, xi–xii, 74–81; structures aligned with, 36–37; timekeeping by, 83–89, 92–93, 103, 145, 203–4n14; visibility of, 46, 59, 77, 84, 85, 88–89, 92, 156, 203–4n14, 204n17. *See also* full moon; months; new moon

Mooney, James, 202n8

morals. *See* virtues

Morning Star: and days of the month, 45; description of, 21, 62–63, 181; George Custer as Son of, 196n15; names for, 61; role of, in Sun Dance, 144, 146, 153, 154; Venus as, 21, 25, 62–63, 146–48, 150, 153, 154, 162

Morton, Ron, 217n15

Mystic Warriors of the Plains (Mails), 16

myths: about creation, 51, 78, 132, 175; about meteors, 121–22, 127–28, 132, 133, 209n10, 210n21; about seasons, 100–102; about stars, 62–63, 69–72, 182, 199–200n10; about Sun and Moon, 74, 75, 84, 120, 202n8; and ethnography, 18, 38, 169; understanding through, 174; in winter counts, 98, 120

NASA, 9, 106, 206n2

National Anthropological Archives, xii, 95

National Museum of the American Indian, Hyde Collection, 92

National Oceanic and Atmospheric Administration, 117, 208n24

Native Americans: astronomy of, xi–xii, 1–4, 8–16, 18, 20–22, 35–43, 61, 76–78, 89, 159–66, 168–70, 173–82, 197n1, 215n2, 216n11, 217n15; belief systems of, 42, 173–79, 215n1, 216n7; ethnography of, 151–54; and science, 173–74; sign language of, 60–61, 77

natural world: cycles of, 86–89, 102–3, 179; effect of Sun and Moon on, 76–77, 83; Lakota beliefs about, 42–43, 49–50, 139, 179; and meteors, 128; and timing of Sun Dance, 144–45; understanding of, 173–74, 176, 177, 179–80, 216n12. *See also* animals; plants; seasons

Nebraska: aurora borealis in, 115; John Bourke in, 152, 153; Lakota territory in, 1, 4–5; landmarks in, 61; month names in, 88; Sun Dance in, 149–51, 155–56, 212n45; view of sky from, 17, 57

nebulae, 71, 201n32

Needles Highway, *8*

Neihardt, Hilda, 194n54

Neihardt, John G., 14, 118, 194n54

Neptune, 33, 148, 150, 160

Nevada, 6, 114

New Age movement, 16, 168, 194n60

New Mexico: archaeology in, 2, 17, 35–36, 156, 204n21; conference

Race Track, 164–65, *165*

radio communication blackout, 119–20, 209n37

Rapid City SD, xi

red: aurora as, 142; and star temperatures, 60, 199n6; symbolism of, 42, 46–48, 60, 79, *80 fig. 10*, 144, 198n13, 201n35

Red Cloud (*Maȟpíya Luta*), 5–6, 47–48, 121–22, 152

Red Cloud Agency, 93

Red Cloud's War, 4

Red Horse Owner, Moses, 95

Red Horse Owner's Winter Count, 95, *97*

Red Rabbit, 115–16

Red Sack, 78

Rehnquist, William, 7

relatives: adopted persons as, 47; in Native American cultures, 62, 175, 199–200n10; rite of making, 50, 116–17; rite to strengthen, 138, 139; sacredness of, 54; stars as, 62, 184; Sun and Moon as, 74–78, 144, 184. *See also* community; humans

Releasing of the Spirit rite. *See* Give Away rite

religion: and astrology, 28, 170; and calendars, 164, 179; circle in, 48, 50; colors in, 46; and ethnography, 18, 169; and Lakota Star Knowledge Project, 167, 168; pilgrimages of, 52; prohibition of Lakota, 6; and science, 175, 216n6; and Sun Dance, 139. *See also* Catholic Church; Christianity; Episcopal Church; gods; Judaism

Remington, Frederick, 150

Reno, Marcus, 5, 149

reservations, 4–6, 159. *See also* Pine Ridge Reservation; Rosebud Reservation

Rigel, 22

Riggs, Stephen Return, 88

Ringing Shield (Lakota elder), xi, 64, 180–82, 200n15

rituals: and aurora borealis, 116–17; book about Lakota, 14; circle in, 50; color in, 46; coordination of, with celestial events, 137, 145, 179; dates of, 28; and meteors and comets, 132, 135; and number seven, 15, 45, 46, 50–51, 138, 198n25; prohibition of Lakota, 6; purpose of, 56; for releasing spirit, 44, 50; and Sun and Moon, 23, 76, 79–81, 114; understanding through, 174, 180, *183*, 183–84. *See also* Sun Dance

roads, 47, 70, 72, 163

Robinson, Charles, 213n58

Robinson, Doane, 209n10

rock, 2, 45, 49, 50, 53, 73, 121, 126, 209n7

Rocky Mountain National Park, 209n8

Rocky Mountain News, 99, 109, 112–13, 207n11, 207–8n18

Rosebud Creek, 5, 148

Rosebud Hills, 149

Rosebud Reservation: Archie Fire Lame Deer on, 159; Doris Leader Charge on, 193n30; Episcopal service on, 214n69; Father Buechel on, 12–13; Give Away on, 44; Lakota reminiscences on, 7; Moon's appearance on, 85; oral history

Sky (*maȟpíya*): appearance of, at night, 49–50, 54, 57–59, 61, 68, 69, 199n1; and connection to earth, 70–72, 79–81, 103, 117, 128, 135, 140, 145, 147, 156, 164–66, 169–71, 174, 176–84, *183*, 217n15; and connection to Spirit, 72, 157, 167, 170–71, 174, 178–84, *183*; as heaven, 48, 70; Lakota beliefs about, 73–74, 176; and number four, 45; shape of, 49–50; sign language for, 61; sizes of objects in, 73, 201n1; symbolism of, 78, 79; watching during Sun Dance, 142–43. *See also* heaven

Slim Buttes, 166

Smithsonian collection, 122, *124*, *129*, 205n28

Snelling, Josiah, 122–26

Snow, Elmer A., 213n54

solar day, 83. *See also* days; sidereal day

solar eclipses, 6, *30*, 106–14, *110*. *See also* eclipses; Sun

solar flares, 33, 119–20, 206n1. *See also* Sun

solstices, 21, 23, 24, 35–36, *37*, *67*, 100, 197n32. *See also* summer solstice

sonic booms, 34, 122, *123 fig. 18*, *123 fig. 19*, 125, 134

South America, 21

south celestial pole, 19

South Dakota: archaeology of, 2; aurora borealis in, 115, 208n24; eclipse in, 111–12; Lakota territory in, 1, 4–5; landmarks in, 61; month names in, 88; sacred site in, 51, *52*; Sun Dance in, 155; view of sky from, 17, 20, 57, 164; winter counts in, 95, 205n27, 205n32

Southwest, American, 17, 18, 35–36, 92, 146, 152, 195n6, 204n21

South Wind, 101–2

spectrometer, 207n11

Spirit: and connection to sky and earth, 72, 157, 167, 170–71, 174, 178–84, *183*; gifts of, 46; release of, 44, 50, 198n25; road of, 70, 72, 163; sacredness of, 53, 54. *See also* ghosts; Great Spirit; Lakota culture: spirituality in

spirits, evil, 112, 181

spirits, good, 60, 132, 181, 199n8

spirit world, 79

Spotted Eagle, 45

Spotted Tail, 6, 129, 149

Spotted Tail Agency, 149, 212n45

spring, 144. *See also* seasons

Spring Creek, 113

Springer, Charles H., 57–58

Standing Elk, 149

Standing Rock Reservation, 6. *See also* reservations

Star Boy, 62, 100–101, 206n36

Star of Bethlehem, 21, 195n8

Starry Night (software), xiv, 8, 106

stars: circumpolar, 19–20, 162, 164, 181; colors of, 32, 60; identification of, 22–23, 62–63; Lakota references to, xi–xii, 59–63, 74, 78, 161–71; magnitude of, 59–60, 71–73, 198–99n29; motions of, 19–20, 24, 65, 103, 181–82; names of, 59–60, 64–69, *65*, 182, 200n17; navigation by, 61; numbers of, 46; in pictographs, 12, *96*, *97*, *108*, 109–11, *110*, *123 fig.*

stars (*continued*)

17, 130, *131*; on Race Track, 164–65, *165*; and relationship to humans, 62, 71–72; rock art of, 2; sacredness of, 52–54, 56, 179–84, 217n22; science of, 174; shapes of, 49, 79; symbolism of, 78, 79, *80*, 143, 144, 147, 156, 177; temperatures of, 60, 199n6; timekeeping by, 84, 103. *See also* asterisms; constellations; *specific stars*

State Historical Society of North Dakota, 134, 211n11

Steltenkamp, Father Michael, 117–18

St. Francis Mission, 12, 78, 85, 205n27

St. John's College (Santa Fe), xi–xii

stone. *See* rock

Stonehenge, 17

stories. *See* myths

Sturgis SD, 51, *52*

summer, 72, 101, 163. *See also* seasons

summer solstice: observation of, 194–95n3; prediction of, 145–47; Sun Dances at, 144–47, 149, 152–54, 157, 180, 212n42; Sun in, 23. *See also* solstices

Sun: and aurora borealis, 115, 117, 119–20; in Buffalo Dance, 142; as center of universe, 17, 114; color of, 60, 106–8; in eclipses, 30–32, 105–6, 207–8n18; Lakota beliefs about, 45, 49, 52–53, 73–78, 114, 139–40, 143–44, 157, 181, 183–84; in Lakota designs, 78–81; motions of, 19–28, 48–49, 73, 83–84, 103, 164, 179, 182, 196n13, 203n1; physics of, 74; in pictographs,

12, *110*, 110–11; puebloan views of, 18, 213n56; relationship of, to comets, 33, 196n23; relationship of, to Moon, 28, 29, *29*, 73–76, 81, 84–86, 201n1, 202n8; resources on, 8–9; Sioux references to, xi–xii, 63; structures aligned with, 36–38, *37*, 137, 156, 214n70; during Sun Dance, 143, 146, 149, 156. *See also* solar eclipses; solar flares

Sun Dance (*Wiwáŋyaŋg wachípi*): 1875 Chadron, 149–51; 1876 Sitting Bull, 148–49; 1881 Pine Ridge, 151–55; descriptions of, 148–55; face and body paint for, 47, 78, 143; fortitude for, 43–44; and Lakota astronomy, xii, 76–77; piercing at, 137, 142; process of, 140–48; prohibition of, 6; purpose of, 114, 138–40; as sacred rite, 50, 51; sites for, 140, *141*, 149, 154–56; structures for, *141*, 141–43, 146, 150–51, 153–57, 180, 214n66; timing of, 137, 144–54, 157, 180, 212n42; in winter counts, 99; written sources on, 11, 16. *See also* rituals

Sundancing at Rosebud and Pine Ridge (Mails), 16

Sundstrom, Linea, 169

sunrise: at Hovenweep, 194–95n3; at Sun Dances, 142, 144–46, 148, 150–56, 212n49, 214n66

sunspots, 117, 119–20

Sutherland, Edwin Van Valkenburg, 213n57

Swallow-Morgan, Sandy, 45

Swan Winter Count, 112, *123 fig. 18*, 130, *131 fig. 21*

U.S. Army (*continued*)
  Lakota, 5, 12, *97*, 138, 139, 149–55,
  213n55; and eclipses, 30, 111–13,
  208n20; journals of, 57–58, 199n4,
  213n55; meteor sightings by, 122–
  26; soldier-scholars in, 213n57; at
  Wounded Knee, 7. *See also* whites
U.S. Congress, 15
U.S. Forest Service, *36*, *37*, 38
U.S. government: assimilation by,
  6, 12, 193n47, 213n55; and Black
  Hills, 7, 51; on Sun Dance, 142,
  151; treaties of, 4–5, 15; in winter
  counts, *97*, 98. *See also* United
  States; whites
U.S. Naval Observatory, 8–9, 102
U.S. Navy, 119–20
U.S. Supreme Court, 7
Utah, 36

Vega, 60
Venn diagram, *183*, 217n24
Venus: as Evening Star, 25, 59; magnitude of, 60; as Morning Star, 21,
  25, 62–63, 146–48, 150, 153, 154,
  162, 212n40; motions of, 24, 25;
  name for, 61; during Pine Ridge
  Sun Dance, 152–53; in sweat lodge
  design, 160
vernal equinox, 23–27, 89. *See also*
  equinoxes
Virgo constellation, 22
virtues, 43–44, 46, 47, 100–101
Vision Quest (*Haŋblécheyapi*), 50-52
visions, 6, 13, 50, 51, 52, 81, 114, 140
Vulcan, 109

Waggoner, Josephine, 205n27

Wahpeton Dakota, 63, 67, 69, 70–71,
  74–75, 114, 134
wakháŋ: of circle, 48, 50; description
  of, 51–56, *183*; in Lakota orthography, xiv; Lakota understanding of,
  xi, 43, 170, 179–84, 217n22; of Sun
  Dance, 78, 139–40, 143–44
Wakháŋ Tháŋka, 55-56, 73, 140, 143
wakíŋyaŋ, 66, 81, 164.
Walker, James R.: on aurora borealis,
  115–16; on Buffalo Dance, 142; on
  circle, 49; on colors, 47, 60, 199n8;
  on eclipse, 106; on meteors, 130–
  32; on month names, 88, 203n13;
  on number four, 44, 100–101; on
  number seven, 68; research of, xi,
  11–12, 161; on Sun and Moon, 73,
  86–89; on Sun Dance, 138, 140,
  143, 145; on times of day, 83; on
  wakháŋ, 52–53, 180–81; on war
  insignia, 81; winter count of, 95
Wallis, Wilson D.: on comets, 134; on
  eclipses, 114; on meteors, 128; on
  moon phases, 85; on sky, 69, 70;
  on stars, 63, 67, 69–71; on Sun and
  Moon, 74–75
Wanáǧi thacháŋku. See Milky Way.
waníyetu, 93, 95
war, 43, 114, 134
Washington DC, 102
water, 45
Wazíya (spirit), 53, 115–16
wazíya wicháȟpi. See Polaris.
west (direction), 81. *See also* directions, cardinal
Westerman, Floyd Red Crow, 193n30
West Point, 152, 208n20, 213n57,
  213n58

Yankton Sioux, 9, 112, 134, 143, 210n24, 215n15

years: and constellations, 164; definition of, 22–24, 86–87, 195n9, 196n18; division of, 100; eclipses during, 105; number of days in, 88–89; records of, 83, 92–101, 102, 103, 179. *See also* winter counts

The Year the Stars Fell (Greene and Thornton), 205n28

yellow, 42, 46–48, 60, 79, 88, *131 fig. 22*, 201n35

Yellow Jacket CO, 36

Yellowstone campaign, 213n54

Young Woman's Puberty Rite (*Išnála awíchalowaŋ*), 50

Yucatan, 17

Zeilik, Mike, 204n21

zenith, 19, 21

Zimmerman, Father, 118

Zitkala-Ša, 60

zodiac, constellations of, 22–23, 162. *See also* constellations

In the Studies in the Anthropology of North American Indians Series

*Wolverine Myths and Visions: Dene
Traditions from Northern Alberta*
Edited by Patrick Moore and
Angela Wheelock

Ceremonies of the Pawnee
By James R. Murie
Edited by Douglas R. Parks

*Households and Families of the
Longhouse Iroquois at
Six Nations Reserve*
By Merlin G. Myers
Foreword by Fred Eggan
Afterword by M. Sam Cronk

*Archaeology and Ethnohistory of the
Omaha Indians: The Big Village Site*
By John M. O'Shea and
John Ludwickson

*Traditional Narratives of the
Arikara Indians* (4 vols.)
By Douglas R. Parks

A Dictionary of Skiri Pawnee
By Douglas R. Parks and
Lula Nora Pratt

Osage Grammar
By Carolyn Quintero

*A Fur Trader on the Upper Missouri:
The Journal and Description of J
ean-Baptiste Truteau, 1794–1796*
By Jean-Baptiste Truteau
Edited by Raymond J. DeMallie,
Douglas R. Parks, and Robert Vézina
Translated by Mildred Mott Wedel,
Raymond J. DeMallie, and
Robert Vézina

*They Treated Us Just Like Indians: The
Worlds of Bennett County, South Dakota*
By Paula L. Wagoner

A Grammar of Kiowa
By Laurel J. Watkins with the
assistance of Parker McKenzie

To order or obtain more information on these or other University of Nebraska
Press titles, visit nebraskapress.unl.edu.

CPSIA information can be obtained
at www.ICGtesting.com
Printed in the USA
LVHW111254101118
596664LV00003B/417/P